JN077480

KYOTO AREA STUDIES ON ASIA
Center for Southeast Asian Studies, Kyoto University
Volume 29

At the Edge of Mangrove Forest

The Suku Asli and the Quest for Indigeneity, Ethnicity, and Development

KYOTO AREA STUDIES ON ASIA

Center for Southeast Asian Studies, Kyoto University

The Nation and Economic Growth:
Korea and Thailand
Yoshihara Kunio

One Malay Village:
A Thirty-Year Community Study
Tsubouchi Yoshihiro

Commodifying Marxism:
The Formation of Modern Thai Radical Culture, 1927–1958
Kasian Tejapira

Gender and Modernity:
Perspectives from Asia and the Pacific
Hayami Yoko, Tanabe Akio and Tokita-Tanabe Yumiko

Practical Buddhism among the Thai-Lao:
Religion in the Making of a Region
Hayashi Yukio

The Political Ecology of Tropical Forests in Southeast Asia:
Historical Perspectives
Lye Tuck-Po, Wil de Jong and Abe Ken-ichi

Between Hills and Plains:
Power and Practice in Socio-Religious Dynamics among Karen
Hayami Yoko

Ecological Destruction, Health and Development:
Advancing Asian Paradigms
Furukawa Hisao, Nishibuchi Mitsuaki, Kono Yasuyuki and Kaida Yoshihiro

Searching for Vietnam:
Selected Writings on Vietnamese Culture and Society
A. Terry Rambo

Laying the Tracks:
The Thai Economy and its Railways 1885–1935
Kakizaki Ichiro

After the Crisis:
Hegemony, Technocracy and Governance in Southeast Asia
Shiraishi Takashi and Patricio N. Abinales

Dislocating Nation-States:
Globalization in Asia and Africa
Patricio N. Abinales, Ishikawa Noboru and Tanabe Akio

People on the Move:
Rural–Urban Interactions in Sarawak
Soda Ryoji

Living on the Periphery:
Development and Islamization among the Orang Asli
Nobuta Toshihiro

KYOTO AREA STUDIES ON ASIA

Center for Southeast Asian Studies, Kyoto University

Myths and Realities:
The Democratization of Thai Politics
Tamada Yoshifumi

East Asian Economies and New Regionalism
Abe Shigeyuki and Bhanupong Nidhipraba

The Rise of Middle Classes in Southeast Asia
Shiraishi Takashi and Pasuk Phongpaichit

Farming with Fire and Water:
The Human Ecology of a Composite Swiddening
Community in Vietnam's Northern Mountains
Trần Đức Viên, A. Terry Rambo and Nguyễn Thanh Lâm

Re-thinking Economic Development:
The Green Revolution, Agrarian Structure and Transformation in Bangladesh
Fujita Koichi

The Limits of Tradition:
Peasants and Land Conflicts in Indonesia
Urano Mariko

Bangsa and Umma:
Development of People-grouping Concepts in Islamized Southeast Asia
Yamamoto Hiroyuki, Anthony Milner, Kawashima Midori and Arai Kazuhiro

Development Monks in Northeast Thailand
Pinit Lapthanon

Politics of Ethnic Classification in Vietnam
Ito Masako

The End of Personal Rule in Indonesia:
Golkar and the Transformation of the Suharto Regime
Masuhara Ayako

Grassroots Globalization:
Reforestation and Cultural Revitalization in the Philippine Cordilleras
Shimizu Hiromu

Conceptualizing the Malay World:
Colonialism and Pan-Malay Identity in Malaya
Soda Naoki

Violence and Democracy:
The Collapse of One-Party Dominant Rule in India
Nakamizo Kazuya

Bali and Hinduism in Indonesia:
The Institutionalization of a Minority Religion
Nagafuchi Yasuyuki

At the Edge of Mangrove Forest:
The Suku Asli and the Quest for Indigeneity, Ethnicity, and Development
Osawa Takamasa

KYOTO AREA STUDIES ON ASIA
Center for Southeast Asian Studies, Kyoto University
Volume 29

At the Edge of Mangrove Forest

The Suku Asli and the Quest for Indigeneity, Ethnicity, and Development

By
Takamasa Osawa

Research Institute for Humanity and Nature/
Center for Southeast Asian Studies, Kyoto University

First published in 2022 jointly by:

Kyoto University Press
69 Yoshida Konoe-cho
Sakyo-ku, Kyoto 606-8315, Japan
Telephone: +81-75-761-6182
Fax: +81-75-761-6190
Email: sales@kyoto-up.or.jp
Web: http://www.kyoto-up.or.jp

Trans Pacific Press Co., Ltd.
2nd Floor, Hamamatsu-cho Daiya Building
2-2-15 Hamamatsu-cho, Minato-ku, Tokyo
105-0013, Japan
Telephone: +81-50-5371-9475
Email: info@transpacificpress.com
Web: http://www.transpacificpress.com

Edited by Cathy Edmonds, Kyneton, Vic., Australia
Designed and set by Ryo Kuroda, Ibaraki, Japan

Distributors

USA and Canada
Independent Publishers Group (IPG)
814 N. Franklin Street
Chicago, IL 60610, USA
Telephone inquiries: +1-312-337-0747
Order placement: 800-888-4741 (domestic only)
Fax: +1-312-337-5985
Email: frontdesk@ipgbook.com
Web: http://www.ipgbook.com

Europe, Oceania, Middle East and Africa
EUROSPAN
Gray's Inn House,
127 Clerkenwell Road
London, EC1R 5DB
United Kingdom
Telephone: +44-(0)20-7240-0856
Email: info@eurospan.co.uk
Web: https://www.eurospangroup.com/

Japan
For purchase orders in Japan, please contact any distributor in Japan.

China
China Publishers Services Ltd.
718, 7/F., Fortune Commercial Building,
362 Sha Tsui Road, Tsuen Wan, N.T.
Hong Kong
Telephone: +852-2491-1436
Email: edwin@cps-hk.com

Southeast Asia
Alkem Company Pte Ltd.
1, Sunview Road #01-27, Eco-Tech@Sunview
Singapore 627615
Telephone: +65 6265 6666
Email: enquiry@alkem.com.sg

ISBN 978-4-8140-0434-8 (hardback)
ISBN 978-4-8140-0435-5 (ebook)

Contents

Maps

Tables

Photographs

Acknowledgments

This book is a revision of my doctoral thesis with the same title submitted to the School of Social and Political Science, The University of Edinburgh, in 2016. The ethnographic data presented is based primarily on twelve months of field research conducted in the village of Teluk Pambang, Bantan subdistrict, Bengkalis regency, Riau, Indonesia, from January to December 2012. Although Teluk Pambang was divided into three administrative villages at the end of my field research and the settlement I investigated has become a new village, Suka Maju, I refer to the village name as Teluk Pambang in this book, as I obtained the data before the new village began working as an administrative unit. In addition, this book includes the results of continuous follow-up field research carried out until September 2019.

It would have been completely impossible to write this book without the warm and generous support and assistance of a number of people in Bengkalis regency. In particular, the Suku Asli and Akit villagers received me as a member of their communities and we spent days together without any distinctions. This experience is a great treasure to me not only as a researcher but also as a person who lived in a different culture and society. Malay and Javanese villagers and regency officials also gave me their views on the Suku Asli. Thanks to their kind cooperation, this book includes multiple perspectives on tribal people's lives and their position in Indonesian politics.

This research was sustained by many Indonesian partners. The staff of Lembaga Ilmu Pengetahuan Indonesia (The Indonesian Institute of Science) and Kementerian Riset dan Teknologi (The Ministry of Research and Technology) permitted my application to research the people and assisted the procedures at government offices. Prof. Nursyrwan Effendi at Andalas University accepted the role of Indonesian counterpart, and a student of his, Pak Irfan Maaruf, looked after my life in Pekanbaru. Dr Nofrizal at Riau University gave me much information about coastal life in Sumatra and an opportunity to make a presentation to the university. His colleagues Dr Romi Joenari and Prof. Isjoni provided me with articles on mangrove forests and other tribal people in Riau. Mr Akhwan Binawan, director of the non-governmental organization Hakiki, provided me with detailed information about the *adat* community in Riau.

In preparing for my field research and writing my thesis, staff and colleagues at The University of Edinburgh gave me great support and assistance—in particular, my supervisors Dr Dimitri Tsintjilonis and Prof. Alan Barnard. Dimitri's enthusiastic and motivational tuition always inspired me with fantastic arguments and deeper explorations of the people's world, and Alan's broad knowledge of indigenous people provided me with ways to connect the issues of being indigenous with international problems. Staff and colleagues gave me tough, detailed, and critical comments, and these comments dramatically developed my arguments. I would also like to thank my two examiners, Dr Kostas Retsikas (The School of Oriental and African Studies, University of London) and Prof. Janet Carsten (The University of Edinburgh). Their comments and constructive criticisms helped focus my argument in a clearer fashion and gave me the opportunity to reformulate some of my ideas to encompass a broader, yet deeper, scope.

Throughout the revision and book edition, staff at the Research Institute for Humanity and Nature (RIHN) and the Center for Southeast Asian Studies, Kyoto University (CSEAS), provided full support and kind advice. At RIHN, Prof. Kaoru Sugihara, Director of Research Program 1, Prof. Kosuke Mizuno and Prof. Osamu Kozan, the leaders of the Tropical Peatland Society Project, and other project members provided a working environment and research funding during the revision process. In addition, I especially appreciate Prof. Julius Bautista at CSEAS and three anonymous reviewers who provided excellent critiques and opinions to improve my description and argument. Mr Shun Teramoto at RIHN redrew my hand-drawn maps. Ms Narumi Shitara at the CSEAS editorial office, Tetsuya Suzuki at Kyoto University Press and the staff at Trans Pacific Press supported the smooth editorial procedures.

In addition, I appreciate Prof. Akifumi Iwabuchi at the Tokyo University of Marine Science and Technology, who first encouraged me to conduct my fieldwork on the eastern coast of Sumatra. Dr Geoffrey Benjamin at Nanyang Technological University and Prof. Sumio Fukami at Momoyama Gakuin University personally sent me very important articles that I had been unable to access. Prof. Tsuyoshi Kato at Kyoto University and Prof. Kazuya Masuda at Kochi University delivered valuable information about ethnicity among Malays in inland areas of Riau.

My work on this book was financially supported by the Japan Society for the Promotion of Science Grants-in-Aid for Scientific Research (Grant No. 17K17729) and the Tropical Peatland Project at RIHN (Project No. 14200117).

Finally, I would like to express deep gratitude to my late parents, who died during my first fieldwork in 2007. By submitting this book, I hope to partially fulfill those duties I forsook when I could not attend your deathbeds.

Takamasa Osawa
Winter 2022, Kyoto

Abbreviations

AMAN	*Aliansi Masyarakat Adat Nusantara* (Archipelagic Alliance of Adat Community)
IKBBSA	*Ikatan Keluarga Besar Batin Suku Asli* (Suku Asli Headman's League)
IKBBSAJ	*Ikatan Keluarga Besar Batin Akit Jaya* (Akit Jaya Headman's League)
KAT	*Komunitas Adat Terpencil* (geographically and politically isolated *adat* community)
NGO	non-governmental organization
OPSA	*Organisasi Pemuda Suku Asli* (Suku Asli Youth Organization)
SKGR	*Surat Keterangan Ganti Rugi* (letter to enable land transaction, issued by village and subdistrict offices)
SKSA	*Surat Keterangan Suku Asli* (the certificate of Suku Asli)
SKT	*Surat Keterangan Tanah* (letter to certify land use issued by village and subdistrict offices)
VOC	*Vereenigde Oostindische Compagnie* (Dutch East India Company)

Positioning Suku Asli as Indigenous Peoples or an *Adat* Community

In January 2012, I was sitting in the director's office of the local DINAS *Kebudayaan dan Pariwisata* (Department of Culture and Tourism) in Bengkalis town to seek information about the Suku Asli villages where I wanted to conduct my fieldwork. I informed the director of my plan to study the 'Utan' (Forest) or 'Orang Utan' (Forest People), an expression used in government documents to refer to the Suku Asli. However, he counseled me not to use the term in front of the people. He said, 'Now they are called Suku Asli, and you should call them so. If you say "Orang Utan" in their village, they get angry.' The term 'Suku Asli' can be translated as 'indigenous people' or 'indigenous tribe.' I was familiar with this, as I had heard it during my fieldwork in 2006 and 2007 in a village of the Akit on Rupat Island, as well as during short trips to Bengkalis Island. In fact, one of my research aims was to investigate how and why the name had been changed and to connect it with my analysis of indigeneity. However, I did not know the name 'Orang Utan' made them angry because many Akit who had a relationship with the Suku Asli had generally used the term.

Several days later, I moved to the village of Teluk Pambang to live in a Suku Asli's house. I avoided using the problematic term for some weeks, but one night I carefully asked my host, Kiat,[1] who was in his late thirties, about why the name had changed. I told him that I had read several government documents in which the Suku Asli were called 'Orang Utan,' and I wondered why. He replied, 'There are no Orang Utan in this village as they are literally people living in the forest. You know, there is no forest in this village anymore.' I could not see his facial expression clearly as the room was lit only by a candle, but I heard his voice becoming higher in tone. I was slightly embarrassed because I knew that his voice became louder when he talked about sensitive topics, such as village politics. I asked him why they had been called this in the past. He continued, 'If there are people who call us this, they do not know this village. When I was a child, people did not live in the forest anymore. We have been Suku Asli from the past until now.' His comments seemed to suggest that the change of name was to replace the exonym 'Orang Utan' with the autonym 'Suku Asli.' I remember thinking that the change of name may not be related to their indigenous identity.

Several days later, I asked the same question to Odang, who was in his early fifties and a famous shaman, or *dukun*, in the village. Odang was smiling, as usual, and answered my question in a calm voice, 'That's right. We were Orang Utan in the past.' During my research, he constantly referred to himself and his people as the Utan in a historical context without hesitation. He continued, 'The name "Orang Utan" is the same as that of the ape and it is unfavorable. We are human. So, the name was changed to "*orang asli*" in recent years.' He usually preferred to use '*orang asli*' or sometimes 'Orang Suku Asli' to refer to himself and his people. '*Orang asli*' can be translated as 'indigenous people' or 'tribal people' in this region, similar to the well-known Orang Asli in Malaysia. At this time, I could not judge whether he used it as a synonym for 'Suku Asli' or for describing their indigenous position. The Akit had also often described themselves as '*orang asli*' when they emphasized their indigenous position. Either way, I thought that the change of name may be related to their indigenous identity.

The next day, I visited Ajui, who was in his mid-forties and a political leader of the Suku Asli on Bengkalis Island. His explanation was a clear and detailed history of their ethnic name:

> The government indeed called us 'Orang Utan' in the past. A long time ago, when our ancestors lived in the forest, they might as well be called 'Orang Utan.' However, the name is wrong now because we live in *kampung* (settlements). Therefore, around 2005, we negotiated with the regency government to change our name. As a result, the name was changed to 'Suku Asli.'

I asked him the reason behind the Suku Asli name. He answered, 'It is because we are *orang asli* in this region. We asked the government to call ourselves *orang asli*. However, the government refused and decided that the new name should be Suku Asli.' The name was changed, based on their aspirations, in negotiation with the government. I was able to confirm that the change of ethnonym was related to their indigenous identity.

Finally, I talked with Koding, who was in his early seventies and was Ajui's father; we talked about the history of the village and his son's explanation of the Suku Asli name. He confirmed Ajui's explanation, adding, 'Now, everything is different. More and more people *jadi* (have become) Suku Asli.' I felt that he viewed the past with some nostalgia, and it struck me that their ethnic and indigenous identity had changed dramatically. The change of ethnic name was not just nominal but was associated with their identity, practices, and position in the region. My initial research explored the change in terms of their ethnic and indigenous identity and found that their society has actually changed in the past few decades.

The four people mentioned above were my best friends in the village, and they appear in my ethnographic descriptions frequently. They lived in the neighborhood, had kinship connections, and communicated with each other constantly. Nevertheless, their nuances of and attitudes toward the various names were neither consistent nor fixed. This is a reflection of historical instability and the recent problematization of their indigenous and ethnic identity in state politics. Despite the lack of definite ethnic boundaries and the fluidity of their identity, they have been categorized in a certain way by the state. In recent years, their identity and position have been problematized in Indonesian politics in terms of indigeneity and, as a result, they have begun claiming their position within the state as an integrated and distinctive ethnic group that is associated with a unique *adat* (tradition) and a particular 'indigenous' identity. The fluctuation of their self-identification shows that it is still a work in progress. However, their ethnic and indigenous identity is certainly transforming.

This book explores the emergence of ethnic identity first and foremost in terms of indigeneity among Suku Asli living on the eastern coast of Sumatra. The emergence of this identity reflects not only their aspirations but also their entanglement with several government development programs or interventions that aim to transform the lives of local people who are more or less in a tribal position. In this process, their identity has been problematized by both the government and themselves, and as a reaction to it, the Suku Asli have embodied their indigeneity.

Throughout these contexts, the most important change has been the development and embodiment of their indigeneity, which, in the context of Indonesia, is imagined, articulated, and recognized in a very particular way by the state, local authorities, and national activists. Alternatively, the Suku Asli have a tacit, non-articulated, and unconscious identity and connection with a place that has been fostered in their history—that is, indigeny. It is through the liaison between indigeneity and indigeny that the Suku Asli have reconfigured their traditional identity and place within the nation state. Focusing on some of the most important manifestations and embodiments, this book attempts to chart the emergence of indigeneity and relate it to the entanglement of the people and the government. Regarding indigeneity from an epistemological perspective, and indigeny as an indigenous ontology, the book describes how people in tribal and marginalized positions come to embody, resist, and transform the government image of 'indigenous peoples' and accomplish their 'modernization'—a modernization demanding, first and foremost, a distinctive and well-bounded indigenous identity.

Indigeneity, ethnicity, and development

Let me begin with a review of discussions about the concepts of 'indigeneity' and 'indigenous peoples' in an academic context, which has contributed to my analytical frame in terms of Suku Asli identity.

Over the past forty years, scholars, activists, and practitioners have attempted to support local, native, and autochthonous people and conceptualize the definition of 'indigenous peoples.' However, indigenous peoples are fundamentally not people who live in a primordial and static state of being. Rather, their indigenous position is determined by their relationship with others and has been dynamically formulated in and through a particular process, as implied in the short ethnographic sketch in the opening to this introduction. This gives us perspective on our relational understanding of indigeneity.

Since the 1980s, the concept of 'indigenous peoples' has become increasingly important at the international political level in a number of challenges attempting to improve the marginalized situation of native or autochthonous peoples. Indeed, the United Nations and the International Labour Organization defined 'indigenous peoples' and emphasized the need to protect their rights in 1986 and 1989, respectively. At this level, the definition of 'indigenous peoples' comprises four points: the priority of land occupation in time, cultural distinctiveness, identification by themselves and others, and the experience of marginalization (Saugestad 2004: 264). The United Nations declared 1993 as the International Year of the World's Indigenous People, and 1995 to 2004 as the International Decade of the World's Indigenous People. It then announced 2005 to 2014 as the Second International Decade of the World's Indigenous People. In 2007, the United Nations Declaration on the Rights of Indigenous Peoples was ratified by the United Nations General Assembly (Merlan 2009; Wawrinec 2010). In accordance with the international conceptualization of indigenous peoples, more and more local, national, and international agents, such as local authorities, non-governmental organizations (NGOs), and international activists, have been involved in the movement to ensure and protect the land rights of local communities.

Indigeneity as a perspective

As a consequence of the rise of the 'indigenous movement,' anthropologists began to criticize the implementation of the universal definition of 'indigenous peoples.' John Bowen (2000) points out the risks in applying the concept—which was conceptualized according to understandings of indigeneity in the settler societies of the Americas and Australia—to non-settler societies of Asia and

Africa, as peoples in the latter regions have moved frequently and the distinction in terms of 'indigenous people' is quite difficult to make. For instance, in terms of the San people in southern Africa, Renée Sylvain (2002) argues that while the international model of 'indigenous peoples' is emerging in their society under the support of an NGO, it prevents the recognition of San cultural identity and replaces the efforts of San activists to fight the legacy of apartheid, racial segregation, and class exploitation because the model ignores their bifurcated history and promotes preservationism and essentialism in the way it treats their culture and ethnicity. In particular, Adam Kuper (2003), whose criticism has sparked intensive debates, points out that the concept of 'indigenous peoples' is based on the obsolete concept of 'primitive peoples,' and questions the empirical validity of the claim to 'be indigenous' in a primordial sense that involves a traditional way of life and a static connection with the land. He warns that the international conceptualization of indigenous peoples involves the risk of essentialism in which people who fail to prove their indigenous position are marginalized and discriminated against even further.

Indigeneity is literally understood as involving 'first-order connections (usually at small scale) between group and locality' (Merlan 2009: 304). Emphasizing the autochthonic sense, some definitions try to specify the people through descriptions of 'what people must be and how people must differ from others' (Merlan 2009: 305). For example, the 1989 International Labour Organization definition of 'indigenousness' is:

> (*a*) 'tribal' people whose social, cultural, and economic conditions distinguish them from other sections of the national community; (*b*) people descended from populations that inhabited the country...and (*c*) people retaining some or all of their own institutions. (Merlan 2009: 305; see also Dove 2006: 192)

Francesca Merlan (2009: 305) sees this kind of definition as 'criterial'; it proposes 'some set of criteria, or conditions, that enable identification of the "indigenous" as a global "kind".' In this scheme, 'indigenous peoples' are defined in association with autochthony, they are pre-modern or 'primitive' and differ from those who are 'modern' and 'civilized' (Cadena and Starn 2007: 7–8). These critiques present the problems that are generated by such specifications of people and the attempts to provide a clear designation of conceptual and practical boundaries between those who are indigenous and those who are not.

In recent studies, more and more anthropologists have seen indigeneity as relational rather than criterial (Merlan 2009; Trigger and Dalley 2010). Merlan (2009: 305) defines 'relational' as emphasizing 'grounding in relations between the "indigenous" and their "others" rather than in properties inherent only to those we call "indigenous" themselves.' From this perspective, indigeneity can be seen not as a fixed state of being but as a process emerging in relationships and dialogues with the 'non-indigenous' in various forms in different parts of the world (Trigger and Dalley 2010: 49), based on 'self-identification, participation and acceptance' (Merlan 2009: 306). In this perspective, the authentic indigeneity of 'autochthony and the pre-modern' is done away with (Cadena and Starn 2007: 8), and indigeneity is understood as something formulated in the transactions between 'indigenous' people and others in each local context.

In this approach, '"indigeneity" as a political concept is like ethnicity' (Barnard, A. 2006: 16). As Fredrik Barth (1969: 9–15) points out, ethnicity is something determined in the transactions between self-ascription and ascription by others, and is not necessarily related to cultural content. In the same way, while indigeneity has a somewhat clearer criterion (rather than in the case of ethnicity) specifying a connection between land and people, it is not necessarily constrained by their autochthony, and their self-identification and identification by others is more essential. In other words, indigeneity is 'fundamentally not a thing *in* the world, but a perspective *on* the world' (Brubaker 2004: 65), the same as ethnicity. Indigeneity is a way of viewing the world which is generated in relation to others. This perspective is necessary to understand the claim of indigeneity especially in Asia and Africa, where, historically, people have frequently moved around different places.

Indigeneity as a reflection of modernity

Geoffrey Benjamin (2002, 2016a, 2016b), an anthropologist who has studied the Orang Asli groups in Malaysia, theorizes the various social dimensions that emerge around the concept of indigeneity, and suggests that indigeneity is something formulated in relation to others. He suggests that the term can be used to label 'the images of the "indigenous" produced by non-indigenous (exogenous) individuals concerned to construct a model of alterity, especially in discussing environmental or traditional-knowledge issues' (Benjamin 2016a: 519). In other words, indigeneity is a form of category and identity that emerges from the perspective of the exogenes in the modern political context. Thus the 'indigenous peoples,' in which 'indigenous' is the adjective of this 'indigeneity,' can be seen as those who adopt and embody the image of non-indigenous people—that is, 'indigenizing' themselves—in and through their communication with non-indigenous, modern people.

Indigeneity stands in association with others' modern perspective and its politics rather than the peoples' traditional way of life or connection with an ancestral land. Some anthropologists describe qualities of indigeneity. In the context of Amazonian Indians, Beth Conklin (1997) argues that the Amazonian manifestation of indigeneity is created in and through active adoptions and demonstrations of the Western image of indigenous people. While it is a strategically effective tool in order to claim the protection of their environment, she concludes that it encompasses a downside in that they reduce their own cultural authenticity to a Western conception of authenticity. Along similar lines, through describing the process by which indigenous people in the Philippines were recognized, Frank Hirtz (2003: 889) suggests that indigeneity is recognized only in and through the modern administrative procedures and representational processes; according to him, 'it takes modern ways to be traditional, to be indigenous' and, by doing so, the 'groups enter the realm of modernity.'

Anthropologists who see indigeneity as relational have tried to explore the dynamic formulation of indigeneity in the 'modernization' context. Laura R. Graham and H. Glenn Penny (2014) focus on the performative dimension of indigeneity, in which they describe the emergent and situational manipulation of indigenous identity and belongings among autochthonous people in communication with non-autochthonous people. The manifestation of indigeneity involves a variety of communication procedures with others, such as the examination of historical facts, the documentation of identity, the legitimation of traditional institutions, and the establishment of foundations and ethnic organizations supported by NGOs and local elites, as well as performances including dances, speeches, and so on. Thus Michael Dove et al. (2007: 131) suggest that 'the rise of interest in indigeneity' is 'both a product of, and a marker of, modernity.' Morgan Ndlovu (2019) critically argues that the performance of indigeneity acted in cultural village tourism in South Africa sustains and reproduces coloniality/modernity at the expense of the interests of the colonized indigenous agency. Indigeneity is a process that emerges in the communication with modernity among people (see also Porath 2002a), and this communication results in their entering 'modernity.' Although the meaning of 'modernity' in these texts varies, it can be summarized by the embodiment of distinctive, well-bounded, and homogenous ethnic identity, the adoption of capitalistic and bureaucratic systems, integration into the nation state, and the social change of the indigenous people, which are brought to indigenous peoples in and through communication with the exogenous modern world.

Indigeneity thus can be seen as a perspective that is formulated in communication with the exogenous outside world. However, autochthonous identity cannot simply be reduced to something constructive, instrumental, or situational, in the same way that ethnic identity has not been understood only in such a way (see Banks 1996). It has a different dimension shared within a local community that is associated with a specific place and their life in the place.

'Indigeny' and 'exogeny'

Benjamin (2002, 2016a, 2016b) suggests the term 'indigeny' for referring to a dimension of indigenous identity that is fostered through 'the continued habitation of the same specific places that one's familial ancestors always lived in' (2016b: 373). According to Benjamin (2016a: 513), indigeny is 'inherited embodiment by *place*'; it 'has to do with *family*-level connections to concrete *place*, and not with the connection of whole ethnic groups (whatever they may be) to broad territories' (Benjamin 2002: 15). In such a place, 'home and workplace are the same, and there is no distinction between family and co-workers' (Benjamin 2016b: 367). In other words, indigeny is a label that can be used to indicate a concrete linkage between people and place that has been formed through the historical sedimentation of people's everyday experiences and inheritances without political processes beyond face-to-face communication. Benjamin also points out that this indigeny is tacit, non-articulated, and unconscious because people's place is their subjective world itself, one that has been inherited from their ancestors through their language and practices. Thus, for people themselves, indigeny can be seen as an emotional, unconscious, and primordial attachment to a land within a small community. It is impossible to see their land as a commodity. At its unconscious and subjective point, indigeny is completely different from indigenism and indigenousness, which are self-conscious political stances that organize the related people collectively and allow them to claim a certain degree of autonomy from the state, or may occasionally be used by the state for its own purpose (Benjamin 2016a: 516, 2016b: 363–9). In this sense, indigeny is a label to conceptualize the ontological dimension of practices and beliefs among autochthonous people (cf. Chandler and Reid 2018).

Conversely, Benjamin (2016a: 513) defines 'exogeny' as 'inherited estrangement from place.' Exogeny is experienced by exogenes 'who moved away from the places inhabited by their presumed familial ancestors,' something which 'characterises a high proportion of the world's population, both rural and urban' (Benjamin 2016b: 364). As their connection with a place is relatively new and temporal, these people 'think of territories as commodities (object) open to exploitation' (Benjamin 2016a: 514). Examining the histories of both settler and non-settler societies, he argues that modernity is formed on the basis of such an exogenous idea.

Here indigeny and indigeneity are clearly contrasted. Indigeny is a non-articulated, unconscious, and subjective connection with a place. It manifests in the practices and beliefs of the autochthonous people, and thus can be regarded as the ontology of their autochthony. On the other hand, indigeneity is something associated with an objective perspective from modern and exogenous others. It is introduced to autochthonous societies and causes social changes that often result in 'modernization.' These social process can be analyzed through epistemological approaches. But, theoretically, it does not mean indigeny and indigeneity are clearly bounded and fixed. This is because social systems and practices, which were imagined by the exogenes, are politically introduced into an autochthonous society, and, then, can be transformed into the non-articulated and subjective beliefs and practices of the people for a long time. Therefore, we can regard indigeneity as a hybrid of indigeny and exogeny. The people, who have maintained their indigeny as everyday experiences and inheritance from ancestors, adopt the idea and image of the exogenes, and, eventually, indigeneity or 'indigenous peoples' emerges in their society.

If so, how are people with indigeny brought to communication with the exogenous world and how is indigeneity embodied in local communities? The main agents are activists, local authorities, and the government, which have adopted the concept of indigenous peoples from national and international contexts, and they intervene in the lives of local communities under the banner of development programs that involve the power of—to echo Foucault—'governmentality' (Foucault 1991; Li 2000, 2007b).

Indigeneity embodied by governmentality

Distinct from sovereignty and discipline, which directly restrict and reform the behavior and knowledge of a population, governmentality is an attempt to shape human conduct by 'educating desires and configuring habits, aspirations and beliefs,' and is especially concerned with the 'well-being' of the population (Li 2007b: 5): 'To govern means to act on the actions of subjects who retain the capacity to act otherwise' (Li 2007b: 17). Demonstrating these quests for the wellbeing of the people themselves, activists, local authorities, and governments try to introduce to the local communities their ideas of how they should live and encourage them to accept the category and identity of 'indigenous people.' As a result, local communities conceptualize their position as indigenous peoples in the state and embody the position in their way of life.

This process is not enacted through imposition but in collaboration between the agents' suggestions and the historical identity and practices of the people. Michael Hathaway (2010: 320) describes the process whereby the Chinese living in Yunnan became 'indigenous' after the 1990s through environmental conservation and rural development programs, and suggests:

> Their work in fostering an indigenous space is neither a top-down imposition of a foreign social category nor a spontaneous bottom-up social movement of social activism. Rather, it works mainly in an intermediate realm, and is being pushed outward by Chinese public intellectuals, tentatively and unevenly.

Tania Murray Li (2000: 151–2) goes one step further and suggests indigenous identity is something 'articulated' in the history of confrontation, engagement, and struggle, referring to Stuart Hall's concept of 'articulation.' According to Li (2000: 151):

> a group's self-identification as tribal or indigenous is not natural or inevitable, but neither is it simply invented, adopted, or imposed. It is, rather, a *positioning* which draws upon historically sedimented practices, landscapes, and repertoires of meaning, and emerges through particular patterns of engagement and struggle. The conjunctures at which (some) people come to identify themselves as indigenous, realigning the ways they connect to the nation, the government, and their own, unique tribal place, are the contingent products of agency and the cultural and political work of *articulation*.

The process by which tribal or indigenous identity is embodied may be seen as this 'cultural and political work of articulation.' However, Li's argument shows that 'historically sedimented practices, landscape, and repertoires of meaning' can be seen as non-articulated, unconscious, and subjective perspectives and practices—that is, indigeny of a local community—as the meaning is obtained in their connection with a place without exogenous political and cultural interventions. Self-identification as indigenous is not simply 'articulated' but manifested on the basis of such non-articulated indigeny.

Combining the relational definitions of indigeneity and Benjamin's (2002, 2016a, 2016b) definition of indigeneity based on an outsider's image, I argue that the indigeneity discussed in recent years is a perspective drawn upon indigeny in and through government development programs, and I would like to explore the transactions between indigenous people and the government in the context of the Suku Asli. In Indonesian politics, the concept of 'indigenous people' is translated as '*masyarakat adat*' or '*adat* community,' which I explore in the next section.

Indigeneity in Indonesian politics

The Indonesian version of indigeneity as a political concept has its roots in the Dutch direct rule. For the purpose of controlling the population effectively, the colonial government divided it into two legal categories: Europeans, and *inlanders* or *bumiputera* ('Natives'). While the Europeans followed Dutch national laws, the 'Natives' were supposed to follow their customary law—that is, *adat* (Fasseur 2007: 50–1; Moniaga 2007: 277; Li 2007b: 44; see also Chapter 5). When the Republic of Indonesia declared independence in 1945, these categories were abolished in the government's attempt to end the racial discrimination derived from them. Thus, in the Constitution of Indonesia of 1945, the government used the term '*orang Indonesia asli*' (real/indigenous Indonesians) (Moniaga 2007: 277). Then, in 1959, under the Sukarno regime, the concept of *pribumi* (sons of the soil; native Indonesians) gained legal standing. The main purpose of establishing this category was to distinguish and protect the rights of autochthonous populations from those who had their origins outside Indonesia, especially the ethnic Chinese who gained power in the Indonesian economy (Moniaga 2007: 277–8; Tsing 2007: 54–5). The *pribumi* category was maintained until 2006, when a new citizenship law was passed (Wawrinec 2010: 102).

Revitalization of '*adat* community'

Although the concepts of 'Natives,' *orang Indonesia asli*, and *pribumi* are related to being indigenous, they differ from the current concept of indigenous peoples because they are concerned with large-scale and national-level connections between population and territory. The government maintained this linkage between the population as a whole and state territory in post-independence Indonesia because being indigenous in this way was meant to 'look back to the anticolonial project and the alliance between elites and peasants that created the nation-state' (Tsing 2007: 54). In other words, the concept was used to integrate the state and bring a number of different people together. However, the small-scale and local-level linkages between people and place (i.e. indigeneity) were conceptualized through '*adat*' and '*adat* community' that was first developed in the Dutch colonial era and later revitalized.

Adat is usually translated as 'tradition,' 'custom,' or 'customary law,' therefore '*adat* community' can be interpreted as 'traditional or customary community.' Under Dutch direct rule, which began in the early nineteenth century, the '*adat* law community' (*adatrechtsgemeenschap* in Dutch; *masyarakat hukum adat* in Indonesian) was recognized by the colonial government and allowed to regulate matters—such as access to farmlands and forests—as customary rights in the outer islands of Java. The community was also associated with the ideal image of a historically continuous and harmonious rural community (Henley and Davidson 2007: 20; Li 2000: 159, 2007b: 50; see Chapter 5). The 1945 Constitution of the Republic of Indonesia confirmed the existence of the *adat* law community (Abdurrahman 2015: 1–2).

The post-independence government, however, pursued centralized sovereignty and did not achieve the effective implementation of customary rights. During Sukarno's regime (1945–67), although the government partly attempted to legally recognize the customary rights of rural communities, it failed due to its lack of power and authority in local areas (Li 2007b: 52–3). In Suharto's New Order regime (1967–98), the government powerfully propelled industrial expansion and the formation of the nation state, in which it grabbed and exploited local lands and resources, conducted transmigration and resettlement programs, and ignored local customary rights (see Chapter 1). During this period, customary laws or *adat*, which had controlled the local use of lands, were depoliticized and reduced to harmless cultural forms like dance, song, architecture, and ritual (Acciaioli 1985; Tsing 2007: 35; see also Chapter 5). The massive exploitation of local lands and resources during the New Order regime raised dissatisfaction among the locals. But social protest was censored in this era, and ways in which the locals could resist government exploitation were limited to those that the government accepted as legitimate (Henley and Davidson 2007). Some local communities tried to negotiate with the government, moderately insisting on their ancestral use of lands and resources, using the term *adat* (Benda-Beckmann and Benda-Beckmann 2011: 183), and some activists and locals emphasized the land rights of rural communities in their attempts to protect natural environments (Tsing 2007: 37). But, in general, these were exceptional cases.

In 1998, President Suharto lost power and the government changed its policies under the slogan of *Reformasi* (Reformation). This change was characterized by 'decentralization,' in which the new polity distributed political power and economic profits to the provinces, regencies, subdistricts, and villages; previously, power and authority were concentrated on the state capital, Jakarta.

In 1999, the *Aliansi Masyarakat Adat Nusantara* (AMAN; Archipelagic Alliance of Adat Community) NGO was founded (Henley and Davidson 2007: 1–2). This organization is involved in international indigenous rights advocacy, has frequently received foreign funding, and uses international media effectively (Henley and Davidson 2007: 7–8). Under the AMAN umbrella, local people who had experienced exploitation of their lands and resources by the government and by government-sponsored corporations began claiming their rights to ancestral land and its resources. AMAN adopted '*masyarakat adat*' (*adat* community) as the translation of 'indigenous peoples',[2] and the locals have mobilized their indigenism under the banner of this Indonesian concept (Li 2000: 155, 2001: 645–6). In accordance with activities by the locals and AMAN, the Indonesian government has been introducing legislation toward protecting the customary rights of the locals (see Chapter 1).

It should be noted here that the Indonesian government has not completely accepted the concepts of indigenous peoples and indigenous rights developed in the international discourses. Since its independence, the Indonesian government has been concerned with large-scale and national-level connections between population and territory, and has negated providing marginalized indigenous peoples with exclusive land rights. Based on this view, the government resisted the implementation of the International Labour Organization Convention 169 in 1989 and the United Nations Year of the World's Indigenous Peoples in 1993 (Bedner and van Huis 2008: 165–9; Persoon 1998: 294–5). Also, even in recent years, although the government ratified the United Nations 2007 Declaration on the Rights of Indigenous Peoples, it emphasized that all ethnic groups in Indonesia are indigenous or native (Bedner and van Huis 2008: 169; Merlan 2009; Tsing 2007: 54). Within the historical and national framework of *adat* community, it has legitimized the customary rights not only of indigenous peoples in international discourse, but also local people as a whole.

In the historical process of this conceptualization, we can see some characteristic features of the Indonesian indigenous movement. First, the movement is characterized by a great quest for *adat* that has been inherited from ancestors in local communities and was once recognized by the Dutch colonial government. Thus David Henley and Jamie Davidson (2007) and Adam D. Tyson (2010) call the Indonesian indigenous movement '*adat* revivalism.' This movement centers on the locals trying to gain their land rights in and through actions to revive or, more precisely, construct their 'traditional' legal orders that were ignored by the post-independence government. Therefore, not only marginalized local groups but also rather 'civilized' and relatively powerful peoples such as the Minangkabau and Balinese participate in this *adat* revivalism (Biezeveld 2007; Warren 2007). Second, this *adat* revivalism is deeply related not only to the legal sphere in terms of land rights but also to the spheres of tradition and culture. This is because the term '*adat*' generally implies not only law-like rules but also morals, norms, rituals, and other cultural practices in everyday life. Furthermore, the state emphasized its cultural aspect rather than the legal ones during the New Order regime. Therefore, ensuring a common and distinctive tradition or culture as *adat* law community is often much more important than one's priority of land occupation in the past, which is the first criterion within the international concept; indeed, local communities actively try to demonstrate their shared and distinctive traditions or cultures. In other words, the Indonesian indigenous movement includes a process of traditionalization or culturalization.

The emergence of governmentality in policies

The conceptualization of indigeneity in Indonesian policies is also related to definitions of and policies connected to autochthonous people in a tribal position. By the term 'tribal people,' I mean the segmentary and decentralized peoples who are not completely subsumed under centralized state control based on their own choice in the state political structure of the 'ruler–peasant–tribal people' relationship (Benjamin 2002: 7–9; Scott 2009: 182–4; see also Chapter 1).[3] Although the expression 'tribal' or 'tribal people' has negative connotations, I do not intend to emphasize their 'primitive' or 'backward' qualities. Rather, 'tribal people' and 'people in a tribal position' are analytical terms used to indicate a particular form of relationship with the state.

Shortly after Indonesia achieved its independence, the Department of Social Affairs in Jakarta designated a category of marginalized tribal people and referred to them as *suku-suku terasing* (isolated tribes). This category was changed to *masyarakat terasing* (isolated communities) in the mid-1970s (Persoon 1998: 287–8). *Suku-suku terasing*, or *masyarakat terasing*, was seen as the main target of government development programs.

Generally, a development program includes a variety of policies and aims. First, it may aim to aid industrial development, involving the exploitation of resources and land, the construction of infrastructure, and the promotion of tourism. Second, it may involve 'development' of the people themselves. These particular programs have covered a great variety of aims: the implementation of immigration and resettlement, the management of land and resources, the legitimization of culture and autonomy, the establishment of educational and medical institutions, the improvement of agricultural techniques, the introduction of industry, and so forth. The people are especially the target of these kinds of programs, which have become some of the most important political issues not only for the Indonesian government, but also for other Southeast Asian governments (Duncan 2004a: 3).

The development programs for tribal populations can be seen as involving one of two agendas: 'raising their level of "civilization"' and 'raising their standard of living' (Duncan 2004a: 3). The aim of the Indonesian development programs has mainly focused on the former agenda, in which the government has tried to socially and culturally integrate them with mainstream rural Indonesians (Persoon 1998: 289; Porath 2010: 275). To achieve this aim, the government implemented three main policies during the Sukarno and Suharto regimes, although their effect was limited. The first one was resettlement programs, in which the government constructed uniformly designed permanent houses and villages, and resettled the people who lived in the forests, mountains, and river or sea coasts. The second policy was the introduction of permanent agriculture to those who were often shifting cultivators in the forests. The third was to encourage them to convert to one of the government-recognized *agama* (religions) (Persoon 1998: 290–4). Through these policies, the government tried to directly constrain and reform the people's behavior, knowledge, and identity, and to assimilate them into 'civilized' Indonesia. For the government, the tribal people's ways of life were 'backward' and 'primitive' and needed to be improved through development programs. The government did not consider the people's historical connections with and emotional attachment to a place. Here, the government failed to see the people's ways of life as part of Indonesian 'cultures,' which the government admitted was an important component of the multi-ethnic nation state.

Since the last years of the Suharto regime, government and public perceptions of tribal populations have been gradually changing. With the rise of the environmental movement between the late 1980s and early 1990s, people living in the forests were regarded as the ones who had managed to live harmoniously with the vulnerable natural environments. From that point onward, they were seen and acknowledged as having 'indigenous knowledge,' through which they maintained harmonious and sustainable relationships with their environment (Dove 2006: 195–6; Effendy 1997, 2002). In 1999, the government category of *masyarakat terasing* was replaced by *Komunitas Adat Terpencil* (KAT; geographically and politically isolated *adat* community) as a result of activities by AMAN (Duncan 2004b: 91) and, as such, their ways of life were connected with *adat* or '*adat* community,' gaining the implication of belonging to idealized and harmonious rural communities—that is, an essential component of the Indonesian nation state. This change of image was also reflected in the way of government intervention in their life. For example, in the government project to designate a national park in Jambi province, the Orang Rimba (the Kubu), who had been seen as one of the most 'primitive' people in Indonesia, were permitted to live in the park with the support of NGOs that emphasized their traditional culture as being dependent on living in the forest (Li 2001). Thus the 'primitive' and 'backward' image of the people has shifted toward something related to *adat* that is an essential component of Indonesian culture.

However, this change of image and policies does not mean that the government stopped its intervention in their lives or permitted complete autonomy and self-determination among them. Instead of the direct constraint and reform of their behavior and knowledge, the government (and NGO activists) began to intervene in the people's lives in a different way—by attempting to educate and reconfigure their habits and aspirations through suggestions of a better way of life (Duncan 2004b; Li 2007b). As I will show in the case of the Suku Asli, this attempt involved various procedures in which the government recognized the usufruct right of ancestral space by the community, legitimized the establishment of an ethnic organization, documented their ethnic background, promoted traditional performances, and integrated their registered religion. These policies were not imposed on the communities; instead, the government only encouraged the locals' actions through setting conditions, advising, and supplying subsidies to encourage them to behave as the government wanted them to behave (Li 2007b: 16). The aim of these approaches was to provide an opportunity for the community to be an *adat* community recognized by the government. Through these policies, the people are involved in the reconfiguration of their position in the state system, and, as Nathan Porath (2010: 269) puts it, they become 'a state-defined "primitive" ethnic minority.'

This change in government development programs can be seen as the emergence of governmentality. The old development programs for tribal populations tried to restrict and reform their behavior and knowledge through resettlement, agricultural, and religious programs. However, as a result of local resistance and the introduction of the international concept, the government tries to control their desire and aspirations through education and support. Here, indigeneity is delivered through governmentality—which regards the manifestation of *adat* as proof of authenticity—to tribal populations who do not always think of themselves as an *adat* community.

The Indonesian government does not place importance on the priority of land occupation in time, which is an essential component of the international concept of indigenous peoples, unlike Malaysia, where such people are comprehensively categorized as 'the Orang Asli.' Instead, the Indonesian government has exerted influences on such people in and through policies related to the concepts of the *adat* community and the KAT, which are closely associated with the politics of development in the modern nation state. Indeed, the Suku Asli have objectified and embodied their indigeneity in and through this kind of politics and its governmentality, as will be described in the following chapters.

The field site: geography and population

Riau province and its people

The province of Riau is situated in the eastern part of Sumatra. It includes about 90,000 square kilometers and has a population of more than six million people. The province capital is Pekanbaru. The western inland boundaries of the province border the West Sumatra province and hilly areas that connect with the mountainous area of the Minangkabau Highlands. Eastward, the altitude gradually lowers and a relatively moderate valley area extends for about a hundred kilometers or so. In this area, the four large rivers of Rokan, Siak, Kampar, and Indragiri run into the Malacca Strait, and the downstream area of each river is low and marshy. Around the estuary areas, there are many islands just off from the mainland, and numerous brackish rivers and channels make up swampy lands, which are covered with mangrove forest. The southeastern coast faces the cross point of the Malacca Strait and the South China Sea, and offshore is the Riau-Lingga Archipelago, which was part of Riau province until 2008. Historically, settlements have been formed along the rivers and their tributaries, and the people depended on water for transportation (Barnard, T. 2003: 12; Kathirithamby-Wells 1993).

Facing the Malacca Strait, which connects the Indian Ocean and the South China Sea, as well as the Indonesian archipelago and the Malay Peninsula, this region has been historically open to outside influences politically, economically, and culturally. In ancient times, the area was controlled by the maritime trading kingdom of Srivijaya. As a trading hub, the kingdom prospered for several hundred years until Srivijaya gradually declined between the eleventh and

Map 1: Coastal area of Riau province

thirteenth centuries. Several Malay kingdoms (such as the Indragiri, Rokan, Pekantua, and Gassib kingdoms) were then established on the eastern coast of Sumatra. At the beginning of the fifteenth century, a successor to Srivijaya, the Melaka kingdom, obtained control of the area and became prosperous during the century. The Portuguese conquered the kingdom in 1511, after which the Johor kingdom (the successor to the Melaka kingdom) controlled the basins of the Indragiri, Siak, and Kampar rivers from the seventeenth century (Andaya 2008: 50–78). In 1725, Raja Kecik, a Minangkabau adventurer, founded the Siak kingdom, which reached the height of its power at the beginning of the nineteenth century (Barnard, T. 2003). In 1858, when the Dutch government concluded a series of new treaties with the sultanates of Siak and Indragiri, these kingdoms lost their sovereignty, but initially had considerable autonomy (Colombijn 2003a: 508–09, 2003b: 338–41).

Under Dutch control, the administrative boundaries were reshuffled. Siak, Indragiri, and the Riau-Lingga Archipelago were combined as an administrative unit. In 1873, Siak was split off from the single administrative unit and established as a new administrative unit, the Bengkalis district. Under Japanese rule between 1942 and 1945, while the Riau-Lingga Archipelago became part of Singapore, Siak (including Bengkalis), Indragiri, and Bangkinang (which had been a part of West Sumatra) were designated as Riau *syu* (province). After Indonesia achieved independence, Bangkinang, Bengkalis, Indragiri, and the Riau-Lingga Archipelago formed the new province of Riau (Colombijn 2003b: 341). Finally, in 2004, the Riau-Lingga Archipelago was split off from mainland Riau as a new province, the Riau Islands province.

The complex geography of Riau province, its position as an international trading center, and repeated changes to the administrative borders have brought about the ethnic diversity of the province's population. At present, the *Orang Melayu* (Malays) are the people who identify themselves as (and are identified as) indigenous in general. However, their society and culture have not been integrated clearly, and, indeed, their identity has been formed by incorporating various populations through a long history of state control (Andaya 2008; Barnard, T. 2003; see also Chapter 1). Since the era of the precolonial Malay kingdoms, the Minangkabau from western Sumatra have immigrated into this area. The Minangkabau established their settlements on the eastern coast and engaged in the exportation of gold, pepper, and, later, the tin that was produced in the western highlands. As members of the ruling class, they were intimately related to the establishment of the Malay kingdoms in the region, and their immigration continues today.

Chinese, Arab, and European traders also visited the area. In particular, from the precolonial era onward, the Chinese established a number of trading posts along the eastern coasts. Their numbers dramatically increased in the mid-nineteenth century when the Siak kingdom delegated timber harvesting to Singaporean Chinese merchants under the *panglong* system (see Chapter 1), and in the 1940s when mainland Southeast Asia was involved in the turmoil of the Japanese intervention. From the early twentieth century, many Javanese also immigrated to this region, first as contract laborers in Dutch times and then as forced laborers under the Japanese. After Indonesia achieved independence, the government also encouraged the Javanese to immigrate to this area. In the last quarter of the twentieth century, a number of Batak from northern Sumatra also came to engage in labor around the oilfields and in acacia and oil palm plantations. In addition to these immigrants, the Bugis from Sulawesi and the Banjarnese from southeast Kalimantan have visited the Riau-Lingga Archipelago and southeastern coastal areas of mainland Riau (Andaya 2008: 88–91; Barnard, T. 2003: 14–15; Colombijn 2003b: 142).

In addition to these peoples, several more groups identify themselves as (and are identified as) indigenous, but have different identities from the Malays. Around the eastern coast of Sumatra, including Riau Islands province and the Bengkalis regency of Riau province, they are called '*orang asli*,' a term that is composed of the Malay words '*orang*' (people) and '*asli*' (original, real, or genuine)—derived from Arabic—and which, according to an Indonesian–English dictionary, has mainly two meanings, 'a native (of a place)' and 'an aborigine' (Stevens and Schmidgall-Tellings 2004: 681). On the eastern coast of Riau, the term is used by the people themselves and neighboring others to indicate KAT comprehensively (see also Porath 2002a: 771, 2003: 3–4; Wee 1985: 41). Although the concept of 'the Orang Asli' has been known in Malaysian politics since the mid-twentieth century (Nicholas 2002), it is unknown when Riau people began to use this phrase. Some Suku Asli elders explained to me that they have used it *dari dulu dulu* (since long ago), but I could not find the phrase in this sense in Indonesian–English dictionaries and documents published before the mid-twentieth century. Nor is it used in Pekanbaru and the western inland regencies of Riau province (personal communication with Tsuyoshi Kato and Kazuya Masuda). It might be a relatively new phrase adopted from a Malaysian concept in the past sixty years (see Wee 1985: 41), or it or its synonym might have been locally used to claim one's native status but then came to be used to specifically indicate a tribal/indigenous position after the 1960s. In any case, among the Suku Asli and neighboring others living around the basin and estuary area of the Siak River, this phrase refers first and foremost to non-Malay tribal/indigenous people; furthermore, it is associated with their identity at present as described and analyzed in the following chapters. I thus use the term '*orang asli*' as meaning, broadly, (1) tribal/indigenous people in Riau, mainly in the form of '*orang asli* groups,' and, narrowly, (2) as a collective name of tribal/indigenous people living around the area of the Siak estuary (i.e. the Suku Asli, Akit, and Rawa), distinguishing it from *suku-suku terasing* and KAT as the government's political terms. On the other hand, Suku Asli is used as a proper noun to indicate the people who were known as Orang Utan in the past.

The Talang Mamak, one of the indigenous groups living in the forest area of the middle reaches of the Indragiri River (Indragiri Hulu regency), a moderately hilly area, cultivate rice on dry fields by slashing and burning rainforest, and grow rubber and coconut trees. They also engage in the collection and trade of *kayu gaharu* (a type of agarwood), hunting in the forest, and fishing on the tributaries of the Indragiri River (Isjoni 2005: 35–81). The Bonai live in the upper reaches of the Rokan River (Rokan Hulu regency). For them, fishing in the tributaries of the Rokan River is an important source of livelihood (Isjoni 2002: 125–34; Pemerintah Propinsi Riau 2005: 22–40). The Orang Suku Laut are traditionally sea nomads and most live in Riau Islands province, but some live around the mouth of the Kampar River (Pelalawan regency) (Pemerintah Propinsi Riau 2005: 22–40). They traditionally depended on the coastal resources and see their living water space as a continuous expanse (Chou 2013). In recent years, they began demanding that the waters that were recognized by the Johor kingdom as belonging to them, and which were inherited from their ancestors, should be recognized by the government (Chou 2003, 2010; Chou and Wee 2002).[4] The Petalangan, who live around the forests of the middle reaches of the Kampar River, are slash-and-burn cultivators of rice on dry fields. While they generally identify themselves and are identified as the Malays, some of them are trying to protect the rainforest area by claiming their historical use of the forests and demonstrating their position as an *adat* community to fight against the encroachment of the forest by oil palm plantations, and have established an ethno-museum and a foundation that receives international support (Effendy 1997, 2002; Masuda 2009, 2012). Around the basin and estuary area of the Siak River, the Sakai,[5] Rawa, Akit, and Suku Asli make their homes. I shall describe them later.

According to a report written by the Riau government (Pemerintah Propinsi Riau 2005), the government recognizes six groups of KAT, which are the main target of government development projects because of their poverty and marginalized position (see Chapter 1).[6] The six groups are the Talang Mamak, Orang Suku Laut, Bonai, Utan (Suku Asli), Sakai, and Akit. According to a report written by the Department of Social Affairs in 1996 (see Isjoni 2002: 17), the populations of these groups were as follows: the Talang Mamak—4816; the Bonai—2070; the Orang Suku Laut (including those in the Riau-Lingga Archipelago)—7750; the Sakai—2955; the Akit—2736; and the Utan—3884. However, these figures seem to be much smaller than actual populations in recent years. According to a survey of the KAT by the Department of Social Affairs in the Bengkalis regency in 2010 (Dinas Sosial Kabupaten Bengkalis 2010: 52–6), the number of households of the Sakai was 2094; that of the Akit, 1504; and that of the Suku Asli, 1439. Therefore, the populations of the Sakai and Akit are around 10,000 people and 8000 people, respectively.[7] In terms of the Suku Asli, there are 1385 households in the Meranti regency (unpublished data obtained from the Department of Social Affairs in Meranti Islands regency in 2012) and some 1000 people who were called the Rawa in Siak regency (see Chapter 1 and Chapter 4), in addition to the figure in the Bengkalis regency above. Therefore, the total population who identify themselves as Suku Asli is estimated at about 15,000 people around the area of the estuary.

Economic and political settings of Riau

Present-day Riau is characterized by three economic, political, and geographical traits. The first trait is the spectacular industrial exploitation of its rich natural resources. At the turn of the twentieth century, rich oilfields were found around Duri city. Throughout the Japanese occupation and post-independence Indonesia, the oilfields and related infrastructure have been dramatically developed. Growing acacia and oil palm is also an important industry. In the last quarter of the twentieth century, the vast rainforests that had covered most areas of the province were transformed into large-scale plantations.

While these industries have generated many employment opportunities for the locals, the capital was controlled by the central government and national and international corporations. In 1989, an international development scheme was set up among Riau, Johor, and Singapore, which formed the 'Growth Triangle.' This international framework was established so that Singapore would be able to utilize cheap resources and labor from Malaysia and Indonesia. In return, Malaysia and Indonesia would obtain capital and technologies from Singapore. In the wake of such economic developments, the province has attracted many migrants from North and West Sumatra, as well as Java, and the landscape of Riau has undergone tremendous change (Chou and Wee 2002: 318–24). Riau is one of the richest provinces in Indonesia.

Second, Riau is a center of Malay ethno-nationalism. Although Riau is regarded as originally the land of the Malays, they have been far from dominant in the economic and political domains as a result of continuous migrations of the Minangkabau and Javanese. This situation resulted in the separatist independence movement of Riau. The kingdoms of Riau and the southern coast of the Malay Peninsula had strong political connections throughout the precolonial era, which forged strong emotional connections between the Malays in Riau and the southern coast of the Malay Peninsula. After the Second World War, the Riau Malays plotted the independence of Riau from the Indonesian republic several times, aiming for the revival of the Sultanate of Johor-Riau. Under Suharto's regime, the celebration of Malay culture was organized through the restoration of historical graves and palaces, and by establishing museums, conducting linguistic and literary research, and organizing conferences (Wee 2002: 498–501). Just after the fall of Suharto, Riau Malay elites tried to seek independence, just like Aceh and Papua, by emphasizing the value and distinctiveness of Malay culture. Unlike Aceh and Papua, no violence was involved, yet they could not win the wide support of citizens and their efforts resulted in failure because the movement could not give clear and persuasive distinctions of boundaries, people, and territory (Colombijn 2003b). At present, this ethno-nationalism among the Riau Malays has changed into a claim for indigeneity and self-determination within the territory.

Third, Riau is one of main arenas for environmental issues in Indonesia. For the past several decades, the area of rainforest has rapidly decreased because of logging and clearing for plantations. In addition, and related to this, the devastation of tropical peatland and its fires have been a serious problem. Peat soils cover the vast area of the eastern lowlands of Riau, and the area was swampy forests in the past. However, over the past decades, peat swamp forests were drained and dried to establish acacia and oil palm plantations. Drained and dried peat soils easily burn because the soil is composed of organic matters. As a result, peatland fires frequently occur during the dry season, and a haze that causes health hazards often spreads over not only the cities and villages in Riau, but also those in Malaysia and Singapore. Several national and international institutions and NGOs are conducting research and campaigns to protect the rainforests and mitigate the peatland devastations (Mizuno et al. 2016).

Through his historical study of the Siak kingdom, Timothy P. Barnard (2003: 1–3) characterized the nature of the kingdom as *kacu* (mixed) (see also Chapter 1). With this word, he summarized the mixed and complex social and ecological situations of the kingdom. Although the situation has changed, the *kacu* feature of the Siak kingdom can still be applied to present-day Riau province. In the complexity and mixture of environments and populations, various identities, cultures, and political and economic agents are competing in this province. In this situation, Suku Asli have sought their indigeneity.

Bengkalis regency and ethnicity

The Bengkalis regency lies on the eastern coast of Riau province, which has an area of about 7000 square kilometers and a population of 500,000 people. Facing the Malacca Strait, this area has historically been the center in Riau for international communications with the outside world. Between the eighteenth and twentieth centuries, the area was controlled by the Siak kingdom. While its political center moved several times, the capital was essentially at Siak Sri Indrapura, which was situated at the middle reaches of the Siak River. When the Dutch government obtained control of the kingdom in the mid-nineteenth century, the Dutch administrative center was moved to Bengkalis town on Bengkalis Island and temporarily controlled the whole area of the eastern coast of Sumatra (Colombijn 2003b: 341). After Indonesia achieved independence, the realm of the Siak kingdom became the Bengkalis regency. Dumai city and the Siak regency were separated in 1999, and the Meranti Islands regency was also split off in 2008. At present, Bengkalis regency consists of the coastal area, mainly Bengkalis and Rupat Island, and an inland area, of which the political and economic center is Duri city. The regency capital is Bengkalis town on Bengkalis Island.

The population of the area is as diverse as that of Riau province, with Malays, Javanese, Minangkabau, ethnic Chinese, Batak, and some *orang asli* groups. In the coastal area, the population of ethnic Chinese is relatively large compared with other regions in Riau because of the introduction of the *panglong* system in the late nineteenth century (see Chapter 1). Some of them live in towns and engage in trading businesses; some live in rural areas and earn their livelihoods from cultivating coconut, rubber, and oil palm gardens and from fishing in the Malacca Strait and inland rivers.

The Sakai are one of the *orang asli* groups who live in the moderately hilly area around the basin of the Mandau River, a tributary of the Siak River (Porath 2000, 2002a, 2002b, 2003). Traditionally, they practiced shifting cultivation of tubers. Today, many Sakai cultivate dry rice and most have identified themselves as Muslims. Throughout the precolonial era, they had a certain connection with the downstream Siak kingdom. They exchanged rainforest products for commodities, such as cloth, salt, and iron, and recognized the sultan as their overlord in return for the sultan's protection of their territory. During the 1930s and the 1940s, oilfields began to be established in Sumatra, and the Sakai's region became a major oilfield. During Suharto's era, the Caltex oil company expanded the oilfields and roads throughout their ancestral rainforest. Oil palm plantations have explosively expanded since the end of the twentieth century. Following the expansion of the oilfields, roads, and oil palm plantations, the Batak, Javanese, and Minangkabau immigrated into the area and built settlements along the roads (Mizuno et al. 2016; Porath 2002a: 771–5). In the post-Suharto era, they began claiming their rights to ancestral lands through negotiations with the government (Porath 2000, 2002a, 2010).

The Rawa, Akit, and Suku Asli live around the coasts and offshore islands. The Rawa live in the low and swampy basin of the Rawa River (Siak regency) on mainland Sumatra. While they were clearly documented in colonial records, they have been confused with the Utan and Akit in following periods. Indeed, they have strong social and cultural connections with the Suku Asli and Akit, as will be explained in the following chapters, and identify themselves as Suku Asli Anak Rawa, allying with the Suku Asli living on offshore islands who were called Utan in the past. In their region, the Caltex oil company has sought oilfields, and an environmental NGO is working to protect the rainforest in alliance with the Rawa.

The Akit live on Rupat Island. Their settlements are concentrated around the coast of the Morong Channel, which runs through the northern part of the island from east to west. Most of them earn their livelihood by harvesting mangrove timber, which is used for charcoal. While the Suku Asli, Akit, and Rawa were or are regarded as different KAT groups in the regency categorization, they have had regular communications and similar cultural and economic traits.

The Suku Asli

The Suku Asli live mainly on islands that are divided by narrow water channels around the Siak estuary, mainly Bengkalis, Padang, Merbau, Rangsang, and Tebing Tinggi islands (except for Bengkalis Island, these islands belong to the Meranti Islands regency). They are Austronesian speakers. Their language, the Malay dialect of this region, and the Indonesian that migrants speak are mutually intelligible.

The Suku Asli have been at a more or less tribal and marginal position. They have a history in which they have avoided state control to a certain extent, and have also avoided becoming Malay. They have been seen as 'primitive' or 'backward' from the state's perspective and are categorized as a KAT. In addition, they are post-foragers. Although several characteristic features are embedded in the label 'foragers' (see Lee 2005: 19–20), I place a strong emphasis on their mobility in their past life: they were people who foraged around the coastal forests along the brackish rivers and channels with canoes, and engaged in fishing, gathering, hunting, trading, and waged labor. Their settlements are scattered over a vast area of the islands. Although they are settled in villages at present, they still maintain some characteristics of their foraging past, such as occasional moves to different communities, little dependence on sedentary agriculture, and rather loose political and social institutions.

Although they have been regarded as a KAT in this region, their identity cannot simply be framed by the category of *adat* community. First, although the state has categorized them as the Utan since the eighteenth and nineteenth centuries, the Suku Asli have formulated an identity that goes beyond the state ethnic categorization. In their foraging ways of life, they have strongly associated with the Akit and Rawa, who were or are categorized as distinct groups by the state. As a result, rather than as Utan, they identify themselves as *orang asli*. Second, their communities have historically incorporated many ethnic Chinese. In the late-nineteenth century, there was a mass immigration of male Chinese laborers into the forest areas where the Utan lived, and they married with Utan females. Their descendants are called *peranakan*, or 'the mixed-blooded,' and they have maintained the Chinese way of ancestral worship and other elements of Chinese culture. As a result, their society has heterogeneous traditional practices and identities. Therefore, it seems to be difficult to see the Suku Asli as an ethnic 'group' in which people share a common identity based on their culture or descent, and they cannot be seen as an ethnic group if we adopt a strict definition (Brubaker 2004: 12; Scott 2009: 256). Even within their community they have heterogeneous traditional practices and histories, but they are moderately connected by the common points of histories, kinships, ancestral lands, and traditions.

Despite this diversity and fluidity of *adat* and identity, in recent years the Suku Asli have developed an 'indigenous movement' emphasizing their position as an *adat* community. In 2005, the Suku Asli established an ethnic organization, *Ikatan Keluarga Besar Batin Suku Asli* (IKBBSA; Suku Asli Headman's League[8]), which has a dual role—it is a headmen's council and the primary means of communicating with the government. In 2006, IKBBSA negotiated with the regency government and succeeded in having its new ethnic name Suku Asli officially recognized—now they are the Suku Asli. Since 2010, they have held periodic ethnic meetings and festivals and demonstrated Suku Asli traditional culture in front of government officials. Around 2011, they designated Buddhism as their traditional *agama*, and in 2013 applied for the usufruct right of the mangrove swamps around which they have traditionally lived, emphasizing that the swamps were their 'ancestral lands.'

The Suku Asli way of manifesting and embodying indigeneity is relatively unique. First, while in many indigenous movement cases in the world, people have confronted urgent issues that could bring about predicaments such as land competition with their neighbors, large-scale deforestation, or the designation of national parks, the Suku Asli are not facing such issues. Second, while international or national NGOs often support and encourage people to protect their rights or environments, no NGOs have worked in Suku Asli communities. Third, while Indonesian indigenous movements are characterized by the recovery of past authority (i.e. *adat* revivalism), the Suku Asli do not seek the revival of past authorities or 'traditional' authenticity. Rather, the trigger for their movement was a government intervention through which they were encouraged to establish an ethnic organization. Subsequently, through this organization, they have tried to communicate directly with the government and establish their new position as an *adat* community within the Indonesian state. In this communication, their ethnic and indigenous identity has been inevitably problematized. They repeatedly face questions from officials and outsiders—who are the Suku Asli and how are they indigenous?

I refer to the people in this book as 'Suku Asli'; however, this name may be disputable, and I considered different names before putting pen to paper. While 'the Utan' was out of consideration, '*orang asli*' was a possible candidate as many people used it, but it seems inadequate as they have nothing to do with the famous Orang Asli in Malaysia, and the Akit, Sakai, and Rawa also identify themselves as *orang asli*. I also considered using the name of the region, but there was no adequate regional name. Finally, I decided to use 'Suku Asli,' which they obtained through their negotiations with the government. Some of them seemed to have pride in the name and I had never come across people who were reluctant to use it. Nevertheless, there was still some hesitation in using this name because Islamic Malays and the Javanese use it (as well as '*orang asli*'; see Chapter 1) in the meaning of 'tribal people' rather than 'indigenous people,' and using 'Suku Asli' in this book might reproduce their marginalized position. To resolve the dilemma, the final decision was to use 'Suku Asli' because it underlines the indigenous position that the people seek; I hope this choice is acceptable for the majority of Suku Asli.

Anthropological and historical issues around the Malacca Strait

Southeast Asianists have been attracted to the topic of ethnic identity and category, as the populations in this area have enormous diversity of society and culture. This has been especially so for scholars who study the regions around the Malacca Strait because this area is characterized by the historical frequent moves of the populations. In classic ethnological approaches, scholars tried to classify ethnic categories and their cultures by focusing on the differences of 'race,' such as 'Negritos,' 'Veddoids,' and 'Proto-Malays,' which were derived from difference in the periods when people migrated to a region from southwestern China or elsewhere (e.g. Winstedt 1961; Loeb 1935). However, over the past three decades, archaeological, linguistic, and human biological evidence has shown that it is hard to explain their sociocultural differentiation by this perspective (Benjamin 2002: 18–19).

Recent scholars have explored issues of ethnic identity and category, focusing on the interactions between agencies of local populations and the state (see Steedly 1999). For example, T. Barnard (2003), a historian studying the eastern coast of Sumatra, explores how the Siak kingdom formed its control over eastern Sumatra on the basis of the *kacu* situation of ethnicity, as mentioned above. A book edited by him (Barnard, T. 2004) scrutinizes the history and diversity of Malays. Leonard Y. Andaya (2008), also a historian studying the Malacca Strait, scrutinizes the core of Malay ethnicity and describes the historical interactions between the Malay states and various local populations. Studies of people in tribal positions, whose identity may have been seen as primordial in public, also adopt a similar perspective. Benjamin (2002: 9) examines the formation of the Orang Asli in Malaysia and other people elsewhere in the Malay world and suggests that 'tribal societies are *secondary* formulations, characterized by the positive steps they have taken to hold themselves apart from incorporation into the state apparatus.' Analyzing the history of mainland Southeast Asia,

James Scott (2009) goes one step further and explains the formulation of tribal populations through their struggles with historical state policies such as taxation, corvée, and slavery.

At an ethnographic level, more and more anthropologists focus on the process of how people embody ethnic categories as their own identity within their societies. Porath (2003) describes the shamanic healing ritual of the Sakai and suggests that the ritual procedures can be seen as a process of the reconstruction of individual and group identity. Cynthia Chou researched Orang Suku Laut communities in the Riau-Lingga Archipelago and has written two books: in the first, she scrutinizes exchange between the Orang Suku Laut and Malays and reveals that their ethnic boundary is configured by their attitudes toward magic and money (Chou 2003); in the second book (Chou 2010), she explores how the Orang Suku Laut developed their attachment to territory in their semi-nomadic way of life on the sea and why they began claiming the right to the territory in relation to state development projects.

In particular, the perspective of Nicholas Long's (2013) work largely contributes to the exploration of indigeneity in this book. He examines Malay identity in Riau Islands province, which was created in 2004 when it separated from Riau province. Considering the fluidity and dynamism of Malay ethnic identification, Long (2013: 18) suggests that 'acts of ethnic identification might be contingent and circumstantial'; however, 'by destabilising the identity of so-called Malays and thereby problematising the category of "ethnicity", it actually reified the "Malayness" they were claiming.' The problematization has caused the people's exploration into 'Malayness,' and new understandings have been emerging in the province.

In the process of the emergence of Suku Asli indigeneity, ethnicity among Suku Asli has also been destabilized and problematized under government interventions. However, unlike the Malay situation, what has been destabilized and problematized is their indigeny, which has been subjectively and unconsciously fostered in their history around the mangrove forest. Their kinship with the ethnic Chinese, connection with coastal land, vagueness of leadership and institutions, flexible and diffuse *adat*, and non-Islamic religion, which have been fostered in their environment and marginalized tribal position, were destabilized and problematized by the government and themselves. In this process, such unconscious and subjective indigeny is partly objectified, and it results in their embodiment of indigeneity. While partly cooperating with and partly resisting the government interventions, the Suku Asli have objectified their indigeny and embodied their indigeneity.

This book contributes to some of these issues of identity and category, especially in relation to indigeneity. More specifically, first, this book contributes to the issues of how the categories of people in tribal positions emerged, how they have maintained their identities, and why the categories were associated with indigeneity. Considering geographic settings, national and regional history, and social and cultural differences, this book reveals a way of transactions between people in tribal/marginalized positions and state politics in the arena of indigeneity. Second, this book deals with the complexity and involvement of various identities. The Suku Asli have heterogeneous identities in their way of life and, furthermore, many people have Chinese identity derived from their ancestry. Exploring the boundaries within their community, as well as with outsiders, this book describes the dynamic transactions of such identities. Finally, this book explores the detailed processes of destabilizing, problematizing, and embodying indigenous identity. The trigger to destabilizing and problematizing indigeneity is state politics. The Suku Asli have not simply adopted the government policies, but have also objectified and abstracted their thoughts and practices based on their indigeny, and eventually reified their integrated indigenous identity in state politics. As a result, indigeneity is created in the community. My argument provides a salient depiction of the emergence of local identity, which could be applied to people in a tribal position not only in Indonesia but elsewhere in the world also.

Field site and methodologies

People and research in Teluk Pambang

I conducted my fieldwork between January and December 2012 (twelve months) in the village of Teluk Pambang,[9] which is situated at the eastern edge of Bengkalis Island. I lived in a Suku Asli house, visited other villages, and sometimes traveled to settlements beyond Bengkalis—including the Rawa region, Rupat Island, and Tebing Tinggi Island—for the purpose of getting to know the Suku Asli (and the Akit and Rawa) living in each place. While most of the ethnographic information in this book stems from this period of fieldwork, I also use complementary data obtained in Rupat, where I conducted fieldwork between July 2006 and December 2007 (eighteen months) in the Akit villages of Titi Akar and Hutan Panjang.[10] In addition, I conducted follow-up research for three weeks in September 2019.

Before the fieldwork, I had several plans about how I would go about collecting data on indigeneity. First, I planned to live in a Suku Asli village. By establishing rapport with the Suku Asli and learning their language, in a village context, I hoped to understand their world more deeply. Second, as my interest was in transactions between the Suku Asli and state politics, I would concentrate on the networks of Suku Asli leaders, as well as government officials. In particular, the broad network of Suku Asli leaders was important. Through my work with Suku Asli leaders, I expected to accumulate significant information on the implementation of government programs in each village. Third, I would seek as much information as I could on Suku Asli *adat*. I would gather and, if possible, make a list of their various *adat* prescriptions and practices, and explore the relationship of *adat* to state policies. Integrating these data, I would explore Suku Asli engagement, struggle, negotiation, and compromise with the state. With one exception, my plans worked out quite well.

My move to a Suku Asli village happened smoothly. My first and strongest supporter was Ajui, the *batin* headman in the Bengkalis regency. He was well respected in the village and the wider area. He managed to arrange my host family and introduce me to a number of elders and *adat* functionaries who were willing and able to facilitate my work. In this context, particularly helpful were Odang and Koding, who had a great deal of knowledge of Suku Asli *adat* and history. I was extremely fortunate to choose the 'right kind' of village—that is, a village that was at the very center of Suku Asli engagement with development programs (something I did not know at the beginning but found out almost as soon as I arrived in the area).

At Bengkalis town, where I had to complete the various administrative procedures for my research permit, I met a number of officials from the Department of Social Affairs. They promised support and provided me with a new report on the development programs for the KAT in the area (Dinas Sosial Kabupaten Bengkalis 2010). They explained the purpose of the various government programs and provided their views on the life of the Suku Asli. After that first meeting, an official took me to the house of a *batin* headman that was the closest to the town. The *batin* was Atang in the village of Selat Baru (see Map 3.1). When we arrived at his house, he was about to attend a wedding ceremony in the village of Teluk Pambang. He took me to the village and introduced me to Ajui and other leaders who had been invited to the ceremony from the village itself and further afield. After talking with them for a while, I found out that Teluk Pambang was the center of the Suku Asli ethnic organization IKBBSA. IKBBSA had the potential to be an excellent focus for my research, and so I asked Ajui to allow me to live in the village. I returned to Bengkalis town and Ajui contacted me by mobile phone a few days later to tell me that he had arranged a host family for me. I moved to the village just a few days after my first visit.

The head of my host family was Kiat, and his family included himself, his wife, and two unmarried sons. He had built a new house made of concrete a few years earlier, and had a room available. Although the house did not have a bathroom or electricity, my stay there was comfortable. Kiat was thirty-nine; he occasionally worked as a temporary laborer in road construction and the logging of mangrove timber. His wife was in her early forties and worked on a coconut plantation owned by Kimdi, an ethnic Chinese in the village. Their sons were in their late teens and worked together with their parents. Just like other Suku Asli, they had received little schooling. Kiat, his wife, and elder son had completed their primary school education. The younger son had graduated from junior high school in the village and wanted to enter high school, but his family circumstances did not allow him to do so—there was not enough money. Staying at their house and accessing the vast network of Ajui's friends and acquaintances, I managed to establish relations with most of the villagers in Teluk Pambang and also to visit leaders' houses in other villages, generally ten to twelve kilometers distant, by motorbike.

Language and communication

From the very beginning of our contact, I could communicate with Suku Asli in (what appeared to be) a mix of Indonesian and Malay, which I had learned during my previous fieldwork in Rupat. Like other KAT in this area (e.g. the Sakai; see Porath 2002a), the Suku Asli in Teluk Pambang speak a Malay dialect that exhibits a number of differences from the Malay and Indonesian spoken by their Javanese and Malay neighbors (different accents, a number of lexical differences, and so forth). Some Suku Asli call it *bahasa Suku Asli* or *bahasa asli* (Suku Asli language). However, the difference was not important. *Bahasa Suku Asli* and Malay are more than mutually intelligible. Furthermore, it varies from place to place even among Suku Asli communities. According to a Suku Asli in Teluk Pambang, it was often more difficult to communicate with a Suku Asli living in a distant community than with a Malay living in Teluk Pambang. Malay villagers in Teluk Pambang also thought Suku Asli spoke Malay. According to them, while the meaning of some Suku Asli words was sometimes obscure, such differences were generally found even among Malay villages in this area. A well-known, albeit slightly old, Malay–English dictionary (Wilkinson 1957) endorsed this opinion, and I could actually find most Suku Asli words in it. On the other hand, it was relatively difficult to find *bahasa Suku Asli* words in Indonesian–English dictionaries published in recent years.

Because of this linguistic similarity, many Suku Asli could easily adapt their accent and expressions to those nearer to standard Indonesian or Malay. They used such adapted accents and expressions not only when they talked with Javanese and Malays in the village, but also when they talked about political topics. My friends, mainly Suku Asli leaders, were good at this. When they talked with me, they seemed to change accent almost unconsciously. While I came to understand their accent and actually use it in daily life by the end of my fieldwork, I mostly communicated with them in the 'mixed' language of Indonesian, Malay, and their dialect because it was easier for all of us to understand. In this book, I have adopted Indonesian orthography to write the expressions of Suku Asli dialect.

Of course, language is highly significant in the context of development and Suku Asli relations with the state. For instance, in later chapters I explore the meaning of words such as *adat* and *agama*. The significance of these words emerged in the political context of unequal relations with outsiders and the need for 'development.' If we were to think of *bahasa Suku Asli* as an indigenous language, *adat* and *agama* are almost certainly not indigenous terms. They reflect the way in which Suku Asli communities were forced to think of their lives in and through terms imported from outsiders in terms of *agama* and *adat*. In many ways, it is this positioning that lies at the heart of this book. It is also remarkable that because of the language similarity with Malay and the linguistic differences among Suku Asli communities, my friends do not distinguish an 'us' and a 'them' based on language. Language, which may often be deeply associated with one's ethnic identity, is by no means a criterion of ethnic identification in their society.

Both in terms of adapting their language and sharing their understanding of the world, Suku Asli leaders were very cooperative with my research. For one thing, because of my previous experience in the area, introducing myself to them and explaining my research was fairly straightforward. From the very first contact at the wedding ceremony, it became clear that they had a good impression of me because of my previous fieldwork. They knew that I had conducted fieldwork in Rupat; they had kinship connections with the Akit and had heard rumors that a Japanese student had researched Akit tradition. As the stories and rumors about my work in Rupat were positive, they appeared to accept me without suspicion. Ajui's support, in particular, broadened my network. He showed me around Teluk Pambang and introduced me not only to Suku Asli but also to Malays and Javanese in the village. When he had meetings or events to attend in other villages, he took me along and introduced me to other Suku Asli leaders. Such leaders kindly explained to me the situation in their villages and welcomed my occasional visits to their houses. Through this network, I obtained much of my ethnographic data on the Suku Asli way of life, history, and engagement with the state—not only in Teluk Pambang but also in other villages.

The leaders' cooperative attitude was also associated with the emergence of indigeneity in Suku Asli society. As I describe in this book, Suku Asli leaders hoped that the government would recognize their community's position as an *adat* community. They almost certainly thought my research, which was supported by the government and dealt with their tradition, could be helpful. In addition, as I describe in Chapter 4, the efficacy of leadership in Suku Asli society is related to communication with outsiders. It may have been significant for them that, through communication with me, they could further their own reputation and the reputation of their village. Of course, this is not to suggest that their cooperation was a simple reflection of local politics. In many ways, they took interest in my research—they appeared to find my questions useful and seemed to relish the opportunity to speak about their community in ways that clarified both their tradition and their quest for a better life.

Beyond my work with leaders, I tried to establish relationships of trust with 'ordinary' people in Teluk Pambang as well. In general, they were also cooperative. My everyday routine involved visiting people's houses and talking about their life histories, economic activities, families, fears, and hopes. I also participated in their economic and religious activities in the village. I followed their work in the rainforest and mangrove forest, trying to learn how they used the forest resources. I attended shamanic séances and asked questions about their cosmology. A great deal of interesting information emerged from these encounters. More than that, little by little, they gave me the opportunity to better understand the information I was collecting from the various leaders by contextualizing their quest for Suku Asli recognition in the everyday lives of ordinary people and the village world.

As a researcher from a foreign country, I thought that some people might have been reluctant to communicate with me. However, I was not a strange person in the village because some people had Chinese ancestors and my East Asian appearance did not stand out among them. My clothes, which were bought in the *pasar* (market) that peddlers held once a week, also helped assimilate my appearance with the people in the village. Furthermore, my identification as a Buddhist seemed to reassure people. We could share food regardless of the halal food restrictions. Almost all Suku Asli in Teluk Pambang registered their religion as Buddhism and seemed more or less emotionally distant from Muslims and Christians, as mentioned in Chapter 2. It was often the case that they accepted visitors from other villages. In Suku Asli houses, I often encountered people who came from distant villages and relied on kinship and friendship (see Chapter 3). The visitor was not always acquainted with community members, so the host introduced the visitors to them, and they usually became friends. I was one of those visitors, and the community opened up to people who were connected or stayed in the village for a while.

At the beginning of my research, I tried to record everything the people talked about in our interviews using an integrated chip recorder and by taking field notes. However, I soon gave up because whenever I switched the recorder on, my interviewees became stiff and unrelaxed. They answered only what I asked and during my notetaking waited wordlessly for my next question. We did not joke or sympathize during the communication, and it was extremely uncomfortable for me, as I wanted to know about their lived experiences and thoughts generated from their everyday life. But such an 'interview' appeared to be completely alien to them. Therefore, I put the recorder away and tried to note down minimal keywords that struck me during our conversations. This strategy seemed to work because once I changed my interview method, people began talking about their experiences and thoughts much more vividly. On returning to Kiat's house, I reconstituted the context of conversations based on these keywords and typed them up on my laptop. The ethnographic facts described in this book were obtained through this process.

Initially, I was a visitor or interviewer, but I hoped I could become friends with at least a dozen Suku Asli. I became especially close to Ajui, Odang, Koding, and Kiat, who all proved extremely knowledgeable about Suku Asli tradition and history, and had experience in engaging with particular state interventions and the world of development. However, it is important to recognize that my friends were generally men. This is because (1) it is men who usually engage in political communication with outsiders and the government and (2) women often hesitated to talk with a foreign male researcher. For instance, when I visited a house, a woman often introduced her husband to me and retreated to a back room. Yet the wives of Kiat and Ajui became good friends of mine. As I had the opportunity to talk with them every day, they managed to share with me their perspectives on the village and life in it.

Nevertheless, in one respect, my initial plan did not work out very well. While leaders in different villages kindly explained to me their village situation and history, I found that it was difficult to explore the significance of this data in detailed ways. A number of repeat visits and interviews were simply not enough. To make it work, I would have had to spend much more time with each one of them and understand their lived experiences in the villages. Consequently, I revised my original plan: instead of trying to obtain data about all the villages (whose leaders I had met), I decided to focus on the situation in Teluk Pambang. As a result, I mainly describe the situation of Teluk Pambang in this book, and information about other villages is used only as complementary data.

Most of my interviews were conducted in an unstructured fashion. When I visited people's houses, I did not have many fixed questions in mind, and I carried on conversations about everyday things without trying to predetermine their direction. If there was something interesting in a particular context, I tried to explore the topic further. In this way, I tried to document, as well as to explicate, people's complex views of their world and, at the same time, to engage with these views as emerging in a form closely related to their everyday lives. In parallel with these unstructured interviews, I conducted a structured survey of the family members (and their backgrounds) of 185 households in the western part of Teluk Pambang (see note 5 in Chapter 2). This survey was necessary for the purpose of clarifying occasional moves, questions of individual descent, and marriage patterns between Suku Asli and *peranakan*.

Beyond interviews and surveys, it is important to emphasize that it was people's readiness to share with me their everyday lives that mattered. I had the opportunity to discuss and observe these lives in many different situations—from visiting Bengkalis town or spending time over coffee on the benches fixed in front of their houses, to working in their gardens or following them in the mangrove forest, I was allowed to learn something about their fears and hopes and, perhaps, share in these a little as well. For this experience, I will be eternally grateful.

Ethnographic approaches

My ethnographic strategy was to bring together the government's images of and interventions in Suku Asli society, and Suku Asli adoptions of and engagements with these images and interventions. As a result of this engagement, the Suku Asli appear to have conceptualized and started to reconfigure and embody their identity, habits, categories, and authenticity. In this book, by analyzing such changes, I explore how the Indonesian version of indigeneity has been introduced to Suku Asli society, what has changed as a result of this introduction, and the kind of actions that are emerging in relation to these changes.

In my ethnographic descriptions, I describe not only the facts of Suku Asli history and their way of life (as it relates to their indigeny) but also their attempts to deliberate their position in communication with neighboring others (as it relates to their indigeneity). As mentioned above, indigeneity is a kind of perspective that was introduced into their world in recent years. The Suku Asli appeared to be unfamiliar with the international concepts of 'indigeneity' and 'indigenous peoples.' Furthermore, at the time of my fieldwork, it seemed that only a few members of local elites knew the terms '*adat* community' and '*adat* law community,' and did not use these terms in a consistent way when explaining their position. Quite often, instead of these terms, they explained their perspectives on who they are through their own experiences and 'cultural logic' (see Long 2009), which have been formed in and through their ancestral practices, historical communications with outsiders, and connections with the land—experiences and cultural logics which, although they have started to change, have not yet been fully objectified in the form of an *adat* community. By describing my conversations with them and exploring their reflections on the concepts of *adat* community or indigeneity, I have tried to reveal how the Suku Asli have started to formulate their own indigeneity. Furthermore, by analyzing such discourses and comparing them with everyday practices, I explore unconscious and subjective attachments, aspirations, desires, and beliefs in the Suku Asli world. These attachments, hopes, and desires are all related to indigeny, and often seem more influential in Suku Asli responses to government interventions than abstract ideas like 'indigenous group.'

Structure of the book

Chapters 1 and 2 focus on the topic of ethnic identity as Suku Asli, which became the basis of the emergence of their indigeneity. While Chapter 1 deals with the state categorization of *orang asli* groups on the eastern coast of Sumatra, Chapter 2 is about identity based on their own perspective, a perspective that has been constituted by their historical experiences. From Chapter 3, I explore the social changes that emerged through the use of indigeneity in their world. Therefore, in the first section of each chapter, I describe the historical background of each topic before the emergence of indigeneity, and analyze the process and results of this emergence in the following sections. Each chapter explores Suku Asli practices and beliefs in everyday life and government intervention related to their historical indigeny and the emergence of indigeneity.

More specifically, Chapter 1 is about the history of the relationship between the state and tribal populations in eastern Sumatra. Some people of eastern Sumatra were categorized as being in a tribal and marginalized position in the process of state formation between the eighteenth and nineteenth centuries, and this category has been transformed into that of 'indigenous people' as a result of the recent changes in Indonesian politics. In Chapter 2, uncoupling the idea of the ethnic category derived from state politics, I describe Suku Asli identity and their historical relationship with the Akit, Rawa, and Chinese. While they have historically shared a clear opposition to Muslims who have their settlements near to those of the Suku Asli, their cultures are far from integrated. Chapter 3 deals with their relationships with space and livelihood resources. Describing their traditional life and the transition of land use in Teluk Pambang, I show a process within which they started to conceptualize their lands as 'descendants' land' and 'ancestral land.' Chapter 4 is concerned with the establishment of the ethnic organization IKBBSA. IKBBSA was established in the recent political atmosphere of decentralization rather than Suku Asli aspirations, but Suku Asli elites have driven the organization of ordinary people and the documentation of their ethnic identity in accordance with the government image of an *adat* community. Chapter 5 analyzes the transformation of their *adat*. More and more people are recognizing *adat* as something related to art or performance under government policies of culturalization, and this tendency encourages ordinary people to form their identity as Suku Asli through participation in these activities. Chapter 6 describes the process of the introduction of Buddhism as their 'ancestral religion.' The adopted image of a distinctive and integrated 'indigenous people' is reflected in their having an *agama*—that is, a religion that is both recognized and supported by the state.

Chapter 1

Under State Politics: State Formation, Ethnic Category, and Development Subjects

In the Bengkalis regency, people generally use the term '*orang asli*' to indicate tribal or indigenous people. When *orang asli* use this term, it seems to signify 'indigenous people' in a neutral or even positive sense. As demonstrated in the ethnographic description in the introduction, some *orang asli* used it with pride in addressing their historical connection with the land and their ancestors. On the other hand, for Malays and Javanese living in towns and villages around *orang asli* settlements, the nuance of 'tribal people' seemed rather strong. Autochthonous Malays do not refer to themselves as *orang asli* because it usually means the Suku Asli, Akit, Sakai, and Rawa. For city dwellers and Malay and Javanese villagers in the region, *orang asli* are people who have less communication with them, maintain their traditional way of life, and thus are basically different from the 'civilized' and dominant population of the Malays, Javanese, and Minangkabau in the region.[1]

The people who are categorized as *orang asli* are also listed in the government's KAT category and are regarded as the main subjects of the government development projects. Isjoni (2002: 20–1), an Indonesian anthropologist in Riau, summarizes the KAT profile: (1) they live in small and segmentary communities and usually depend on the natural resources around them; (2) therefore, they have poor material culture, are not really associated with *agama*, and follow their own *adat* without receiving benefits from the state *penbagunan* (development) projects (see also Dinas Sosial Kabupaten Bengkalis 2010: 1–5). These images show *orang asli* as 'primitive' and 'backward' people who have maintained the 'old' ways of life inherited from their ancestors in peripheral areas, and who have not been 'civilized' in modern Indonesia. In other words, *orang asli* have been seen as 'tribal people' in a primordial fashion.

However, recent studies point out that tribal populations in Southeast Asia have not existed or maintained themselves in a primordial way but have been formed in the politics of the state. Benjamin (2002) defines tribal people as people living in 'particular socio-political circumstances of life' within state politics and suggests that all tribal societies are 'secondary formulations' therein. Negating the claim that they follow 'the dictates of some collective inborn drive' or hold 'total collectivities' as ethnic groups in a primordial fashion, he emphasizes that 'being tribal' is a result of the 'individual choice' of the people in locating themselves in the state system (Benjamin 2002: 8–12). Scott (2009: 127–77) also suggests that the people living in the 'hilly areas' of mainland Southeast

Asia became 'tribal people' in politics and the economy in the process of state formation, and describes the fashion in which they ran away from state raids and the imposition of slavery, corvée, and taxation. If we consider historical and ethnographic records, we can see that these arguments apply to the situation of *orang asli* in eastern Sumatra as well. In the process whereby the state extends its power as it seeks more resources, labor, and tax revenue, some people living in its realm become *orang asli*. Thus the position of *orang asli* is formulated in transactions between state politics and people's choice (see also Chou 2020).

In this chapter, I would like to focus on the position of *orang asli* in state politics and explore this mainly using information from historical and ethnographic records. The essential tools or arts for the state in governing the population are identification, categorization, and certification. The state can objectify the people with whom it needs to intervene and can control them more effectively and easily (Li 2000; Scott 1998, 2009). This technique of objectification is important particularly to control tribal populations kept more distant from direct state control than the 'civilized' populations. By identifying and categorizing them, the state can show not only how they should be but also how the 'civilized' population in the state should be. Such politics have formed the present-day *orang asli* image.

Orang asli under the precolonial and colonial state

The maritime states, Melayu people, and *orang asli* groups

Let us begin with the formation of the early maritime state in the Malacca Strait, which goes back to the period of the ancient kingdom of Srivijaya. The Malacca Strait has been the principal maritime route connecting China, India, and the Middle East for the past 2000 years, and the communities along its shores continue to benefit from the trade (Andaya 2008: 50). After China became a powerful state and expanded its maritime trade in the first millennium, the importance of this area as a trade transit point increased. In particular, the port cities of southern Sumatra gradually developed because the southern area was the end point of the northeast monsoon winds that provided tailwinds for the ships from East Asia (Andaya 2008: 51). The ancient Hindu-Buddhist kingdom of Srivijaya thus emerged around the area of present-day Palembang in southern Sumatra. Changing its capital repeatedly, this maritime trading kingdom ruled the area for several centuries and exerted its influence on the ports of Sumatra, the Malay Peninsula, western Java, and mainland Southeast Asia (Andaya 2008: 78). Srivijaya control gradually declined from the eleventh century, and by the thirteenth century the area of southern Sumatra was subservient to the Javanese kingdoms of Kediri and Singasari (Andaya 2008: 57–9). At the beginning of the fifteenth century, Srivijaya was succeeded by the kingdom of Melaka, which was established by people who claimed they were descendants of the Srivijaya royal family. This kingdom rapidly became a prosperous trading center in the strait during the fifteenth century, supported by the Emperor of the Ming dynasty of China. The kingdom was conquered by the Portuguese in 1511 (Andaya 2008).

Andaya (2008: 67–8) summarizes the characteristic features of the Srivijaya kingdom between the seventh and fourteenth centuries as follows:

> (1) an entrepot state involved in maritime international commerce; (2) a ruler endowed with sacred attributes and powers; (3) governance based on kinship ties; (4) a mixed population with specific and mutually advantageous roles in the economy; (5) a realm whose extent was determined not by territory but by shifting locations of its subject.

In short, the power of the Srivijaya kingdom was concentrated on controlling ports, maritime commerce, and its populations, but not on the territories that the states in the following eras were interested in (Anderson 1990). In other words, the political power of the Srivijaya was not really exerted as far as the peripheries of the realm; for example, the 'upstream' of the port center or isles and inlets of the coasts and their populations. These characteristics transferred largely unchanged to the Melaka kingdom (Andaya 2008: 68).

The term 'Malay' or '*Melayu*' (in Malay) is very ancient, but was not associated with people or ethnic identity. Various texts recorded in foreign countries between the seventh and fourteenth centuries mentioned terms related to *Melayu*, but Anthony Reid (2004: 3–4) suggests these terms were an old toponym associated with Srivijaya. In *Sejarah Melayu*, a Malay text composed between the fifteenth and sixteenth centuries, the term '*Melayu*' is used as a placename, an adjective of king, a kind of *adat*, a synonym of Melaka city, and for the subjects following the king of Melaka, but it was not used as an ethnic category. Then, through the conquest of Melaka and the resulting dispersal of the population, the culture of the kingdom (such as language, dress, and Islam) spread across the former realm of the Srivijaya kingdom, and the people related to these cultures were gradually categorized as '*Orang Melayu*' (Reid 2004: 7–8). '*Melayu*' appears as one of the various ethnic labels in Dutch colonial records in the eighteenth century before its categorization was developed under the British colonial control of the Malay Peninsula in the nineteenth and twentieth centuries (Reid 2004: 8–14).

Andaya (2008: 59–60) analyzed records of the Melaka and Johor kingdoms and infers the spread of Malay identity since the period of the Srivijaya. According to him, Malay identity was initially associated with the state polity—that is, the people subject to Srivijaya (whose successors were identified as 'the Malayu people'[2]). The Melaka kingdom developed control over the Malacca Strait and South China Sea through the reinforcement of the ruler–subject relationship, a maritime trading network, and kinship alliances. The elite in the remote ports adopted styles and ideas from Melaka because they symbolized the kingdom's legitimacy as rulers. For example, the language used in Melaka became the trade and diplomatic lingua franca throughout the strait and the South China Sea; Islam, to which the Melaka royal family converted in the mid-fifteenth century, was introduced through the kingdom's sphere of influence (Andaya 2008: 71). Such a prestigious status as Malayu prevailed not only among the elites but also among their subjects through the expansion of kinship networks until the late eighteenth century (Andaya 2008: 71–7).

Although direct records before the sixteenth century of the people who are now called *orang asli* on the eastern cast of Sumatra are extremely scarce, some historical studies argue their relationship with the state. First, there were people who lived in places where the maritime port state could not adequately exert its power. These people were usually found in the inland areas, and such political center–peripheral relationships are expressed in the schema of 'upstream' and 'downstream' or 'hill' and 'valley' in studies of Southeast Asia (e.g. Bronson 1978; Kathirithamby-Wells 1993; Li 1999; Scott 2009). The coastal space of eastern Sumatra, with its numerous isles and inlets, also had spaces where state control was barely exercised (Barnard, T. 2003). In both cases, such spaces and populations were related to the present-day *orang asli* groups. Second, although they lived in the peripheral area of the state's realm, they had a certain connection with the state. For the maritime trading state, products harvested in the forest area (such as camphor, benzoin, and beeswax) were precious commodities, and the people harvested the products and exchanged them with the state's subjects (Andaya 2008: 221; Kathirithamby-Wells 1993: 80). However, third, they were not much subjected to state control.

It is certain that some groups came under state control before the sixteenth century. For example, the Orang Suku Laut supported the establishment and extension of the Melaka kingdom by acting as militia in the maritime world and received titles from the kingdom (Chou 2003: 24–9, 2010: 40–50). However, around the estuary area of the Siak River, many of the coastal forest dwellers were not subsumed in the polities of the Melaka–Johor kingdoms (Barnard, T. 2003: 18–19). In these peripheral areas, they maintained their autonomy and traditional way of life in the fashion of hunter-gatherers and shifting cultivators without strong political systems. In short, their position was economically connected with but politically separated from state control.

Therefore, in the process of expanding the Malay identity, some of these forest dwellers did not adopt the Malay identity of the state polity, and non-Malay identity was formulated in relation to the people who had Malay identity. On the periphery of the Malay Peninsula, on the one hand, such people would have been the ancestors of the Orang Asli in present-day Malaysia. Yet there were also such people on the coast of Sumatra. They might have been the 'Veddoid' and 'Negrito' populations (Loeb 1935: 290–5; Moszkowski 1909), indigenous Austronesian speakers who lived at places far away from the political centers, the sea nomads living in boats (Chou 2010 42–6), or even the Malays who had fled state control to avoid raids, taxation, and slavery (Hamidy 1991: 134; see also Scott 2009: 127–77).

Although these people must have been related to the ancestors of present-day Suku Asli and other *orang asli* groups on the eastern coast of Sumatra, it seems difficult to suggest that they are direct ancestors. This is because these peoples would have frequently moved from place to place during this era and many of them were absorbed in the state, becoming 'the Malays' in the following periods. As Benjamin (2002: 8–9) pointed out, more than a few such peoples became the Malays following state control and the adoption of the Malay identity. For example, some Kubu became Malays before the nineteenth century (Andaya 2008: 205), and some Utan became Malays in the early nineteenth century, as mentioned below.

The Siak kingdom and subordination to the state

After the Portuguese conquest of Melaka in 1511, the Malay kingdom was divided in two—the Johor kingdom on the southern coast of the Malay Peninsula (where the royal family of the Melaka kingdom fled) and, on the northern edge of Sumatra, the Aceh kingdom, which had succeeded the Samudera/Pasai kingdom, a part of Srivijaya (Andaya 2008: 114–18). While the new Johor kingdom was targeted by the Portuguese and the Aceh kingdom during the sixteenth century, the center of Malay culture and international trade in the Malacca Strait was dominated by the Aceh kingdom. The kingdom became prosperous as Middle Eastern traders sponsored it, and, as a result of the close communication, Malay identity was increasingly associated with Islam between the sixteenth century and the first half of the seventeenth century (Andaya 2008: 108–45). The Dutch East India Company (*Vereenigde Oostindische Compagnie*;

VOC) took control of the trade in Java around the first half of the seventeenth century, and the Dutch Republic obtained power in the Indonesian archipelago. The VOC assisted the Johor kingdom and occupied Melaka in 1641, and it achieved dominance over trade in Sumatra, instead of the Portuguese. In 1718, Raja Kecik, possibly a Minangkabau adventurer, took over the throne of the Johor kingdom with support of Minangkabau, Malay, and Orang Suku Laut communities in eastern Sumatra (Barnard, T. 2003: 55–6). In 1722, a son of the former Sultan of Johor retrieved the throne from Raja Kecik with the support of the Bugis from southern Sulawesi. Raja Kecik fled to the coastal area of eastern Sumatra and established the Siak kingdom (Barnard, T. 2003).

During this period, with the increase in the number of European traders, the eastern coast of central Sumatra emerged as an important supply center of timber for shipbuilding. At the end of the seventeenth century and the beginning of the eighteenth century, the VOC and Johor kingdom signed a series of treaties for trading in timber (Barnard, T. 1998: 90), and the VOC tried to obtain timber in this region. In harvesting the timber, it was necessary to seek the cooperation of local communities for the safety of operations and the ability to trace the species of wood suitable for shipbuilding. The Siak kingdom tried to control the forest and coastal dwellers to harvest timber. Between the eighteenth century and the mid-nineteenth century, the forest and coastal dwellers were subsumed under state control (Barnard, T. 1998: 92).

The earliest description of the forest and coastal dwellers around the mouth of the Siak River appears in Dutch and British articles. Balthasar Bort (1927: 177) refers to the indigenous people living around Bengkalis Island in the mid-seventeenth century as 'a Malay tribe of very uncivilised people, who live with their wives and children in their vessels among the islands roving hither and thither.' The people seem to be related to the Orang Suku Laut, who live mainly in the Riau-Lingga Archipelago at present. William Dampier (1906: 41–4), who sailed around the world and visited Melaka in 1689, recorded that Captain Johnson, who had gone to Bengkalis Island to buy a sloop, was killed on the coast between Bengkalis and Rupat islands in an ambush at night by 'a band of armed Malayans' using canoes, and that a headman of the Johor kingdom at Bengkalis gave an account of it by arguing that the government could not control the 'wild unruly Men, not subject to Government.' These records show that there were people who were not subsumed under the government polity in this region, and that they maintained their autonomy in the seventeenth century.

About a century later, one group of such 'folk' appears in a Dutch record as, more or less, the subjects of the Siak kingdom (Barnard, T. 1998: 91–3). In 1763, VOC officials at a post on Gontong Island at the mouth of the Siak River attempted to construct fences to protect the post from hostile forces, and they asked the king of Siak at that time, Raja Alam, to dispatch laborers to assist in cutting wood and constructing fences. Soon after the request, a group of the 'king's folk' arrived and helped with the construction. After a certain period of labor, however, the 'king's folk' refused to work any further despite the officials assuring them of payment for their work. Raja Alam sent his son to negotiate with the intransigent laborers (see Barnard, T. 1998: 92–3). This event indicates that some of the forest and coastal dwellers were under the control of the kingdom to some extent in this era. The government gradually reinforced control over these forest dwellers, and eventually the Siak rulers declared that they could supply a large amount of timber through their control by the early nineteenth century (Barnard, T. 1998: 93).

It is remarkable that most of the forest and coastal dwellers were not completely subsumed under state control even after the state declared control. They maintained their position and identity as non-Malay and avoided strong state control even after the nineteenth century, since their labor in the forest and its products were important to the state in maintaining its commercial and political power. For the government, the existence of tribal populations in peripheral areas was necessary—they were the suppliers of forest products to the state and, as a result, were not absorbed into the state. Rather, they enjoyed their autonomy and traditional ways of life in the forest, and they maintained their identity as distinct from Malays. Their position was transformed into ethnicity in the manner of state control in the following period.

Tribal position in the state formation

Benjamin (2002: 8) explains the formulation of the tribal position in the Malay world by employing the typological schema of 'tribal people–peasant–ruler' in the state. Rulers are people such as priests, tax collectors, soldiers, and kings, and peasants are 'those who allow their lives to be controlled by agencies of the state, which they provision in exchange for a little reflected glory but no counter-control' (Benjamin 2002: 9).[3] On the other hand, 'tribal people' are those who 'stand apart from the state and its rulers, holding themselves culturally aloof' in a fashion in which they accept the state system only to some extent (Benjamin 2002: 9, 15–16). This applies to the situation of people in tribal positions living in the coastal area of eastern Sumatra. The rulers and peasants were Malays. The people who were not always subjugated to the state can be seen as the non-Malay, and this non-Malay became the basis of the category of present-day *orang asli*. In this meaning, '*orang asli*' and '*Melayu*' or '*Orang Melayu*' can be seen as antonyms in the way the various group classifications developed. However, it should be noted that the binary relationship is the case only when we focus on the *orang asli*–Malay relationship. When we consider the context of their relationship with others, such as the Javanese and Bataks, the *orang asli* and Malays may claim their close relationship and have hybrid versions of identity: for example, some Orang Suku Laut identify themselves as '*Orang Melayu asli*' (Lenhart 1997: 153–4). There are people called '*Melayu Sakai*' in Sakai communities (Porath 2003: 5) and the Sakai may see the Malays as a sibling group (Porath 2019a: 146). While Malay and *orang asli* can be seen as two poles of the classification, the boundary between them is fluid and not substantial, depending on the context. Emphasizing cultural similarity, Benjamin (2019) summarizes the relationship between tribal people, peasant, and aristocrats in the Malay world as 'a Cline of Malayness.'

Scott (2009) discusses the ethnogenesis of diverse tribal people of mainland Southeast Asia by focusing on the political and economic relationship between the people and the state, as well as the specific geographic setting. According to him, the communities of tribal people, who live in the hilly areas with mosaic-like distributions, were formed by those who rejected state control or fled from the state that tried to extort labor and taxes from them. In this transaction between the tribal people and the state, the hilly parts of inland Southeast Asia, called Zomia, played an essential role for the people as a shelter, and prevented the exertion of the state power that dominated the valleys and coastal areas. While Scott's argument focuses on mainland Southeast Asia, this seems to apply to the formation of the tribal position on the eastern coast of Sumatra as well. In the development of the state polity, the people avoided state intervention in their lives, and their position as tribal people was formed. The numerous isles, inlets, and channels covered by mangrove forests in this region could provide shelter. In this coastal forest, the people tried to maintain their distance from state control, practicing the less-integrated semi-nomadic ways of life in which the state hardly intervened. Their mobility, unintegrality, and distance from the political center were sustained by their low-population density (cf. Trocki 1997: 87); by the complex geography of the low and marshy lands penetrated by numerous channels, rivers, and their tributaries; and by the cultivation of sago palm as the staple food, which does not need intensive collective labor (Barnard, T. 2003: 11–26).

However, there would also have been a certain difference between the situation of the tribal populations in the mainland and coastal areas, as the political and geographic settings were different. Paddy cultivation in the valley areas sustained the mainland state, and its power mainly focused on organizing populations and labor. Therefore, the state tried to strengthen its power and wealth through raids and by taking slaves (Anderson 1990; Colombijn 2003a: 448–99), and people fled to the hilly areas in which the state barely exerted its power (Scott 2009). Elsewhere, the maritime state in eastern Sumatra, which is generally unsuitable for paddy cultivation, was not only interested in a supply of labor but also in commodities that could be harvested in the forest and the sea. Although the state led slavery and piracy raids in coastal areas and exerted its power to the coastal areas to a certain extent, it did not try to absorb peripheral populations living in the forest and coastal areas into the political and agricultural centers. Rather, it tried to control the population by leaving them in the forest and coastal areas and maintaining trading communications (Barnard, T. 2014). So, while the peripheral populations were embedded in hierarchical and regional systems, they maintained some autonomy in the form of being legitimated by the state in the nineteenth century.[4] Andaya (2008: 17) summarizes their situation: 'Their ethnicization was…a deliberate effort to preserve a way of life that guaranteed their advantage and eventual survival from the intrusions of their numerically dominant Malayu neighbors.'

Currently, many *orang asli* living upstream in east and south Sumatra, such as the Sakai, Bonai, and Talang Mamak in present-day Riau and the Orang Rimba and the Suku Anak Dalam (or Kubu) in present-day Jambi, are thought to be derived from the Pagaruyung kingdom in western Sumatra. They have oral histories that imply their historical connections with the Pagaruyung kingdom and are more or less characterized by Minangkabau culture and the matrilineal descent system (Isjoni 2002; Porath 2003; Sandbukt 1984). Yet, with regard to the Akit, Utan, and Rawa in the coastal areas, there is no evidence implying their direct connection with the Minangkabau, and they have had little communication with upstream groups like the Sakai. Rather, it is more likely that they would have relations with Orang Suku Laut groups generally in the Riau-Lingga Archipelago.

Formation of the ethnic category

The polity of the Siak kingdom and Dutch government

Raja Kecik fled to Siak and established the Siak kingdom in 1723. During the eighteenth century, the kingdom developed around the port of Siak Sri Indrapura and gained control over communities and ports not only in the Malacca Strait but also in the South China Sea by means of the charisma of its rulers, control over the commerce between ports, formation of kinship alliances between powerful communities and alliances with the VOC, and by carrying out attacks and raids against hostile groups. By the end of the eighteenth century, the kingdom had reached its peak (Barnard, T. 2001: 339–40, 2003: 116–23; Kathirithamby-Wells 1997: 230–2), and the Anglo-Dutch treaty of 1824 allowed the Dutch to exert their influence on the Siak kingdom. In 1858, the Netherlands East Indies government and Sultan Ismail signed a treaty in which the kingdom was subsumed under the rule of the Dutch colonial government (van Anrooij 1885: 270–1). Further treaties were signed during the late nineteenth century whereby the rights of taxation and some territories were handed over to the Dutch colonial government. In this process, the kingdom ceded Bengkalis Island, on which the government established its capital in 1875 to control the eastern coast of Sumatra (van Anrooij 1885: 308).[5] The Dutch government indirectly controlled the other areas through the Siak government. According to the treaties, the rights of taxation, such as import and export duties and passenger tax, were transferred from the kingdom to the government. This system of control continued until 1942, when the Japanese occupied the archipelago.

The early polity of the Siak kingdom was characterized by the '*kacu*-ness' of its population (Barnard, T. 2003). As mentioned in the introduction, *kacu* means 'mixed' or 'not pure' in Malay (Barnard, T. 2003: 1) and implies the coexistence of the Malays and Minangkabau in the kingdom. After the sixteenth century, an increasing number of Minangkabau migrants flowed into the eastern lowlands from the western highlands and the Pagaruyung kingdom. This immigration was characterized by the pursuit of new trade–economic opportunities that connected the western highlands with the Malacca Strait.[6] They formed their settlements upstream on the Indragiri and Kampar rivers, and traded gold, pepper, and forest products such as camphor, bezoar, and benzoin,[7] and then tin (Andaya 2008: 88–91; Barnard, T. 2003: 12–18; Kathirithamby-Wells 1997). Raja Kecik is thought to have been one of these immigrants, and the immigrants strongly supported the establishment of the kingdom. People of Minangkabau descent formed the elite section of the kingdom, and intermarried with indigenous Malays in the eastern lowlands. For the Johor–Melaka Malays, who were seen as the true holders of the throne of the Malay state and as the 'pure' Malay population, the Siak kingdom was *kacu*. The elites of the Siak kingdom also recognized this. However, in the process of the state formation in the eighteenth and nineteenth centuries, the Minangkabau and the Malays formulated a combined identity as the 'Siak Malays' (Andaya 2008: 68–75; Barnard, T. 2001: 339–40).

Kacu also implies the actual diversity of the ways of life in the region, which has environments that include hinterland hills and vast forests, large rivers and their labyrinthine tributaries, long channels, tidal mangrove swamps, and numerous islands and inlets. Such a complex geography sustained diverse ways of life and the mobility of the population, including the Minangkabau, the Malays, and other forest and coastal dwellers (Barnard, T. 2003: 2–3). The Siak kingdom required a state system to integrate and control such diverse populations and geographic environments.

Based on this *kacu* population, the kingdom established a hierarchical structure of the polity between the eighteenth and nineteenth centuries. An official of the Dutch colonial government, Hijmans van Anrooij (1885: 311–53), describes the situation in detail. The population was divided into two categories under the sultan—the sultan's subjects and the *empat suku* (or four clans), who were the people of Minangkabau descent and the elites of the kingdom. Their headmen or *datuk* were regarded as contributors to the state establishment and enjoyed a position equal to that of the sultan. They controlled their subjects, most of whom had their roots in western Sumatra, and, with almost complete economic and political autonomy, were obliged to support the military affairs of the kingdom.

The remainder of the population came under the sultan's rule and was divided into three classes—the *anak raja*, *hamba raja*, and *rakyat raja*. The *anak raja* (king's children) were literally the sultan's kinsfolk. Although they possessed high titles and constituted the noble class in the kingdom, their economic and political power was not substantial. The *hamba raja* (king's subjects) were the ordinary citizens of the state, the Muslim Malays who were loyal to the sultan. While they had various rights in terms of land possession and fishing, they were obliged to pay taxes and were under the sultan's control. The third class, the *rakyat raja* (king's folk), was the lowest class in the state, and kept their traditional headman, or *batin*. This category was further subdivided into two classes—the *rakyat tantera* and *rakyat banang*.[8] The *rakyat tantera* were 'nominal' Muslims who had converted to Islam a short time earlier and included the Orang Talang (the present-day Petalangan) living in the forest of Pelalawan region; the Rakyat Laut (the Orang Suku Laut), who went back and forth along the coasts; the subjects of the four *batin* on Bengkalis Island (who are regarded as the ordinary Malays today); and so forth. The *rakyat banang* were non-Muslims; they were the Sakai, Akit, Utan, and Rawa. Because the *rakyat tantera* were Muslims, they were recognized as possessing the communal forest or *utan tanah*. However, because the *rakyat banang* were not Muslims, Islamic law considered the forests they inhabited as the sultan's possession.

Van Anrooij (1885: 324, 337) suggests that the boundaries between the *hamba raja* and the *rakyat raja* and those between the *rakyat tantera* and the *rakyat banang* were based on the degree of their belief in Islam. Yet religion is not an exclusively significant criterion to decide the people's position. Although religion was part of the polity, it was not one of its foundations (Barnard, T. 2001: 333, Colombijn 2003a: 510–11). Given the fact that the highest class, the *empat suku*, obtained its privileges through contributions to the state establishment, its contributions seem to have been much more important than religion. Thus hierarchical classifications were based on the communities' loyalties and contributions—that is, the degree of subordination—to the state.

While the vertical boundaries reflected the degree of subordination to the state, the horizontal categories were established based on the region where the people lived. The kingdom legitimated local headmen of the communities as formal headmen in the polity and controlled the population through them. The *Bab Al-Qawa'id*, which was published in 1903 and codified the polity of the Siak government, addressed the headmen of each region in the kingdom (see Junus 2002: 69–76). The kingdom legitimated around two hundred headmen, and they had various titles such as *datuk, penghulu,* and *tua-tua*. These titles were addressed in sets, including a placename and the name of a community. The subjects of each headman were referred to as the headman's '*anak buah*,' which means nephew and niece (or, more broadly, collateral descendants, in Malay) (van Anrooij 1885: 288). In the net of vertical and horizontal boundaries created by the state, people who lived in peripheral inland and coastal forests gradually became marginalized from the people subordinated to the state during the two centuries of the Siak kingdom and the Dutch colonial government. In his voyage diary in the mid-nineteenth century, J. S. G. Gramberg (1864: 503–04), a Dutch official, presented the poverty of the Utan living around Bengkalis Island in terms of their clothes and houses. Their marginalization in relation to the Malays was already clear.

Although van Anrooij describes the position of the *rakyat raja*, especially the *rakyat banang*, as marginalized and discriminated against in the state hierarchy, they were not marginalized or discriminated against in a simple and fixed fashion. First, while the social structure was a hierarchical one, the boundaries of each class were vague and fluid; people could move to different categories through conversion and marriage. Indeed, some Utan living on Tebing Tinggi and Rangsang islands converted to Islam and obtained the status of the *rakyat tantera* before the end of the nineteenth century (van Anrooij 1885: 353). In the same way, the subjects of the four *batin* on Bengkalis Island, who had been seen as *rakyat raja* in the Siak kingdom, have called themselves (and been seen as) ordinary Malays or *hamba raja* since before the independence of Indonesia. Second, *rakyat raja* were essential to the rulers' authority in the state. The state and the various populations had much respect for the *rakyat raja* owing to the strong supernatural powers or *ilmu* (magic) they were believed to possess. The rulers of the Siak kingdom tried to absorb their supernatural powers through trade relations and marriage and to use it as a part of their charismatic authority, or *daulat* (Andaya 2008: 216; Barnard, T. 2003: 27–9; see also Chapter 5). Finally, although Islamic law did not recognize the land rights of non-Muslims (i.e. the *rakyat banang*), their rights were recognized to some extent at the local level. For example, according to Suku Asli elders, when the Javanese migrated into the area in which the Utan lived, they had to ask the Utan headman for permission to live in the area (see also Chapter 3), which means that their customary land rights—as indigenous people who were thought to have lived in the region before the state formed—must have been respected at the local level to some extent. Interestingly, although the *empat suku* were the elites of the state, they did not possess the communal forests because they were immigrants from western Sumatra and were not indigenous to this region (van Anrooij 1885: 317).

Suku as a regional political unit

In the Siak polity, the concept of *suku* played an essential role. At present, for general city dwellers this term implies 'tribe' or 'inferior culture' of rural areas (Benjamin 2002: 16–17; Wilkinson 1957: 1129–30). However, in the Siak kingdom the term clearly differed from the negative implication. In fact, '*suku*' was used with the meaning of 'clan' or 'community' in the *Bab Al-Qawa'id*,[9] and the elites of the kingdom (i.e. the *empat suku*) were also referred to as '*suku*.' The term was used to indicate local communities neutrally as a political unit under a headman, and even now is often used without any negative connotations not only by *orang asli* but also the Malays, Javanese, and Minangkabau in the rural areas of Riau.

The term '*suku*' would have been introduced to the Siak polity by the Minangkabau immigrants from western Sumatra.[10] According to Joel Kahn (1993: 155–60), the Minangkabau term can be translated as 'clan,' which is characterized as being matrilineal. In Minangkabau communities, *suku* was the basic social, political, and regional unit. Each *suku* had a collective name and a single *panghulu* (headman),[11] who, in the colonial era, controlled the selling and buying of paddy fields. The fields were regarded not only as the individual property of a female, but also as common property of the *suku* members as a whole.[12] Based on this idea, the Minangkabau elites in the Siak polity would have adopted the term '*suku*.' The kingdom established categories based on the (imagined) kin group as *suku* that was composed of the *anak buah* of a headman, gave collective names to each *suku*, and legitimated the control of their territory. By doing so, it controlled the population and obtained commodities harvested in the forest. The local headmen were granted the right to control their communal forest as a territory. In this process, the Malays and *orang asli* groups living in coastal areas, who had a bilateral or non-lineal descent system, would have been categorized as *suku*, even though they did not have a matrilineal clan. In any case, the people who lived in peripheral forests and coasts were integrated and differentiated as the regional political unit of the *suku* under the Siak polity.

In this period, the kingdom was interested in not only controlling labor but also territory as a result of the influences of the VOC and the Dutch colonial government (cf. Duncan 2004a: 6–7). In accordance with this shift in interests, the kingdom would have needed to control the ports and settlements, where it could control the population and obtain regular taxes, as well as the peripheral coasts and forests where people lived. The kingdom tried to control such peripheral areas as its territory by legitimating the people living in the areas and maintaining the boundaries with other kingdoms (Porath 2003: 15). In this process, to control the population easily and effectively it was essential for the state to array the population on the map and characterize them by giving them collective names (Scott 1998: 1–83). *Orang asli* groups were also given collective names and headmanship based on the regions that they inhabited as the regional political units of Siak polity.

In designating boundaries on the criterion of region in this manner, the Siak kingdom ignored the people's social and cultural boundaries, communication, heterogeneity, or homogeneity. As a result, the horizontal boundaries among the people were very flexible. This was especially the case among the people living in the coastal islands, who frequently moved from place to place via the sea, channels, and rivers. Thus, not surprisingly, some Dutch observers, who would have been interested in the social and cultural characteristics of *orang asli* groups, emphasized their lack of understanding of the differences between the Akit, Utan, Rawa, and others. For example, van Anrooij (1885: 352) pointed out the vague distinction and significance of mobility between the Utan, whom the Siak kingdom had regarded as living in islands around the Siak estuary, and the Rawa, who were regarded as living around Rawa River in mainland Sumatra, as follows: 'There seems to be no essential distinction between them. At least, the Rawa are the Utan living along and near to Rawa River. They are going back and forth, sometimes from the mainland to the islands of the opposite shore, and then to the mainland again.' J. Tideman (1935: 14) also addressed his supposition that the Rawa might be another name for the Akit. He also stated that the Utan in the Siak kingdom were the same people as the Mantang (Orang Mantang) living in the present-day Kampar regency, who are regarded as a regional group of the Orang Suku Laut (Chou 2010: 6–7).

In addition, Hans Kähler (1960), a German ethno-linguist, refers to the heterogeneity of the people called the Utan. Kähler visited the two Utan villages of Tandjung Səsap and Djanggut on Tebing Tinggi Island in 1939 and, in a few pages, sketched the customs (such as marriage, funeral, pregnancy, and circumcision) of each village. The important fact is that he divided the descriptions of the two villages into different sections, and described different cultural practices. Furthermore, the vocabularies of the two villages he recorded in his book differ to some extent. The kingdom would have attempted to reduce such unintegration and heterogeneity among similar and mobile populations into the category of the Utan in order to govern them more easily and effectively through the hierarchical and regional political structure.

The term '*suku*,' which is used in the present ethnonym Suku Asli, was formulated in the Siak kingdom. Although this term may be used to imply 'backward and primitive tribal people' in modern Indonesia, it was a regional political unit based on kinship or a class of the state hierarchy rather than ethnicity in a primordial fashion. The unit of *suku* was not always concerned with cultural and social boundaries. 'Suku Utan,' 'Suku Akit,' and 'Suku Rawa,' which have often been used to indicate them, are the collective names articulated and imposed by the state for regional distinction of the units, despite the fact that their social and cultural boundaries were vague and fluid.

The process and degree of subordination

The implications of the state's imposition of collective names on *orang asli* groups in the Dutch colonial records correspond with the oral history of the Akit. The Akit living in Rupat recognize that a sultan of the kingdom gave them the collective names 'Akit' and 'Utan' and their territories. They have a relatively detailed oral history about their immigration to Rupat, subordination to the kingdom, and receipt of their collective names.[13]

Akit ancestors came to this island somewhere *dari timur* (from the east).[14] They frequently moved from place to place by canoes, and eventually entered the territory of the Siak kingdom. However, animals such as tigers and elephants were a threat, so they moved to Padang Island and lived there for a while, but they were still threatened by wild animals, so they moved again. They found a safe place on Rupat Island, which the Orang Rempang already inhabited.[15] The Orang Rempang agreed to concede the land in exchange for gifts of silver and gold. As the ancestors did not have such gifts, they went to Bukit Batu and asked the Datuk Laksamana (a Malay title of the Siak kingdom) to support them. He accepted their request but asked them to support the construction of an *istana* (court) at Bukit Batu in exchange for the gifts. He divided them into three groups for labor as follows: the group that cut down the trees in the forest—the Suku Utan (the group of the forest); the group that made rafts using the timbers and transported them to the destination—the Suku Akit (the group of the raft); and the group that constructed the paths and cleaned the rivers for timber *mehatas* (transportation)—the Suku Hatas (the group of the *hatas*). After completing the labor, they received the gifts from the Datuk Laksamana and obtained the land in Rupat. The sultan of the kingdom also recognized their right to live in the place. Suku Akit obtained the area 'upstream' of the Morong Channel, which penetrates Rupat Island; namely, the present-day village of Hutan Panjang. Suku Hatas took the area 'downstream'; namely, the present-day Titi Akar. (These groups live in Rupat and both groups identify themselves as the Akit today.[16]) Suku Utan received the place of Tanjung Padang on Padang Island, or, in a different version, Bantan, the northern coast of Bengkalis Island. The state legitimated their *batin* headmen and they have since lived in these respective territories.

These events occurred at the turn of the nineteenth century,[17] but the extent to which the oral history reflects historical facts is uncertain because it does not explain the origin of the Utan living in distant places such as Rangsang and Mendol islands. In addition, a different view of the origin of the name 'Akit' is based on their custom of building a house on a raft.[18] It seems probable that there were similar but distinctive *orang asli* groups around this region. As part of the process of state control, the state exerted its control to these people and re-allied the populations, giving them either the name of 'Akit' or 'Utan,' which would have been ambiguously used to indicate coastal or forest dwellers. What is certain is that the Akit in Rupat and part of the Utan or Suku Asli at present in Bengkalis recognize that they obtained their position as *suku* in the kingdom, their territory, and collective names through these events.

The peoples of different regions would have also been subsumed under the control of kingdoms in more or less similar ways. Nevertheless, the degree of subordination to the kingdom varied. For example, the people who lived in the inland forest of the Pelalawan kingdom and conducted the slash-and-burn cultivation of dry rice were subsumed under the polity accepting the name 'Orang Talang'—'*talang*' refers to a settlement or space in the forest (Hamidy

1987: 22–3)—and had somewhat closer relations with the kingdom than other forest and coastal dwellers. They regularly paid taxes for rice and beeswax to the state, and they converted to Islam relatively earlier (van Anrooij 1885: 337–42). The Pelalawan kingdom recognized their *pebatinan* (district; chiefdom) as their customary territory (Effendy 2002: 369; Masuda 2012: 246–8). At present, they essentially identify themselves as Malay (Masuda 2012: 60–2).

In addition, the people on the upstream Mandau River, a tributary of the Siak River, were called 'Orang Sakai.' While there are many views on the sense of '*sakai*' (Porath 2002b: 98–100), it implied 'slavery and debt bondage' in the past (Porath 2003: 4; see also note 5 in Introduction), and forest dwellers in different regions of the Malay world are often referred to by the same collective name (Porath 2000: 177). They were important to the Siak kingdom in terms of military affairs because they lived sparsely in the boundary area between the Siak and Rokan kingdoms. Although the Orang Sakai engaged in trade, they were under less control from the Siak kingdom and they rarely paid the taxes that they were obligated to pay in the form of forest products (van Anrooij 1885: 347–50; Porath 2003: 1–25).

The degree of subordination to the Siak kingdom of the Utan, Akit, and Rawa was almost the same as that of the Sakai, although they were obliged to supply timber to the sultan (van Anrooij 1885: 359) and the rule was reinforced regularly. At present, the Akit and Suku Asli do not seem to remember any regular taxation or corvée imposed by the state except for the corvée mentioned above and occasional tributary communication with the sultan (see Chapter 4). Although they lived near the seacoasts, where the state could access them relatively easily, the state control was limited as their settlements were scattered along the coasts and across the labyrinthine rivers covered by thick mangrove forests. The state was interested only in controlling the lands as territory for timber in this region rather than the population. Therefore, after the middle of the nineteenth century, the Siak kingdom established a system to obtain resources and taxes from Chinese and European enterprises, not the *orang asli*, as mentioned below.

Although this seems to be an unreliable census, van Anrooij (1885: 358–60) provides population numbers of Sakai, Akit, Rawa, and Utan in the late nineteenth century: the Sakai—4000 to 5000 people; the Akit in Rupat—around 200 people; the Rawa around Rawa River—from 20 to 130 people; and the Utan—about 200 people on Padang Island, 300 people in Merbau, and 600 to 700 people on both Tebing Tinggi and Rangsang islands.

The *orang asli* communities did not always accept the collective names because the state-designated categories were exonyms used by outsiders. On the one hand, the Akit accepted the name 'Orang Akit' relatively early, and appear to have used the collective name without resistance, together with *orang asli*, to date. On the other hand, the Sakai identified themselves as *Orang Batin* (people under the headman) in the past, and refer to themselves as *orang asli* or *orang kampung* (village dwellers) at present. Porath (2002a: 771, 2003: 3–4) identifies them as 'upstream Mandau people' when he mentions them before the 1960s, since they accepted the collective name 'Orang Sakai' only after this period. In a similar way, the people called 'Orang Utan' on Bengkalis Island resisted being called this because the expression was directly connected not only with forests but also with apes. They called themselves *orang asli* or even 'Orang Akit' when they needed to use their collective names, while accepting the status or class of Suku Hutan in the state polity (see also Chapter 2 and Chapter 4).

Although the acceptance of collective names varied, it should be noted here that some groups have adopted the names. In recent years, they have claimed their rights under the banner of the provided name (e.g. Porath 2000), which means that the names are associated with their indigenous identity. The ethnic categories and collective names were articulated by the state, but can change into something empirical and unconscious related to their place through history—that is, something related to their indigeny.

Early records of the Utan and involvement in trade

Although *orang asli* political communication with the state was rather limited, their life was far from isolated. Their connection with the state in the economic sphere was continuously maintained, as they engaged in trade. In the mid-nineteenth century, some European writings mentioned a group called the Utan as the suppliers of sago and forest products. The 15 February 1827 issue of the Singapore Chronicles mentions the Utan living in 'Appong,' present-day Mendol Island (see Map 1):

> At Appong the Sago is made by Orang Utan, or people of the woods—who speak a jargon of Malayan, are not Mahometans [Mohammedans], and eat the hogs, deer, &c. with which their island abounds and the maritime malays who visit them for sago, are obliged to be always upon their guard, and not unfrequently wait 2 Months for a cargo...if they take money to purchase they get it much quicker, but require additional caution in making advances. There are said to be about 350 souls, and that the produce might be put down at 3000 piculs a year.—The most of these people are dependants of Siak and Campar, the Chiefs of the former place exercising a system of extortion and rapine enough

> to induce any other class of people less accustomed, to desert the place.—The cultivators in the other places are Malays and much superior, tho' their exports are severally less—and trafficking with them is not so dangerous or uncertain.

As far as I know, this is the first account that mentions the 'Orang Utan' living on the islands of the estuary areas of the Siak and Kampar rivers. Mendol Island is within the area that the Utan have historically moved around, and some present-day Suku Asli on Bengkalis Island have relatives and friends on this island. In addition, J. H. Moor (1837: 98) briefly describes the population living between Rangsang and Bengkalis islands, who were also engaging in the cultivation of sago:

> [These islands are] partly inhabited by Malays but chiefly by another race not yet converted to mahomedanism. Rantao [present-day Rangsang], a low marshy island, produces by far the larger quantity of raw sago which is imported into Malacca and Singapore, for the manufacture of pearl sago, and has become, within the last few years, so large and important an article of export to Europe. The unconverted race now mentioned, and not the Malays, are the sole cultivators and preparers of the sago.

In this article, the collective name of the 'unconverted race' is not mentioned, but it must be related to the Utan. In addition to sago, they engaged in the trade of forest products such as wild boar meat and the ivory of elephants and rhinoceroses (Barnard, T. 2003: 26).

The trade of various forest products with outsiders gradually converged in harvesting timber. In 1824, the Johor kingdom ceded Singapore to Britain, and Singapore rapidly became a prosperous trading center within Asia. The dramatic rise in the population led to an increase in demand for timber for the construction of buildings, so the eastern coast of Sumatra became an important supply center. The Siak kingdom granted the rights to harvest timber in its realm to Singapore at the beginning of the 1850s (Barnard, T. 1998: 94–5). This system is the *panglong* system—'*panglong*' means 'timber' in Hakka Chinese (Tideman 1935: 19; Barnard, T. 1998: 94) or 'enterprise' (van Anrooij 1885: 307). The term is still used in Suku Asli–Chinese society in Bengkalis, but it mainly means the 'charcoal hut,' which produces charcoal for export. In this *panglong* system, about one-and-a-half million hectares of forestlands along the eastern coast were designated as *panglong-gebied* (*panglong* area) and the Siak government designated the harvesting and export of timber to European and Chinese companies in Singapore and Bengkalis town (Masuda et al. 2016:

164–5; Tideman 1935: 3). In exchange, the government obtained taxes for each laborer sent by the companies. Almost all the laborers were Chinese men who were employed from southern China (van Anrooij 1885: 309; Tideman 1935: 18–20). As a result, many Chinese timber mills and laborers moved to the forest areas in this region. The immigration of ethnic Chinese was of such a large scale that the Siak government tried to regulate the number of immigrants at the end of the nineteenth century (Tideman 1935: 19–20).

The forests of the Utan, Akit, and Rawa territories were involved in the *panglong* area, probably because their land rights could be ignored according to the principle that the non-Islamic population could not possess land in the Islamic kingdom. After the Chinese companies penetrated their forests, the Utan, Akit, and Rawa were also employed as laborers. In exchange, they obtained cloth, iron tools, rice, and money from the Chinese merchants. The dealings involving timber for construction were gradually reduced in the twentieth century because of the Great Depression from the end of the 1920s (Tideman 1935: 21), the unrest caused by the Japanese incursion into Southeast Asia in the 1940s, and probably a reduction in the number of suitable large trees. Therefore, the timber trade diminished in the mid-twentieth century.[19] Instead, the importance of trade in charcoal, which is made from mangrove timber and exported to Singapore and Malaysia, has increased. Until very recent years, the logging of mangrove timber was the main source of cash income for most of the Utan or Suku Asli, Akit, and Rawa (see Chapter 3).

After the introduction of the *panglong* system, the *orang asli* in the Siak estuary established kinship and close economic and political connections with the ethnic Chinese. Some Chinese men married *orang asli* women, and are the ancestors of *peranakan* in present-day Suku Asli, Akit, and Rawa communities. According to Tideman (1935: 14), one of the *batin* headmen among the Rawa in the 1930s was an ethnic Chinese. The connection between the Suku Asli, Akit, and Rawa communities and the ethnic Chinese has been reinforced for a century, and formulated a specific ethnic identity and category in their society (see Chapter 2).

To sum up, in terms of the state control of the Siak kingdom and the Dutch colonial government, the state related to forest and coastal dwellers by employing them as laborers in the forests and on the coasts, and subsumed them under state control. The state gave them collective names, territories, and headmanships. Therefore, 'the Sakai,' 'the Akit,' 'the Rawa,' and 'the Utan' are ethnic categories given by the Siak kingdom while ignoring actual indigenous identification and practices. However, the categorization of populations in this period focused more on forming the state polity encompassing the *kacu* populations as a whole rather than on controlling the specific populations in peripheral and marginal locations. While the state succeeded in making the forest and coastal dwellers its subjects, it did not directly intervene in their lives except for the purpose of categorization and territorialization, and almost ignored the people. The people accepted the legitimatized territory and headmanship that were beneficial for them, but some groups did not accept the collective name. They maintained their autonomy or segmentation in relation to the state and retained their marginalized position while accepting the Chinese incomers through marriages. In this way, the relationship between tribal people and the state, characterized by economic connection and political separation, was maintained until the twentieth century, though their relationship was much reinforced under the rule of the Siak kingdom.

The relationship changed after Indonesia gained independence. The group and headmanship categories changed from regional political units or classes to become essential elements of the objectives of development programs in Indonesian government policies. As a result, the government began to intervene directly in their lives.

As the subjects of development policies

Formation of the nation state and *masyarakat terasing*

With a short period of Japanese occupation (1942–45) and the Indonesian War of Independence (1945–49), the archipelago declared independence in 1945 as the Republic of Indonesia and achieved it in 1949. Afterwards, Indonesia experienced regime changes, with Sukarno's Old Order (1949–67), Suharto's New Order (1967–98), and the present post-Suharto regime (1998–). The government of this vast nation state, which is divided by the sea and includes diverse populations, faced the necessity of integrating the rural populations into 'the Indonesians,' so it intervened in their lives under the banner of 'development.'

During the Sukarno and Suharto regimes, government policies were characterized by centralized sovereignty, and the government tried to control the local population, territory, and resources by claiming the priority of the state and ignoring the rights of the local populations. During the Sukarno regime, although the government tried to legally recognize the customary rights of rural communities based on the idea of the *adat* community that was formed during the Dutch colonial era, it failed to implement reforms because the bureaucracy was limited in its ability to exert authority in local areas (Li 2007b: 52–3; see also Chapter 5). For example, according to the Basic Agrarian Law of

1960 (No. 5/1960 on Basic Agrarian Principles), when customary land rights and national law contradicted each other, it was customary law that had to be amended. The state had the right to regulate and exploit all natural resources (Porath 2000: 182). It is also remarkable that the rise of anti-communism in the late 1960s brought about the reinforcement of control over peripheral areas. There were considerable government interventions in local societies because the government feared that the peripheral areas and their populations might become a hotbed for communism (Duncan 2004a: 8).

During the Suharto regime, the pursuit of centralized sovereignty was strengthened further. President Suharto took office in 1968 and referred to himself as the *Bapak Pembangunan* (Father of Development) (Heryanto 1988: 20–1). This 'development' meant, primarily, the 'modernization' of the state or rising economic profits and the construction of infrastructure. Under the development programs, many mines, oilfields, and industrial companies were established, and many roads, dams, plantations, and factories were constructed. The various development schemes were designed primarily to pursue economic profits only for the government and the limited number of people associated with it. When the government claimed to achieve more 'efficient' usage of land, many Indonesians in rural areas received no benefits, and even lost their ancestral lands (Li 2007b: 58). The Basic Forestry Law of 1967 (No. 5/1967 on Forestry Basic Provisions) provided legal standing for the state to designate the forest areas as state forest, and 143 million hectares of land (70 percent of the total land mass of Indonesia) was categorized as state forest in the 1980s (Moniaga 2007: 279). This law was generally interpreted as claiming that all rights over forest areas resided in the state (Henley and Davidson 2007: 11). In addition, this kind of development program had the purpose of 'civilizing' peripheral populations with the aim of limiting the influence of communism rather than raising the standard of living. Porath (2002a: 791) cites the following comment made about the regime by a Riau Malay intellectual: 'the Suharto government wanted the land without its peoples (*Riau tampa orangnya*).'

Under these development schemes, the government (mainly the Department of Social Affairs) set up the category of, first, *suku-suku terasing* (isolated tribes) and then *masyarakat terasing* (isolated communities) (Persoon 1998: 287–8). The purpose was to classify those people who lived in peripheral areas and were regarded as 'backward' and 'primitive' and to integrate them with 'rural Indonesians' (Duncan 2004a:1–5; Persoon 1998: 287–9; Porath 2010: 275). At first, few people who were living in extreme poverty were regarded as *suku-suku terasing*. In particular, the Kubu or the Orang Rimba in Jambi and the Mentawaians in the islands of West Sumatra were referred to as such people. The government implemented projects to improve their lives, though the impact was limited (Persoon 1998: 287). The number of *suku-suku terasing* dramatically increased between the mid-1960s and 1980; while it was estimated at 30,000 people in the mid-1960s, it increased to 1.7 million in 1980 (Persoon 1998: 288). In accordance with the increase, the category was changed to *masyarakat terasing* in the mid-1970s. These peoples were the main targets of the development programs implemented by the Department of Social Affairs.

It is remarkable that the categorization of *suku-suku terasing* or *masyarakat terasing* did not have strict criteria and was a product of government imagination (Persoon 1998: 289). Probably, the category was first established by the central government in a top-down fashion based on the image of the people in 'primitive' and 'backward' situations. Province and regency governments then reported some groups in their regions to Jakarta as *suku-suku terasing*. In this process, local governments seem to have identified the groups based on the category of local histories. They defined the people whom they had regarded at a tribal or marginalized position during the precolonial and colonial eras as *suku-suku terasing*, and ignored the people's actual economic situation, ways of life, self-identification, and changes. The dramatic increase in the number of *masyarakat terasing* seems to have resulted from this process. In other words, the precolonial and colonial categorization of people who were not subjugated to the state was inherited and consolidated by the categorization of *suku-suku terasing* or *masyarakat terasing* in post-independence Indonesia.

The local government of Riau designated the locals as *suku-suku terasing* or *masyarakat terasing*, clearly under the influence of the classification formed in the colonial era but not necessarily considering the people's actual economic situations and sociocultural boundaries and mobility. According to a report written by the Riau government in 2005 (Pemerintah Propinsi Riau 2005), the government recognized six groups as the KAT: the Akit, the Bonai, the Orang Suku Laut, the Utan, the Sakai, and the Talang Mamak.[20] The Talang Mamak and Bonai lived in the realms of the Indragiri and Rokan kingdoms, respectively, in situations similar to the people at the tribal position in the Siak kingdom, while the Malays were not included in the list at all, although some would have lived in similar economic conditions. As a result, although the *suku* system in the Siak kingdom was abolished, the colonial era hierarchical classification and the names of the groups have remained as the formal political category in postcolonial Indonesia, thereby transforming the people involved into the subjects of the development projects.

The main development project imposed on the people of the *suku-suku terasing* or *masyarakat terasing* was resettlement and the construction of houses (Duncan 2004b: 93–4; Persoon 1998: 290–1). The government brought together the forest dwellers living in sparsely populated areas, moved them to newly constructed settlements near the coasts or roads that were made accessible by the government, and encouraged them to establish a community as rural Indonesians. By doing so, the government could control them easily and effectively, obtain forest resources without any concern for the inhabitants, and prevent the rise of communism. In addition, the government encouraged many Javanese and Balinese, who were regarded as 'civilized' rural populations and lived in densely populated areas, to immigrate to the peripheral areas inhabited by *masyarakat terasing*. By doing so, the government could fill the population-devoid areas in the territory and bring 'modernization' and 'civilization' to the *masyarakat terasing* through communication between the migrants and the local populations.

In Riau, resettlement projects targeting *suku terasing* or *masyarakat terasing* were also rolled out. For example, just before independence, oilfields began to be established in the Mandau region, and the Sakai forests became a major oilfield. To access the oilfield, the Caltex oil company began to construct roads throughout the rainforest. Following the expansion of the oilfields and roads, North Sumatrans (the Bataks), Javanese, and West Sumatrans (the Minangkabau) migrated to the area and built settlements along the roads. Many Sakai sold their lands to such immigrants, and moved to the settlements near the roads that gave them easy access to various sources of income. The government often constructed settlements with Islamic mosques where the Sakai could pray together (Porath 2002a). In the same way, an oil company made a foray into the forest areas along the Rawa River between the 1980s and 1990s. The government and the company assembled hundreds of people who had previously been scattered through the forest and had been called the Rawa in the Siak kingdom, and constructed a new administrative village on the sea coast. Yet, in the islands of the Siak estuary, including Bengkalis and Rupat Island, the government did not conduct the resettlement of the Akit and Utan, although projects for Javanese immigration into these islands have been intermittently implemented since the 1970s (see Chapter 3). In addition, the government occasionally constructed dozens of new houses near the roads and coasts as small development projects for the Akit and Utan.

The people who were in the lowest class in the Siak kingdom were transformed into *suku-suku terasing* as the subjects of development programs in the government quest for control of the land and resources and 'civilization' of the people. The word '*suku-suku*,' the plural form of '*suku*,' simply shows their position in the state; the word refers to 'primitive and backward tribes,' rather than its neutral meaning in the Siak kingdom. Although the government category later changed to *masyarakat terasing*, *suku terasing* had been used to indicate 'primitive' and 'backward' people. According to Porath (2010: 270):

> as an ideological tool by which the nation-state interacts with tribal peoples, development gives the target group certain definitions of who they are *vis-à-vis* the rest of national society, who they should be and how they should achieve it. These definitions are rooted in the modernist's ideological mirror of primitivism and underline the more explicit developmental dichotomy of progressed *versus* not progressed and rich *versus* poor.

In short, their categorization and position were determined in relation to the 'civilized' ordinary Indonesians in the process of state formation after independence, much like the position of *orang asli* in relation with the Malays in the precolonial kingdom. However, the difference was this new political categorization involved, more or less, direct intervention in the people's lives. Through such interventions, the government tried to control them in a manner more suited to the agenda of creating the nation state in the modern world.

Post-Suharto era: *adat* community and tribal position

Since the end of the Suharto regime in 1998, government development policies have changed to 'decentralization.' New legislation and international support have provided opportunities for local communities, including people in tribal or marginalized positions, to govern the use of their resources locally, something that was impossible under previous regimes. For instance, between 1998 and 2003, the World Bank backed this movement by loaning Indonesia funds worth US$1 billion for the purpose of restructuring and empowering local communities 'damaged' during the New Order (Li 2007b: 230–1). As a result, some people in tribal positions, such as the Punan, Orang Rimba, Meratus, and Dayak, have been able to access new resources and social services (Erni and Stidsen 2006: 302–3; Wollenberg et al. 2009). The government is making efforts to raise the living standards of local populations and to provide education as to how they can achieve their desires and aspirations. This is a dramatic change in the government's attitude compared with the development projects in earlier periods.

Under these political changes, people who had experienced exploitation and marginalization during the older regimes began to organize local power to claim their right of autonomy, land, and resources. In particular, AMAN is the most influential organization focusing on matters of indigenous rights. This organization was established as an alliance of local communities in 1999 mainly by people living in Kalimantan. It rapidly developed over the archipelago and took the role of serving 'as an umbrella organization for the member organizations that would formulate specific programmes to carry out its demands' (Acciaioli 2007: 299). Lobbying for the recognition of local rights in Indonesian state politics, AMAN is at the center of the movement that tries to change government development schemes, and has begun supporting activities on behalf of local communities, including tribal and marginalized people. AMAN has provided local communities the chance to seek an increase in their livelihoods and establish their new position in the Indonesian state. Supported by AMAN, some local authorities and communities have been able to intervene in government development programs (which the government previously planned without consultation) to ensure that they receive the benefits (Henley and Davidson 2007: 1–7).

These movements have made remarkable progress in demonstrating the rights of an *adat* community. By adopting this concept, many activists and local authorities have tried to identify themselves as authentic Indonesian rural communities, and have tried to convince the government to legitimate their rights. The concept of an *adat* community is linked to the transnational concept of 'indigenous peoples,' which has been conceptualized at the international political level. AMAN required the government to deal with the rights of the *adat* communities according to international guidelines for indigenous peoples (Henley and Davidson 2007: 2–5) and to reinforce the legal position of '*adat* community,' and it succeeded in reflecting the concept of '*adat* law community' in some policies.

Although there are many problems and issues in terms of *adat* community rights, the government has also began to recognize—or, at least, give more respect to—'traditional' access to and maintenance of lands and resources among local communities. The government revised a series of national laws concerned with land use, such as the Basic Forestry Law, between 1999 and 2004 (Bedner and van Huis 2008: 184–90; Fitzpatrick 2007: 139–42), and the land rights of local communities based on *adat* were ensured in realms where they did not collide with the national laws and government policies. Furthermore, over the past several years, the government has sought to officially recognize *adat* law communities and grant them special status, rights, and entitlements. In 2012, a Constitutional Court decision (No. 35/PUU-X/2012) raised the legal status of *hutan adat* (*adat* forest), which has been used by an *adat* law community in relation to state forest designated by the Basic Forestry Law of

1967 and its successor, the Forestry Law of 1999 (No. 41/1999 on Forestry) (Warman 2014). In 2013, the Indonesian parliament discussed a draft law to recognize and protect the rights of *adat* law community,[21] in which five points were decided as the criteria for specifying an *adat* law community: to have a shared history as an *adat* community; to own *adat* territory or customary land; to have *adat* law; to possess *adat* property, relations, and artefacts; and to have a customary governance system (Hauser-Schäublin 2013: 10; see also Arizona and Cahyadi 2013: 56). These criteria were reflected in several pieces of legislation issued in following years. For example, the Village Legislation of 2014 (No. 6/2014 on Administrative Village), which reinforced the competence of administrative villages, also defines '*adat* law community.' This law defines an *adat* law community as one that maintains one or more of the following traits: it shares an identity as a group; it has a customary governance system; it has its own customary property or objects; it possesses customary norms (Abdurrahman 2015: 71–2).

These attempts to recognize the rights of an *adat* law community are ongoing. Although the draft law to recognize and protect the rights of an *adat* law community has been discussed continuously, as of the end of 2021 it has not been passed (see Nugraha 2019), and encroachment on customary land by the government and government-sponsored companies has not yet ceased (Mizuno et al. 2016). There have been tensions and conflicts between the state and the locals in terms of land rights in many regions, even after the government amended some laws. AMAN still challenges the government to provide recognition and support for the communities, especially in peripheral areas, and continues to increase its membership today.[22]

However, we can say for sure that the Indonesian state itself has been involved in its quest for *adat* communities. Within the politics of decentralization, the present-day government has begun to define the criteria of the *adat* law community and is creating and dispersing the image of it by conferring land rights to such communities. Therefore, the government is a powerful agent in the creation and integration of the *adat* law community idea, and the movement struggles cannot be reduced to a simple scheme of the state versus the locals. This is especially the case for some local communities that are not supported by national and international activists. In such situations, the locals have tried to create the social integration imagined by the state based on *adat* by (re)organizing their past relationships to related peoples, circumscribing their territories, reinforcing their local rules, facilitating rituals and arts, and empowering traditional political organizations.

In this movement, the public view of people in a tribal position has also been changing. They are regarded as not only having been exploited by state development projects in post-independence Indonesia, but also as clearly needing to maintain their 'traditional' ways of life and knowledge, or *adat*. Therefore, activists try to support them and protect their rights as a symbol of the movement. In accordance with the change, the KAT replaced the designation of 'tribal people' as *masyarakat terasing* in 1999 (Duncan 2004a: 91). '*Terpencil*' in the KAT title (Komunitas Adat Terpencil) is a synonym for '*terasing*,' but it implies political marginalization rather than geographic isolation. In addition, their traditional ways of life and knowledge, which have gone along with the natural environment, gained respect (e.g. Colombijn 2003b; Effendy 1997, 2002; Li 2001). Accepting to some extent the urgings of this movement, the government began implementing development projects for people in tribal positions with respect for traditional practices and beliefs.

In Riau, the position of *orang asli* groups changed in accordance with the rise of Malay ethno-nationalism. Riau province experienced exploration of land and resources by Jakarta and the mass immigration of Javanese and Minangkabau during the Suharto regime. After the fall of Suharto, local authorities and Riau Malay intellectuals, who included many local officials, tried to regain autonomy and self-determination based on Malay values and institutions. In this movement, they facilitated Malay ethno-nationalism by redefining local cultures and traditions as Malay *adat* (Colombijn 2003b: 343–51). *Orang asli* cultures and traditions were also redefined as part of Malay culture in this movement. For example, just after the Suharto regime, the Petalangan (or, as they were known in the past, the Talang) began claiming their ancestral land rights over the forest, which the government development projects were encroaching upon. Intellectuals in Riau began to be active in their support of this movement, and the Petalangan obtained subsidies and support from the local government and international foundations. In this process, their tradition and culture, which had been seen as different from 'civilized' Malays in the colonial era and ignored as a version of rural Malays in post-independent Indonesia, became recognized as a symbol of Riau Malay culture (Effendy 1997, 2002; Masuda 2009).

Similarly, the people at a more tribal position, especially the Sakai and Talang Mamak, have also been pushed to the fore in the local autonomy movement because they are considered to have maintained the culture and tradition that modern Malays have lost. The Sakai have been honored for their spiritual and environmental knowledge, and the Talang Mamak have been recognized as the maternal kinsmen of the king of the Indragiri kingdom

(Colombijn 2003b: 349). The Utan, Akit, and Rawa were not included in the mainstream of this movement, probably because they are not Muslims. In the rise of Malay ethno-nationalism, Islam is considered essential for regarding Malays as an integrated ethnicity, and Malay intellectuals do not emphasize the significance of non-Islamic *orang asli* such as the Utan, Akit, and Rawa. However, the local government may recognize their traditions and autonomy according to the changing political atmosphere.

Although the Sukarno and Suharto regimes wanted to integrate the 'primitive' and 'backward' people into the mainstream Indonesian population, successive recent governments have come to regard them as the ones who have maintained their respect for regional traditions or cultures. The government has begun to take a somewhat positive view of their autonomy and their social and cultural differences. In these policies, the government has begun configuring the image of *adat* communities and, in line with this image, has educated people's desires, aspirations, and habits. Accordingly, *orang asli* in Riau are beginning to positively demonstrate their position as *adat* communities or indigenous peoples, and to accept the support of the activists and the government.

In the post-Suharto regime, we can see the emergence of governmentality in government development interventions with tribal populations. During previous regimes, development projects took the form of large-scale exploitation of rural land and resources while ignoring the benefit of local communities. In addition, the government had tried to transform people in tribal positions into 'ordinary' rural Indonesians through resettlement while ignoring their traditional ways of life. These development projects seem to have directly restricted and reformed the behavior and knowledge of local populations. In other words, the government tried to control people's conduct. In addition, the government affirms and respects the local autonomy based on *adat* and tries to embed the people in the polity that maintains it. As a result, local communities, including people in tribal positions, have positively pursued the improvement of their livelihood and their position in local and state politics. In other words, echoing Foucault's definition of governmentality, the government has come to control the 'conduct of conduct' of the people (Li 2007b: 12–13). Therefore, recent development schemes planned by the government and NGOs appear to include a governmental ethos that was ignored in the past.

This governmentality does not affirm all kinds of autonomy and rights among locals. The autonomy and rights that the government may permit are only what fits the government image of a local community—that is, an *adat* community. In an *adat* community, individuals should share the thoughts and practices inherited from their ancestors and so maintain historically continuous and harmonious social connections (see Introduction). Only when the people can show this 'traditional' character of their community can they obtain economic and political benefit. Thus, in the new policies, demonstrating historical continuity as an *adat* community is becoming increasingly important for local communities. In this arena, culture and identity emerge as important factors in order to be recognized as an *adat* community. For example, among the Dayak people in Malinau in East Kalimantan, actors at the regency level are creating new links with other regency and village actors, and, by doing so, are trying to consolidate their power and demonstrate their traditional rights to natural resources. The basis of these links is their Dayak identity; thus 'ethnicity has come to play a more important and political role in how people define and align themselves *vis-à-vis* others' (Rhee 2009: 46–56). However, it is often difficult for people in a tribal and marginalized position to do this. First, most of the people did not have literary records until recent years, and it is impossible to show a written record of their history. Second, the people often have heterogeneous social structures in which *adat* is diverse, and their communities are often far from politically and culturally integrated (Li 1999). This differs from the image of an *adat* community that the government seems to demand.

Despite such difficulties, the people have begun configuring the image of a historically continuous community. In this process, they are trying to conceptualize and elaborate their *adat*, choose and declare their identity, and designate and claim their territory. By doing so, they can fit the government image of an *adat* community and try to obtain a certain legitimated position in state politics. Governmentality is stimulating local agency to affirm people's position in a way acceptable to the government's view. Thus the people are adopting and demonstrating their position as an *adat* community—that is, indigenizing themselves in accordance with the image created in the government imagination of how they should be. In other words, their conduct needs to be 'traditional' and 'indigenous.' However, this is not a passive process, and they exert their agency in between indigeny and state governmentality. As Adam Tyson (2010: 4) states, 'Becoming indigenous is not only instrumental and ephemeral, but also...based on conviction and the sustained capacity for self-improvement.'

In summary, the state has taken an essential role in the formation of a tribal or *orang asli* position in eastern Sumatra. In the long historical process, the Malay identity was linked to subordination and loyalty to the precolonial state, and people who did not adopt the identity—that is, 'non-Malays'—gradually formed a tribal position. During the eighteenth and nineteenth centuries, the state fixed the ethnonyms and territories of the non-Malays and embedded them in the polity, but left them as they were for economic and political reasons. After the independence of Indonesia, the state designated them as needing to develop their way of life and to become ordinary rural Indonesians. In this process, the state adopted the precolonial and colonial ethnic categories, and the tribal position was fixed. However, in the recent decentralized regime, their position has begun to be respected and honored as a symbol of autonomy and tradition connected with the concept of an *adat* community. Peoples in tribal positions, who had been seen as 'primitive' and 'backward,' have been increasingly regarded as indigenous peoples, which, by implication, involves people whose rights should be protected.

It is remarkable that ethnicity among *orang asli* groups is deeply related to the ethnic category that the Siak kingdom developed and imposed in its politics and economy. Also remarkable are the meanings of development that the post-independence government attached to their ethnicity. Because these categories and meanings come from the imagination of outsiders, the images are simplified and do not always coincide with the actual practices, thoughts, and aspirations of the people themselves, who actually have an indigenous and ethnic identity inherited from their ancestors—that is, indigeny. In any case, their attempts to show the position of their *adat* community in present-day Indonesian politics are very recent as they involve the problematization of their indigenous and ethnic identity and the embodiment of the *adat* community reality that the government imagined.

Chapter 2

Identity as Non-Muslims: *Orang Asli*, *Peranakan*, and Ancestral Worship

Despite government-designated ethnic names and imagined categories for the purpose of control, the Utan, Akit, and Rawa have their own understandings of who they are and an understanding of their historical and practical experiences—that is, non-articulated, subjective, and unconscious identities embodied in and through their practices and languages. The main issue of this chapter is to explore such categories and identity at some remove from the government categories.

The Suku Asli are basically those who were called the Utan in the government categorization scheme. In 2006, the government recognized the change of ethnic name from 'Utan' to 'Suku Asli' as a result of activities by their ethnic organization (for this process, see Chapter 4). The term '*suku asli*' is equivocal. Its literal meaning in Indonesian is 'indigenous people' or 'indigenous tribe,' with the same meaning as '*orang asli*.' Indeed, the Suku Asli may use this term to indicate any indigenous or tribal people in Indonesia and in the world. However, this usage is rare and is unrelated to their identity. When they use it with the implication of identity, it mainly indicates three different categories of people. First, in the broadest sense, it has the same meaning as *orang asli* living around the estuary area of the Siak River. The Utan, Akit, and Rawa are included in the term, and they use it to distinguish themselves from the Malays, Javanese, and so on.[1] Second, it indicates the people who were called the Utan, which the government recognized as KAT and which I explore in this book. In this usage, Suku Asli are one of the *orang asli* groups and are distinguished from the Akit and Rawa. Third, in the narrowest sense, it is used to distinguish the 'real' from *peranakan* Suku Asli within Suku Asli communities. In this context, 'Suku Asli' indicates the 'real' Suku Asli, and its antonym is '*peranakan*' (the people who are the descendants of Chinese men and Utan women). The ambiguity of the term 'Suku Asli' seems to derive from the fact that it is a relatively new term that has been adopted in recent political engagements.

It is not a complex matter, however, for the Suku Asli to show who they are. If asked about the essence of being Suku Asli, they tend to emphasize their connections based on *nenek moyang* (ancestry), which they express in the phrase, '*Nenek moyangnya sama*' (We have the same ancestors). This view elicits an analysis that Suku Asli have been integrated by common ancestry. However, in considering their actual practices in detail, we find that their identity does not really depend on their ancestry. In general, they do not care about actual genealogies when distinguishing 'us' and 'others,' and they categorize people with different ancestry as Suku Asli. If this is the case, how have they distinguished 'us' and 'others' and maintained their differences from the other ethnic groups around them? This question is related to their actual practices and thoughts of ethnic and indigenous identity. In this chapter, I explore Suku Asli identity and categorization in terms of ethnicity as it was formed outside the state's definitions.

Identity and the category of Suku Asli

'We have the same ancestors': the Suku Asli, Akit, and Rawa

Let me start with a description of conversations with one of my friends in 2012. One afternoon, I talked with Odang while sitting on a bench on the front terrace of his house. In Suku Asli houses, one or two benches are usually fixed on the front terrace. In this space, one can feel the breeze, so the Suku Asli often use the front terrace for handiworks, cooling off, and chatting with neighbors. It was the most comfortable place for me to chat with people and it was my routine every afternoon, while riding a motorcycle on a paved road, to look for a person sitting on a front terrace so that I could talk with them.

As I have mentioned, Odang was a famous shaman or *dukun* in the village. He was a 'real' Suku Asli, who did not have Chinese ancestors, and he had much knowledge of *adat* and took the role of the *kepala adat* (*adat* manager) in the Teluk Pambang branch of IKBBSA. Although he was an incumbent of IKBBSA, he was not involved in the political activities of the ethnic organization. He was frank and friendly, and I especially relied on him as his views and opinions seemed to reveal actual life among Suku Asli.

On that day, I had a question prepared in advance. I began explaining my experience to him. During my fieldwork among the Akit in Rupat, I had heard their oral history, according to which the Akit and Utan were originally the same group until the sultan divided them into different groups. As I discuss in the introduction to this book, Odang recognized that his people were '*Orang Utan*' in the past, so I used the term frankly. After talking about their oral history, I asked him whether he thought that the Suku Asli and Akit had the same ancestors. He answered, 'Right, I know that the Akit have such a story. Maybe, it is true.' As his daughter had married a man living in Rupat, he knew the history. He continued:

> But what I heard from elders is slightly different. According to them, our ancestors lived in the Rawa region. Then they moved to islands such as Bengkalis and Rangsang. Some of them moved to Rupat, and they are the Akit. Probably, that story was created when our ancestors were moving. Anyway, we have the same ancestors.

According to him, after their ancestors moved to Bengkalis Island, they were recognized as Utan by the Siak kingdom. He estimated that the period was some one hundred years ago.

Both the Suku Asli and Akit recognize that they have the same ancestors. This view is not only based on the oral history but also on their historically continuous practices. Present-day Suku Asli, Akit, and Rawa have many anecdotes of individuals moving between distant communities in the recent past. For example, according to Akit people, a former *batin* headman of the Akit in Rupat who lived around the beginning of the twentieth century was an Utan from Bengkalis Island. Also, a Rawa stated that the Utan headmen on Tebing Tinggi Island had frequently visited the Rawa region in the past. This was also relevant to Odang's life history. He was born in a village on Rangsang Island, which is approximately thirty kilometers east of Teluk Pambang, where most of the population was Suku Asli. Although he had been a fisherman in his home village, he was employed by a Chinese middleman, or *touke*, and engaged in logging and cargo work in several places. When he worked as a mangrove timber logger in Selat Akar, on the east coast of Padang Island, he became acquainted with a woman who was born in Teluk Pambang and was visiting a kinsman's house. He married her and they moved to Teluk Pambang at the end of the 1980s. He built a house on the land of her parents and still lived there. One of his daughters married an Akit living in Rupat. Other people have similar stories, and they have strong networks over the distant islands and beyond the ethnic categories of the Suku Asli, Akit, and Rawa. As a result, they seem to feel a deep connection that goes beyond the categories of Suku Asli, Akit, and Rawa.

In the same way, I asked Koding the same question as Odang, in which I presented the Akit story and asked about the origins of Suku Asli in Teluk Pambang. Koding was a *peranakan* Suku Asli, and his paternal grandfather was a Chinese laborer from Teochew.[2] His wife's sister was Odang's wife, and he was the father of Ajui, who was the *batin* headman of IKBBSA. He was born and has lived in Teluk Pambang all his life and knew the history of the village thoroughly. He was also a famous *dukun* in the village. He was usually working in the coconut garden around his house, so almost every evening, just before dinner, I visited his house and talked with him. I loved chatting with him—

sitting on the bench, having coffee, and smoking together in front of his house—as his talk about the past was fascinating.

Koding did not know the Akit story and regarded the Suku Asli in the village as being from the Rawa region. He said, 'The Akit work in *kerja bakau* (mangrove logging) just like Suku Asli, right? So, probably, they have the same ancestors with us.' He categorized the Akit as having the same ancestors based on their dependency on mangrove logging. Their oral history, historical moves, and engagement in mangrove logging create the flexibility of identity experienced among the Suku Asli, Akit, and Rawa.

Another day, I was talking with Odang again, and it was a chat about everyday things rather than an interview. In the conversation, he said his plan was to move to Rupat some years later and live in a house near his daughter. Hearing his plan, I somewhat jokingly asked, 'If you live in Rupat, are you Akit or Suku Asli?' He laughed at my question and considered it for just a moment. Then he answered, 'The Akit are also *orang asli*. So, it's the same. But it's okay to call me Akit if I live in Rupat. I have family there, and probably I may well become an Akit.' I asked, 'Does *orang asli* mean Suku Asli?' He laughed again and answered, 'Yes. They are *sama saja* (just the same thing).' He usually used '*orang asli*' to refer to Suku Asli.

His comments have some important points in terms of identity and group categorization. First, he stated, 'The Akit are also *orang asli*,' and he used '*orang asli*' in the same meaning as 'Suku Asli.' Indeed, in terms of the relationship between the categories of the Suku Asli, Akit, and Rawa, people often comprehend one category as another. Generally, the Suku Asli identify the Akit and Rawa with Suku Asli and call them 'Suku Asli.' However, the Akit in Rupat usually refer to Suku Asli and Rawa as 'Akit' and occasionally 'Utan,' especially in a historical context. In short, these categories are flexible and mutually inclusive. To indicate which people are intended, speakers usually use a set consisting of an ethnic name and a placename. For example, Suku Asli may call the Akit 'Suku Asli Rupat,' and Akit call Suku Asli in Bengkalis 'Orang/Suku Akit Bengkalis.' Second, and related to this, they tend to classify people based on the place where they live. Odang said, 'But it's okay to call me Akit if I live in Rupat.' During my fieldwork in Rupat, I met people who had been born in Bengkalis but identified themselves as Akit. A Suku Asli in Teluk Pambang said to me, 'Akit live in Rupat, Rawa live around Rawa River, and Suku Asli live in Bengkalis [and other surrounding islands].' Yet people who move from one place to another can easily change the name of the group that they belong to in accordance with the place. Therefore, their way of identification differs from the definition of KAT by the state.

The state defines the Suku Asli and Akit as different groups in the KAT, in which the people are seen as maintaining distinctive *adat* inherited from their ancestors and as being distinctive and independent ethnic groups. Suku Asli and Akit identities are much more flexible and decided by the place in which one lives. In other words, in terms of self-identification, the identities of Suku Asli (the Utan), Akit, and Rawa are regional—not ethnic—identities that may often be defined by sharing or not sharing descent and culture.

In addition, Odang's preference to use '*orang asli*' seems to imply his real feelings about ethnicity. He knew that 'Suku Asli' was a name recognized by the government, but that this name circumscribes the people within region and tradition. His identity related to ethnicity was more flexible and expansive, going beyond the Suku Asli, Akit, and Rawa. Many other Suku Asli also prefer '*orang asli*' to 'Suku Asli,' and Akit and Rawa people often identify themselves as *orang asli*.

In my fieldwork in Teluk Pambang and Rupat, as well as during my short trip to the Rawa region, I often asked about the relationship between the Akit, Suku Asli, and Rawa. While people often pointed out their cultural and historical similarities and differences or concrete kin relationships, they usually concluded with a similar expression to Odang's comment above—'We have the same ancestors'—in which they expressed the comradeship and connection among the Suku Asli, Akit, and Rawa. This image is backed by the fact that they have historically moved from one community to another and married with each other.

The categories and identities of Suku Asli, Akit, and Rawa do not have strict ethnic boundaries between them, and they distinguish these categories only on regional criteria. They recognize that they have the same ancestors and similar cultural traits. This means that they have a flexible and borderless identity that goes beyond the regional categories of Suku Asli, Akit, and Rawa—that is, *orang asli* identity—which can be seen as an ethnic identity. This identity has clear boundaries in relation to the Malays.

Boundary with Muslims

In Chapter 1, I described the historical relationship between *orang asli* and Malays, and how people subordinated themselves to state control and adopted the Malay identity—and how people who were not completely subjected to state control were *orang asli*. Therefore, the boundary must have been flexible and ambiguous in the first step of forming the categories. This explains the reason why *orang asli* and Malays share some cultural practices. For example, although there is some difference in vocabularies and pronunciations, the dialects of the Malays and *orang asli* are mutually intelligible. Also, the traditional instruments used in rituals, such as resin incense and *tepak sirih* (*sirih* boxes), and performances such as *silat* (Malay martial arts or dance) are common among them.

In the process by which the state implemented the hierarchical system in the nineteenth and twentieth centuries, the boundaries were gradually institutionalized and fixed. Van Anrooij (1885: 324) describes the communication between *hamba raja* (Malays) and *rakyat raja* (*orang asli* and part of present-day Malays) as follows: 'According to *adat*, *rakyat raja* are not allowed to eat together with *hamba raja*, and the latter do not give daughters to the former or obtain them from the former in marriage.'[3] This indicates that the Malays avoided communication with *orang asli* in the hierarchal system of the Siak kingdom.

The *orang asli* also institutionalized the avoidance of communication with the Malays, and their avoidance of marriage with the Malays at present clearly shows the significance of the boundary between them and the Malays. Today, marriages between Suku Asli and Malays are very rare. When I questioned some Suku Asli whether they permitted their children to marry Malays, their faces always showed embarrassment. Indeed, if a Suku Asli, either man or woman, marries a Malay, they are no longer regarded as Suku Asli. The person essentially lives as a Malay in the partner's Malay community, and communication with Suku Asli kinsmen and friends is limited.

One day, when talking with Odang, I asked him the reason why Suku Asli have rejected marriage with Malays. I pointed out that, to me, their culture and language seem to be mutually similar. Odang said:

> Maybe, Suku Asli and Malay ancestors are the same, and the Malays were also a kind of *orang asli* in the far past. However, their ancestors converted to Islam. This is different from our ancestors…Our ancestors were not Muslims, and we have never believed in Islam. The people who *masuk Islam* (became Muslim) have to throw away our *adat*. They do not respect Suku Asli ancestors anymore and have to leave the Suku Asli community.

His comments seem to clearly summarize how Suku Asli have distinguished 'us' and 'others' and maintained their differences. At first, Odang emphasized the difference in ancestry. Although he recognized the possibility that Suku Asli and Malays had the same ancestors in the remote past, he divided the ancestors into two—those who had converted to Islam and those who had not converted and, along these lines, regarded Suku Asli ancestors as different from those of the Malays. Although some other people insisted that their ancestors were completely different from those of the Malays, they generally claimed their difference from the Malays was because of differences in the ancestors' religion. In addition, they avoid marriage not only with the Malays but with Muslims. Indeed, they avoid marriage with the Javanese, who immigrated into this area at the turn of the twentieth century.

According to my survey of more than three hundred households of Suku Asli, Javanese, and Malays in the western part of Teluk Pambang, only two Suku Asli women had married Muslim men. They converted to Islam, and the Suku Asli said that they were no longer Suku Asli. Their communication with Suku Asli was extremely limited. In addition, in the case of a Javanese man who married a Suku Asli woman, the husband changed his *agama* registration to Buddhism and the Suku Asli recognized that he *masuk Suku Asli* (became Suku Asli). Therefore, what the Suku Asli have tried to avoid is the introduction of Islam into their community rather than marriage with Malays itself. This avoidance is a rigid one, and I met no Suku Asli who believed in Islam or had a spouse believing in Islam in Teluk Pambang.

Finally, Odang explained the reason why Suku Asli avoid marriage with Muslims. It is because people who marry Muslims have to abandon their *adat*, which in Suku Asli society indicates, first and foremost, rituals involving ancestral worship (see Chapter 5). Under Islamic law, the spouse of a Muslim has to convert to Islam (Clarke 2000: 287), thus Suku Asli regard those who marry Malays and Javanese as abandoning their *adat*. In other words, in Odang's comments, in order to be Suku Asli it is essential to follow their *adat*.

Avoiding marriage with Muslims is a practice held in common by the Suku Asli, Akit, and Rawa, and they generally provide explanations that echo Odang's comment. For them, the categories of *orang asli* and Muslim are different and mutually exclusive. Indeed, they strongly reject being called 'Malay' in spite of their cultural and linguistic similarity. Therefore, *orang asli* identity has a clear boundary in relation to the Malays and Javanese, which reflects their non-Islamic religious practices.

Along similar lines, generally for the Malays and Javanese in Riau, marriage with an *orang asli* partner is undesirable. This is because they perceive the *orang asli* as having strong supernatural power and knowledge of magic (Chou 2003: 52–72; Porath 2003: 108–09)—something that makes them dangerous. Indeed, Malays and Javanese living in the villages and towns sometimes asked me about the Suku Asli practices of magic and advised me to be careful. For them, a marriage is acceptable only when the *orang asli* partner has converted to Islam and abandoned his or her magical power and practices.

Interestingly, when compared with other *orang asli* groups around Riau, the boundary with the Malays and Muslims among the Suku Asli, Akit, and Rawa seems remarkably strong. As far as I know, all other *orang asli* groups, such as the Sakai, Orang Suku Laut, Orang Rimba, Bonai, and Talang Mamak, have accepted Islam and Malays to some extent, although they also have a history in which they more or less rejected Islam and marriage with Malays in the past. For example, in Sakai society, most people identify themselves as Muslim and see Malays as 'siblings' (Porath 2019a: 146). The term '*Sakai Melayu*' indicates the mixed ancestry between the Sakai and Malays (Porath 2003: 5). For them, being Sakai is not really exclusive in relation to being Malay and Muslim. Even if it is merely nominal, many *orang asli* in eastern Sumatra register their *agama* as Islam at the government administrative offices.

The boundaries with Islam and Malays among the Suku Asli, Akit, and Rawa communities seem to have been much weaker in the past than they are today. The fact that quite a few Utan communities converted to Islam before the mid-nineteenth century backs this assumption (see Chapter 1). Why has the boundary with Muslims and Malays been institutionalized in such a strong way only among *orang asli* society in the Siak estuary? This seems to be related to their connection to the Chinese and, furthermore, to the core of their ethnicity. I will return to this question in the last section of this chapter.

Relationship between the 'real' and *peranakan* Suku Asli

Peranakan Suku Asli or Akit

In the comments above, Odang emphasized the significance of maintaining *adat*. However, this does not mean that Suku Asli practices related to *adat* are culturally integrated or normative. On the contrary, their *adat* is often vague and does not encompass legal or judicial characters that are imagined in the concept of an *adat* law community. Furthermore, in their ritual practices of *adat*, some people distinguish their ancestry from other Suku Asli. Nevertheless, they regard *adat* as essential to distinguish Suku Asli and others. What is their *adat* and how do they distinguish 'us' and 'them'? These questions concern the relationship between the 'real' and *peranakan* Suku Asli.

My first encounter with a *peranakan* was during my fieldwork in Rupat in August 2006. I had visited the village of Titi Akar and stayed at the house of the village headman. The headman of the administrative village was an Akit, who had worked in the role for a long time and was respected not only by the Akit but also by the Javanese in the village. Shortly after I started living in the house, the headman's son-in-law, Adi, became my guide at the request of his father-in-law. He was about the same age as me, was very kind, and knew a lot about village life. More importantly, Adi could mercifully understand my poor Indonesian, and he soon taught me Indonesian and Akit dialect. At the beginning of my fieldwork, I was always with him. Around two months later, I attended an Akit funeral and that night I asked Adi about the funeral procedures I had witnessed. I asked detailed questions, and Adi became embarrassed and answered, 'I do not know because I'm a *peranakan.*' I asked him what '*peranakan*' meant, and he answered, 'It is *semacam orang Cina* (a kind of Chinese). I have Chinese ancestors.'

I was completely confused at Adi's words because I thought he was an Akit. I knew that in Titi Akar there were several ethnic Chinese living around a landing jetty who were traders and transported goods between Indonesia and Malaysia. Their houses were made of brick, they seemed to be wealthier than the Akit, and they spoke Chinese. Although there was no clear boundary between Chinese and Akit settlements, the houses of ethnic Chinese were concentrated around the jetty and those of the Akit were scatted over hinterlands. However, there did seem to be some social boundaries between them. The reason why I was confused was that none of the points above applied to Adi. He spoke Indonesian and Akit dialect but could not speak any Chinese, and his parents did not use the Chinese language. They were fishermen and I did not think that they were wealthier than other Akit. Furthermore, Adi had introduced me to several Akit but he had not introduced me to anyone in the Chinese settlement, which he only visited to buy necessities and to ship items. I asked him, therefore, if he was Chinese. He answered, 'No. I'm not Chinese. The Chinese live in the cities. I'm Akit, but I'm a *peranakan* Akit.' I asked, 'Are the people living around the jetty also Akit *peranakan*?' He said, 'Well, they are *peranakan* as well, but they are *peranakan Cina* (*peranakan* Chinese), not Akit.'

Through my fieldwork, I gradually learned the category of *peranakan* in Akit society and the relationship between the Akit and the Chinese. On commencing my fieldwork in Teluk Pambang, I found the categories and relationships in the village were the same as those of the Akit, the most common of which I describe below.

The formation of *peranakan* Suku Asli

The term '*peranakan*' in Malay originally meant 'local-born' or 'native' (Tan Chee-Beng 2004: 34; Wilkinson 1957: 27). However, in Indonesia, the term was specifically used for ethnic Chinese and indicated 'local-born Chinese' in relation to 'China-born Chinese,' as they were distinguished in terms of legal rights during the colonial era. Since Indonesian-born Chinese became the majority of the total Chinese population in mid-twentieth century Indonesia, the term has been used to indicate 'acculturated Chinese' with emphasis on the cultural sense (Suryadinata 1978: 2). In the twenty-first century, increasing numbers of ethnic Chinese prefer to identify themselves as *peranakan*, as this address includes the implication of being Indonesian (Reid 2009). However, the definition and identity of *peranakan* varies from place to place in accordance with the local situation of the Chinese, because the identity and category of *peranakan* has been generally formed by local relationships between the ethnic Chinese and native populations (Coppel 2013: 347).

On the east coast of Sumatra, *peranakan* describes, first and foremost, the mixed ancestry between the ethnic Chinese and Indonesian-origin populations such as Malay, Javanese, and *orang asli*. In general, while those who have only Chinese ancestors are referred to as ethnic Chinese (*Orang Tionghua*; *Orang Cina*), those who have both native and Chinese ancestors identify themselves and are identified as *peranakan*. The people I refer to as '*peranakan* Suku Asli' (*Suku Asli peranak*; *peranakan*) are part of those *peranakan* who relate to Suku Asli ancestors. While *peranakan* or *peranakan* Chinese may live in Chinese communities and maintain the Chinese language, the *peranakan* Suku Asli have generally lost the Chinese language and live in Suku Asli communities.[4] The only point that differentiates them from the 'real' Suku Asli (*Suku Asli*; *Suku Asli asli*; *Suku Asli betul*) is that they have maintained Chinese surnames inherited through the paternal line and conduct rituals in the *peranakan* or 'Chinese' way. It should be noted here that I find no special meaning in the adjective 'real' (*asli*; *betul*) when related to indigeneity. Only when I asked whether the person mentioned was *peranakan* or not did they identify it either with the expression '*Suku Asli asli*' or '*Suku Asli betul*' situationally. Usually, both 'real' and *peranakan* peoples identify themselves as Suku Asli and share almost all aspects of everyday life without any distinctions.

The emergence of the *peranakan* Suku Asli is related to the manner of Chinese immigration in this region. As I mentioned in Chapter 1, a mass Chinese immigration occurred through the state's implementation of the *panglong* system between the late-nineteenth and early-twentieth century. A large number of Chinese entered the rural forest areas on the east coast of Sumatra for the purpose of harvesting timber. In this immigration, two kinds of Chinese visited the forest where the Utan, Akit, and Rawa lived. First were the traders who formed settlements in some towns of eastern Sumatra or who were dispatched from companies in Singapore and Melaka. They mainly engaged in the management of harvesting forest products and their export. Their numbers were relatively small and most went back to their home areas after their work was complete. However, some settled in the rural areas and became local middlemen or *touke*. They had connections with trading towns and maintained social and commercial ties with the Chinese. The second kind comprised the many temporary laborers, or 'coolies,' who engaged in physical labor in the forest under the *touke*'s management. They were from various areas in southern coastal China and were exclusively men.

The Chinese migrants established trading posts on the banks of brackish rivers that had sufficient depth for ships and were near the hinterland forest. Some of these areas overlapped with the space where the Utan, Akit, and Rawa lived. The Utan and Chinese lived in the same or nearby settlements, and the middlemen often employed the Utan as laborers. Some Chinese laborers married *orang asli* women because the number of Chinese women was very small.

The Chinese laborers were transients who had temporary contracts with *touke* and the companies, and most of them left the forest areas after they completed their work. According to Suku Asli elders, some moved to Chinese communities in the region, together with their Utan wives and children. They lived as members of a Chinese community and their descendants maintained the Chinese language and culture. They are *peranakan* but are often referred to specifically as *peranakan* Chinese, and they did not have strong social ties with Suku Asli and spoke Chinese language within their family. There were also some laborers who went back to China or moved to Chinese communities, leaving their wives and children behind, and some laborers who settled in the forest areas together with the Utan and died there. In these cases, the children were usually raised by the mother and the mother's kinfolk in a matrilocal way. These children have married Utan or other *peranakan* living in the forest areas for some generations. My 2012 research revealed that many *peranakan* Suku Asli in their fifties to seventies had Chinese-migrant ancestors as their grandfathers or great-grandfathers. However, their marriages with the ethnic Chinese, who are usually *touke*, are relatively rare because *touke* are few in number and have a tendency to look for spouses among their Chinese connections. Through the repeated marriages, their physical appearance is the same as Suku Asli; they have lost the Chinese language and most of their Chinese culture, and they have engaged in the same economic activities as Suku Asli.

The Suku Asli distinguish descent based on the criterion of whether one has a Chinese *sei* (surname) or not. Conversely, the Utan have a bilateral kinship system and do not distinguish paternal and maternal kin in terms of kinship terminologies, marriage avoidance, and the right of inheritance. They prohibit marriages with bilateral kin, and one cannot marry anyone who in alleged to have any consanguineous relationship. This is still the case among present-day 'real' Suku Asli, and, naturally, they do not have surnames that signal one's specific descent. On the other hand, the ethnic Chinese have a patrilineal kinship system and distinguish paternal and maternal kin (Clarke 2000; Tan Chee-Beng 1982, 1988; Tan Yao Sua and Ngah 2013). The *peranakan* Suku Asli also have this system and have Chinese surnames passed through the paternal line. They prohibit the marriage of a couple who have the same surname even when they do not have any consanguineous relationship, but often allow marriage between cross-cousins. They also have kinship terminologies that distinguish paternal and maternal kin.

At a marriage between the 'real' and *peranakan* Suku Asli, the wife and the children follow the husband's custom. For example, when a woman with a surname marries a male without a surname, the female's surname disappears, and she and the children follow the marriage rule of the 'real' Suku Asli. When a male with a surname marries a female without a surname, the female acquires the husband's surname and she and the children follow the rule of the *peranaka*n Suku Asli. As these marriages have occurred frequently, all 'real' Suku Asli have close consanguineous or in-law kin among the *peranakan* Suku Asli, and vice versa. Every *peranakan* household recognizes its own Chinese surname. Suku Asli generally know that a household in their local community is either 'real' or *peranakan* Suku Asli.

There are *peranakan* in Akit and Rawa communities as well (*Akit/Rawa peranak*), and the number is sizable. According to my survey in Rupat and Bengkalis, 30 to 40 percent of all Suku Asli or Akit households had Chinese surnames. However, in Teluk Pambang, about 70 percent of all Suku Asli households had Chinese surnames.[5] The reason that this village shows such a high rate, according to villagers, is because there was a timber mill managed by an ethnic Chinese until the 1950s, and many ethnic Chinese continuously moved to this village from the towns of Bengkalis and Selat Panjang (on Tebing Tinggi Island), where there are large Chinese communities.

'Real' and *peranakan* Suku Asli are close kinfolk and intimate neighbors, and share almost all aspects of everyday life. Both have engaged in mangrove logging as their main livelihood and obtained cash income by supplying the timber to *touke* (see Chapter 3). When they need the support of other people, as in hunting and construction of buildings, they cooperate with each other without any distinctions associated with descent. They participate in each other's rituals and support their preparation, although, as I explore in detail in the next section, their practices differ. It is true that some *peranakan* Suku Asli are in a better economic position than the 'real' Suku Asli, as they have maintained relatively close social ties with *touke* and have been able to obtain work. However, it is also the case that the economic situation of many *peranakan* is almost the same as the ordinary 'real' Suku Asli.

Sharing Suku Asli and Chinese 'cultures'

Although the *peranakan* Suku Asli appear to have lost almost all Chinese language and identity, they have maintained their Chinese culture in some spheres. One such sphere is their kinship system and terminology. As mentioned above, the *peranakan* Suku Asli have inherited a patrilineal kinship system. While they prohibit the marriage of a couple with the same Chinese surname, they permit marriage between cross-cousins—although, in practice, this rule is much influenced by that of the 'real' Suku Asli.

As discussed in the introduction, Kiat was the head of my host family. He was a *peranakan* Suku Asli and had been born in the village. According to him, there had been quite a few cases of marriage with maternal kin among *peranakan* in Teluk Pambang in the past. However, at present, *peranakan* do not want to engage in such marriages because some have not gone well. According to him, such couples suffered divorce, infertility, or a child's death. Although he emphasized the failed cases, it seems more probable that *peranakan* in this village adopted 'real' Suku Asli bilateral marriage avoidance.

Interestingly, the marriage avoidance of the 'real' Akit differs from that of the 'real' Suku Asli; they prohibit marriages between paternal cousins and permit ones between cross-cousins, just like *peranakan* do. Although it is unclear whether the Akit acquired this marriage avoidance from their ancestors or adopted it from *peranakan*, it is a fact that marriages between cross-cousins are very common among both 'real' and *peranakan* Akit in Rupat.

In addition, the Suku Asli maintain Chinese kinship terminologies. They have two kinds of kinship terminologies derived from that of the Utan and Chinese, which are characterized by bilateral and patrilineal kinship systems, respectively (see Tables 2.1 and 2.2). Generally, it is said that the 'real' Suku Asli should use the Suku Asli way of kinship terminology and the *peranakan* Suku Asli should use the *peranakan* one. However, the terminology is used in a mixed way in practice. For example, Odang was called *akong* ('grandfather' in Chinese) by his wife's sister's son's children. I asked him why he was called by the Chinese term even though he was a 'real' Suku Asli. He recognized that it would have been better to refer to him as *nek* ('grandfather' in Suku Asli), but he stated that using the Chinese term was all right because '*akong*' was more useful than '*nek*.' According to him, while '*akong*' can clearly indicate 'grandfather,' '*nek*' indicates either 'grandfather' or 'grandmother' and is vague if used in conversation. He concluded, 'There are some ways to call family relatives in this village. The terms are different but the meaning is the same.' In addition, it is remarkable that, in the kinship terminology of *peranakan* (Table 2.2), 'real' Suku Asli terms are adopted in the forms of address of juniors in the same generation and descendants. This means that they maintain a Chinese form of address only for ancestors. According to them, this is because they need to respect elders and ancestors.

Another sphere that the 'real' and *peranakan* Suku Asli share is their religious practices and beliefs. In Suku Asli society, two kinds of specialists can directly communicate with supernatural existences. One is the shaman (*dukun, bomo asli*) derived from Utan culture. Shamans can be possessed by *datuk* (a type of spirit living in forests at the confluences of rivers and the headwaters of tributaries and controlling other spirits) and send their souls to distant places or the other world (see Chapter 4). The other specialists are the Chinese spirit mediums (*bomo cina, kiton*), who can be possessed by Chinese deities such as *Kwan tei* (Guan Yu) and *Kwat'im* (Guanyin), with Chinese costumes and instruments (Photographs 2.1 and 2.2). Both kinds of specialists hold séances to heal illness or pray for the peace of a settlement. Both 'real' and *peranakan* Suku Asli can become one or both of these specialists—indeed, there are many such people.

Sacred places are maintained by both specialists. Such places are called *keramat* in 'real' Suku Asli and *datuk kong* in Chinese.[6] Around the Raya River of Teluk Pambang, four *keramat* were inherited from Utan ancestors, which were managed by *dukun*. Three were also used as shrines for Chinese deities, and *kiton* also joined in the management of these places. While both expressions are still used in Teluk Pambang, calling the sacred places *datuk kong* is more usual than *keramat*, even among 'real' Suku Asli. However, there were many *datuk kong* in which only Chinese deities were enshrined in Teluk Pambang because *peranakan* households may establish their own *datuk kong* at the corner of their homes.

In the same way, the 'real' and *peranakan* Suku Asli appear to have two different perspectives on the fate of the human soul. One day, I talked with Odang in his house about the spirits of the dead. I asked Odang where the soul of the dead goes and where the ancestral souls come from at rituals. He said:

> I don't know. But elders said to me that after a person died, one's *roh* (soul) separates from one's *badan* (body). And, then, the soul goes in and out the house in which one died for seven days. Therefore, we have to leave the entrance door of the house open during the days. After that, the soul is gradually going upward and stays in the upper space of the house until the fortieth day. I do not know where it is then going. Some people say it is going to the *atas dunia* (upper world)...But if we call the *nenek moyang* (ancestral souls) by burning incense, they certainly come and receive offerings.

Our topic moved to the influence of the dead on everyday life. According to Odang, the spirits of the dead do not intervene in people's everyday life; therefore, their ancestral souls also do not protect or impede everyday life. It is other spirits living around or passing through the settlements, rather than ancestral souls, that may exert influences on everyday life, such as *orang bunyian* or 'people' (invisible human beings; see also Chapter 3), *datuk*, *setan* (evil spirits), and *jin* (jinn; there are both benevolent and malevolent kinds). While *jin* is an Arabic or Islamic concept, it is often used as a name of spirits that shamans employ. For example, one of Odang's supporting spirits had the name of *Jin Putih* or While Jinn.

In general, Suku Asli remember their ancestors only when one has been met in the past. Thus they usually remember ancestors' names as far as grandparents on both sides. In the rituals, they offer meals for ancestral souls. The meals are for all ancestral souls rather than specific ancestors. Ancestral souls neither protect descendants from misfortune or disease nor bring peace and welfare to them. More important agents that influence everyday life are invisible human beings, *datuk*, *setan*, and *jin* living around and passing through a settlement. In the conversation above, I asked Odang the reason why the Suku Asli hold ritual feasts for ancestors. According to him, 'It is for respecting our ancestors. It is not a matter whether they will help or not.' For them, rituals are practices or institutions inherited from the past, and their importance lies in 'paying respect.'

After the conversation above, Odang added, 'But this is the ['real'] Suku Asli case. In the case of the Chinese dead, the soul may intervene in our life.' Chinese interpretations of ancestors differ from the Suku Asli way, and, indeed, I often heard and observed the *peranakan*/Chinese view of ancestral souls. For instance, I saw that some *peranakan* fathers repeatedly teach their small children the names of the paternal grandfathers of several generations back as far as they knew them, or made a list of the ancestors and put it on the wall behind the *tepekong* (altar). A *peranakan* explained to me that the ancestral souls were living in a different world that was almost the same as the 'real' world. Therefore,

	Reference		Address	
Relationship (Generation)	Male	Female	Male	Female
Grandparents' generation				
Lineal	*Nek*	*Nek*	*Nek*	*Nek*
Collateral	*Nek*	*Nek*	*Nek*	*Nek*
Parents' generation				
Lineal	*Bah*	*Mak*	*Bah*	*Mak*
Collateral				
General	*Pak*	*Mak*	*Pak*	*Mak*
Eldest	*Pak-tua*	*Mak-tua*	*Paktua*	*Maktua*
Second	*Pak-long*	*Mak-long*	*Paklong*	*Maklong*
Third	*Pak-anyang*	*Mak-anyang*	*Paknyang*	*Maknyan*
Fourth	*Pak-ngah*	*Mak-ngah*	*Pakngah*	*Makngah*
Fifth	*Pak-ci*	*Mak-ci*	*Pakci*	*Makci*
Sixth	*Pak-anak*	*Mak-anak*	*Paknak*	*Maknak*
Youngest	*Pak-usuh*	*Mak-usuh*	*Paksuh*	*Maksuh*
Affinity				
Spouse's parents	*Mertua*	*Mertua*	*Bah*	*Mak*
Ego's generation				
Lineal				
Seniors	*Abang*	*Kakak*	*Bang*	*Kak*
Juniors	*Adek*	*Adek*	*Dek*	*Dek*
Collateral				
Seniors	*Sepupu*	*Sepupu*	*Bang*	*Kak*
Juniors	*Sepupu*	*Sepupu*	*Dek*	*Dek*
Affinity				
Spouse's siblings	*Ipah*	*Ipah*	*Ipah*	*Ipah*
Spouse's sibling's spouse	*Meyen*	*Meyen*	*Yen*	*Yen*
Children's generation				
Lineal	*Anak*	*Anak*	N/A (name)	N/A (name)
Collateral	*Anak penak*	*Anak penak*	N/A (name)	N/A (name)
Affinity				
Children's spouse	*Menantu*	*Menantu*	N/A (name)	N/A (name)
Grandchildren's generation				
Lineal	*Cucu*	*Cucu*	N/A (name)	N/A (name)
Collateral	*Cucu*	*Cucu*	N/A (name)	N/A (name)

Note: the collateral parent data was collected in Teluk Pambang.

Table 2.1: Kinship terminology: the Suku Asli way

	Reference		Address	
"Relationship (Generation)"	Male	Female	Male	Female
Grandparents' generation				
Patrilateral	*Guakong*	*Guama*	*Akong*	*Ama*
Matrilateral	*Laikong*	*Laima*	*Akong*	*Ama*
Parents' generation				
Lineal	*Apa*	*Mak*	*Apa*	*Mak*
Patrilateral				
General (seniors to father)	*Apek*	*Ako*	*Apek*	*Ako*
General (juniors to father)	*Acek*	*Ako*	*Acek*	*Ako*
Eldest	*Tuapek*	*Tua-ko*	*Tuapek; Apek*	*Ako; Tuako*
Second	*Di-pek; Di-cek*	*Di-ko*	*Apek; Acek; Dipek; Dicek*	*Ako; Diko*
Third	*Sa-pek; Sa-cek*	*Sa-ko*	*Apek; Acek; Sapek; Sacek*	*Ako; Sako*
Fourth	*Shi-pek; Shi-cek*	*Shi-ko*	*Apek; Acek; Shipek; Shicek*	*Ako; Shiko*
Fifth	*Go-pek; Go-cek*	*Go-ko*	*Apek; Acek; Gopek; gocek*	*Ako; Goko*
Matrilateral				
General	*Aku*	*Ai*	*Aku*	*Ai*
Eldest	*Tua-ku*	*Tuai*	*Aku; Tuaku*	*Ai; Tuai*
Second	*Di-ku*	*Di-i*	*Aku; Diku*	*Ai; Dii*
Third	*Sa-ku*	*Sa-i*	*Aku; Saku*	*Ai; Sai*
Fourth	*Shi-ku*	*Shi-i*	*Aku; Shiku*	*Ai; Shii*
Fifth	*Go-ku*	*Go-i*	*Aku; goku*	*Goi; Goi*
Affinity				
Spouse's parents	*Mertua*	*Mertua*	*Apa*	*Mak*
Ego's generation				
Lineal				
Seniors	*Ahia*	*Aci*	*Ahia*	*Aci*
Juniors	*Adek*	*Adek*	*Adek*	*Adek*
Collateral				
Seniors	*Sepupu*	*Sepupu*	*Ahia*	*Aci*
Juniors	*Sepupu*	*Sepupu*	*Adek*	*Adek*
Affinity				
Spouse's sibling	*Ipah*	*Ipah*	*Ipah*	*Ipah*
Spouse's sibling's spouse	*Meyen*	*Meyen*	*Yen*	*Yen*
Children's generation				
Lineal	*Anak*	*Anak*	N/A (name)	N/A (name)
Collateral	*Anak Penak*	*Anak Penak*	N/A (name)	N/A (name)
Affinity	*Menantu*	*Menantu*	N/A (name)	N/A (name)
Grandchildren's generation				
Lineal	*Cucu*	*Cucu*	N/A (Name)	N/A (Name)
Collateral	*Cucu*	*Cucu*	N/A (Name)	N/A (Name)

Notes: the prefix '*Tua*' means 'old' in Malay. The prefixes '*Di*' to '*Go*' mean 'two' to 'five' in Chinese. I used Indonesian expressions in this table based on advice from *peranakan* Suku Asli, regardless of the four tones of Chinese pronunciation.

Table 2.2: Kinship terminology: the *peranakan* way

Photograph 2.1: *Dukun* at a séance

Photograph 2.2: *Bomo Cina*; *Kiton* at a séance

Photograph 2.3: A *keramat* (with no *datuk kong*) and offerings for *datuk* (Raya River)

Photograph 2.4: A séance held at *datuk kong* that was built at a *keramat* (Raya River)

they were obliged to offer meals to them and provide money and consumables by burning *kertas mas* (paper money). If they ignored the obligations, their ancestral souls became angry and did not protect the peace of the descendant's house. As a result, misfortune and disease might be caused. A *peranakan* described the meaning of the offerings: 'If we do not provide food and money for the ancestors, how do they live? If our children will not do it, how can I live after my dying?' His comment implies that their cosmology involves a strong connection between their ancestral souls and the living or the descendants that is realized through 'Chinese' ancestral rituals (Clarke 2000: 289).

While there are two interpretations of ancestral souls and their significance, the actual interpretation adopted is generally dependent on individuals. For example, some days after the conversation with Odang, I talked to Koding, a *peranakan* Suku Asli, about what I had heard from Odang. As I was talking about the topic of ancestral souls, he nodded in agreement. I asked him whether there was a case where *peranakan* ancestors may have intervened in everyday life. He answered, 'Right, but it's an opinion of some *bomo cina*.' According to him, the spirit mediums of Chinese deities occasionally attributed the cause of disease to the lack of respect for ancestral souls or to the malevolent souls of the dead. However, he concluded, 'It's a Chinese way. I don't know which is true. But I have not experienced that the ancestral souls intervene in our life.'

In terms of these kinship systems and religious beliefs, one or both are adopted depending on social connections. A 'real' Suku Asli who has only a small number of *peranakan* kin and neighbors may take only 'real' Suku Asli ways, but those who have many *peranakan* kin and neighbors may take both 'real' and *peranakan* Suku Asli ways. The *peranakan* Suku Asli also adopt one or both ways in a similar fashion.

The distinction of ancestral worship

Although they do not distinguish 'real' and *peranakan* Suku Asli in kinship terminologies and religious beliefs, the practice of ancestral worship has remained an essential criterion for the distinction. This is because, according to Suku Asli elders, *peranakan* were under the control of the local Chinese *kapitan* or manager before the independence of Indonesia. When *peranakan* held wedding and funeral ceremonies, a *kapitan* was called and managed the ceremony in the Chinese way. Although the role of *kapitan* was abolished after independence, the custom of holding ceremonies in the Chinese way has continued.

There are two ways to conduct *acara* (rituals)—the *acara Suku Asli* (*adat*; Suku Asli way) and the *acara peranak/Tionghua* (*peranakan*/Chinese way). 'Real' Suku Asli hold rituals in the Suku Asli way, which can be characterized by its similarity to Malay culture. The basic rituals are weddings, funerals, *kenduri* (anniversary of the dead), and the feast of the *tujuh likur* (New Year). In these rituals, they perform *silat*, play music with drums, viola, and flute, eat areca nuts and betel leaves kept in a *sirih* box, burn resin incense, and wear Malay-style dress, including the sarong. In addition to these basic rituals, *sunat* (circumcision) was held in the past. This ritual included a large feast, traditional dances, music, and ceremonies, and an elder performed the circumcision. *Sunat* was essential for boys before getting married; marriages of males who had not undergone this ritual were not allowed or recognized by the community. In Teluk Pambang, although all 'real' Suku Asli husbands aged over forty were circumcised before their marriages, the ritual had not been held for a few decades because, according to them, it is too costly. However, in Akit communities in Rupat, circumcision is still conducted as an essential life ceremony, which is held almost every year as a large ceremony in which neighbors cooperate.

Peranakan Suku Asli conduct their rituals in the *peranakan*/Chinese way, in which they use Chinese symbols such as *hyou* (incense sticks), red color, Chinese letters, *kertas mas*, and sometimes short Chinese phrases. In addition to weddings, funerals, and anniversaries of the dead, they hold the feast of *imlek* (Chinese New Year) and seasonal rituals based on the Chinese lunar calendar. At the entrance of their houses, they also have an altar on which Chinese deities and their ancestral souls are enshrined. Many ethnic Chinese have the tablets of their ancestors at these altars. However, *peranakan* generally do not. They place an icon of a Chinese deity and, occasionally, put a piece of red paper on which the ancestors' names or Chinese words are written to pray for the peace of the household (cf. Tan Chee-Beng 1982: 36–7, 1983: 218). They worship their ancestral souls and Chinese deities every morning and evening. Each member of the household burns incense sticks and prays for the peace of the house in front of it every morning and evening. Their way of ritual is related to Chinese folk religion, which is often described as *Konghucu* (Confucianism) in Indonesia (see Chapter 6).

'Real' Suku Asli households generally do not have an altar in the house, nor do they practice everyday worship, seasonal rituals, or a large feast at *imlek* as seen in the *peranakan*/Chinese way. *Peranakan* males should not be circumcised, and their households do not hold a large feast at *tujuh likur*. These distinctions are strict ones, and they do not permit mixing of rituals.

One day, I was in Ajui's house listening to Koding and Odang chat. Ajui, who was in his late forties, was a son of Koding; thus he was a *peranakan* Suku Asli. He was the most powerful leader of the Suku Asli on Bengkalis Island and held the role of regency *batin*, the top IKBBSA role in Bengkalis regency (see Chapter 4). Sitting on chairs in the living room, Koding and Odang were talking about a wedding ceremony that would be held on the weekend in the village of Penebal, an hour from Teluk Pambang by motorbike. Even though it seemed to be a celebratory event, the atmosphere appeared somewhat strained. From their chat, I found that they had been invited to the ceremony in order to perform *silat* and to play the viola. Odang was a good performer of *silat* and Koding was a viola player, and they always performed when wedding ceremonies were held in Teluk Pambang. Listening to their talk, I cut in with a question—'So, it's a wedding of a ['real'] Suku Asli bride, right?'—because I knew that *silat*, viola, and drums were performed only in a wedding ceremony for a Suku Asli bride, not a *peranakan* bride. Odang answered, 'No, it's a *peranakan* wedding.' This seemed odd and I asked Odang why *silat* and viola were to be used in a *peranakan* bride's wedding ceremony. He answered, 'That's the problem.'

According to Odang, the bride was a Penebal-born *peranakan* and worked in Jakarta. She would marry a Javanese bridegroom who lived in Jakarta. Although there were some *peranakan* households, her community in Penebal was ethnic Chinese and had no performers of Suku Asli music and *silat*. Planning to hold the wedding ceremony at her house, her family had asked Ajui to introduce Suku Asli performers in order to show *kebudayaan Suku Asli* (Suku Asli culture) to the groom and his family, and Ajui had asked Koding and Odang to perform. However, in their conversation, Koding and Odang were talking about how *tek baik* (not good) and *luar biasa* (unusual) performing Suku Asli dance and music would be, and they obviously appeared hesitant to be involved. Although they complained for a while, they finally agreed because Ajui had requested it.

On the wedding day, I visited the site. In front of the bride's house, tents and a stage were set up, and many people were visiting. Indonesian pop music was played by a band on the stage for a few hours, and then the Suku Asli performances began. The host family invited not only Odang and Koding but also several performers from a Suku Asli community in Selat Akar, Padang Island, and they performed a song and dance on the stage. After their performance, there was an intermission. Together with Koding, I visited a *peranakan* house very close to the site to have a rest. Sitting on the floor, Koding spoke to the 'old man' of the house who appeared to be an old friend of his: 'Look, *ini macam capcai!*' (it's a kind of chop suey!), he said. Following his comment, the old man nodded with a somewhat bitter smile. I could not understand his comment, and asked, 'What do you mean?' Koding answered, 'You saw that there was an altar in the [bride's] house, right? She is actually a *peranakan*. However, they use ['real'] Suku Asli way. Everything is mixed! So, I said, "it's chop suey." It's not good. It's a mistake.' His face looked serene and smiling as usual, but his words were obviously critical. Another day, I asked Koding why he complained about the use of the Suku Asli way of performances at the wedding. According to him, 'It is because *peranakan*'s ancestors were the Chinese from China. So, we should pay respect for the Chinese ancestors' (*Kami harus menghormati nenek-moyang Tionghua*).

Ancestral worship is involved not only in wedding ceremonies but also in funerals, anniversaries, and New Year feasts. In these ceremonies, Suku Asli perform a ritual in which ancestral souls are called to the site and have meals prepared for them. In doing so, they inform the ancestral souls of a descendant's marriage or death and they pray for the ancestors' peace in the other world. 'Real' Suku Asli descendants are expected to call their 'real' Suku Asli or Utan ancestors using the Suku Asli procedures of ritual, and the *peranakan* descendants are expected to call their *peranakan* or Chinese ancestors using the *peranakan*/Chinese procedures. It is disrespectful to ancestral souls for descendants to mix the two ways and ignore the inherited practice of their ancestors.

Thus Suku Asli avoid mixing the two types of rituals. This means that they avoid the confusion of their ancestry and distinguish 'real' Suku Asli and *peranakan*/Chinese ancestors. It is certain that the image of 'having the same ancestors' is multilayered: it is possible that while one expresses that the other has the same ancestor in the remote past, one can simultaneously believe that the other has a different ancestor in the near past. Therefore, this does not completely contradict their image that Suku Asli have the same ancestors. However, it can be said, at least, that Suku Asli identity does not depend on unilateral ancestry. Furthermore, it also can be said that their *adat* is not a single and integrated one. There are two ways of ancestral ritual, which is an essential component of *adat* in their community, and they have practiced them. Therefore, their categorization of 'us' and 'others' and identity as Suku Asli is not really sustained by a single ancestry or the practices of common *adat*.

Basis and limits of identity

Exclusion of Islam and acceptance of *peranakan*

The reason why the *peranakan* Suku Asli have maintained their *peranakan*/Chinese way of ancestral worship may be related to the manner of acculturation of the ethnic Chinese in the Malay world. There are many *peranakan* communities in Indonesia, Malaysia, and Singapore. For example, the *peranakan* of Melaka in Malaysia have Malay ancestors in their maternal line and have lost their Chinese language, acculturated with Melaka Malays, and identify themselves as the *baba*, distinguishing themselves from the Malays and 'pure' ethnic Chinese (Tan Chee-Beng 1988, 2004). The Tirok Chinese *peranakan* in Terengganu have adopted Malay-like language, food, and dress, but identify themselves as ethnic Chinese (Tan Yao Sua and Ngah 2013). *Peranakan* in Java have lost the Chinese language and their connection with *totok* (China-born Chinese or 'newcomers'), and they have a distinct and independent identity from both the Javanese and Chinese (Hoadley 1988; Tan Giok-Lan 1963; Willmott 1960). In all these cases, identities and patterns of acculturations vary from place to place, yet the thing in common is that they maintain Chinese ancestral worship. For Chinese migrants, it has been an obligation to worship their ancestors, essentially Chinese paternal ancestors (Clarke 2000; Tan Chee-Beng 1982, 1988; Tan Yao Sua and Ngah 2013).

With the strong attachment to the Chinese way of ancestral worship, Chinese migrants in Southeast Asia have generally rejected Islam not only by rejecting conversion but also by controlling social belonging. Among the *peranakan* Chinese in Malaysia, people who convert to Islam are eliminated from membership in the community, and '"Chinese" and "Malay" are mutually exclusive categories' (Clarke 2000: 290). In Indonesia, the situation is almost the same; in accordance with the rise of a strict doctrine of Islam in the Indonesian archipelago after the mid-eighteenth century, a 'religious barrier' has prevented intermarriage between the ethnic Chinese and Muslims (Skinner 1996: 64–6). These membership and kinship controls appear to be the same among the Suku Asli.

The reason why *orang asli* communities around the Siak estuary have a strict and institutionalized boundary with the Malays and Muslims seems to be related to the rejection of Islam among the *peranakan* and Chinese. Before the mid-nineteenth century, the Utan would have rejected Islam and becoming Malay to a certain extent, yet the boundaries between them and Malays or Muslims would likely have been much weaker than they are today, and a few Utan might have identified themselves as Muslims or Malay. However, in the late-nineteenth century, when the *panglong* system was introduced, the Chinese migrants looked for non-Islamic spouses and mainly married Utan, Akit, and Rawa women, since, on the eastern coast of Sumatra, the dominant groups of Malays, Minangkabau, and Javanese were all Muslims and only *orang asli* were non-Islamic. The *orang asli* accepted such Chinese-origin members through mutual communication and cooperation with them. In the process of forming kinship with the ethnic Chinese, the Utan adopted the Chinese way of membership and kinship control and excluded Muslims from their community, and the rule became an institution among *orang asli*. As a result, for the Suku Asli, Akit, and Rawa, '*orang asli*' and 'Malay' or 'Muslim' would have become mutually exclusive categories.

The regions of other *orang asli* groups, such as the Sakai, Orang Rimba, and Talang Mamak in eastern Sumatra were not involved in the *panglong* system, and the numbers of Chinese migrants were limited. Therefore, they have accepted the Malays and Islam to a certain extent, and, for them, the categories of '*orang asli*' and 'Malay' or 'Muslim' have not been exclusive.[7] It is probable that if the Chinese had not immigrated in the mid-nineteenth century, the identity among the Suku Asli, Akit, and Rawa would have been dramatically different and the categories of 'Suku Asli' and 'Malay' or 'Muslim' might not have been mutually exclusive.

'Real' and *peranakan* Suku Asli recognize their difference of ancestry and cultural practices. If this is the case, why do the *peranakan* Suku Asli identify themselves as Suku Asli, and not as Chinese or *peranakan*? Indeed, some studies of the ethnic Chinese in Malaysia show that their Chinese identity has been reproduced and maintained through ancestral worship because mutual participation and cooperation in the ancestral rituals integrate them as a Chinese community (Clarke 2000: 288; see also Chan 2005: 102; Tan Chee-Beng 1982: 48). Even though the *peranakan* Suku Asli recognize their different ancestry, they have a reason to emphasize their common ancestry with 'real' Suku Asli, and this seems to be related to the position of ethnic Chinese in Indonesia.

The political distinction between 'native' and Chinese-origin populations in Indonesia began in the early colonial era. In the eighteenth century, the VOC government categorized Javanese-born Chinese (or 'old comers') as *peranakan* and regarded them as Dutch citizens. On the other hand, they categorized Chinese-born Chinese (or 'newcomers') as *totok* and regarded them as foreigners. After the independence of Indonesia, the government categorized the *totok* as *Warga Negara Asing* (foreigners) and provided them with limited citizenship (Suryadinata 1978: 94–6). The *peranakan* have constituted a *peranakan* identity as distinct from *totok*, who did not have full citizenship (Skinner 1959; Tan, Mely G. 1997). In the mid-1960s, the Indonesian government suppressed the members of the Communist Party of Indonesia following the 30 September Movement in which many ethnic Chinese who were believed to have close connections with communism were killed by the military. In the Suharto regime, while the ethnic Chinese were the dominant power in the Indonesian economy, in the process of the formation of the nation state they were marginalized, discriminated against, and stigmatized as people who had a foreign origin (Chua 2004). Chinese schools were closed and representations of Chinese culture in public spaces were banned by the government. Although the oppressive policies ended in accordance with the *reformasi* (reformation) in 1998, the discrimination and marginalization of the ethnic Chinese and their identity has continued. As a result, more and more Chinese-related people identify themselves as *peranakan*, abandoning their identity as Chinese in contemporary Indonesia (Reid 2009).

Although these harsh national policies against the ethnic Chinese did not directly influence the *peranakan* Suku Asli, they have experienced some of the fallout. According to Koding, during the 30 September Movement he heard that many ethnic Chinese were killed on Babi Island, an uninhabited islet near Rupat Island. Also, during Suharto's regime, the *peranakan* Suku Asli did not place Chinese altars at the entrances of their houses and held as few ceremonies and rituals in the *peranakan*/Chinese way as possible. Even today, they know that it is potentially unbeneficial or is even risky to claim their Chinese ancestry or clearly manifest Chinese culture. By identifying themselves as Suku Asli, they can demonstrate their native or indigenous position much more strongly than by identifying themselves as *peranakan*. In other words, the *peranakan* Suku Asli have been in a dilemma in which they have recognized their Chinese ancestry in rituals but emphasized their Suku Asli ancestry in politics. The emphasis on common ancestry among the Suku Asli has been constituted not only by the historical kinship between the 'real' and *peranakan* Suku Asli, but also by the political emphasis on Suku Asli ancestry among the *peranakan* Suku Asli.

The 'real' Suku Asli, however, would have accepted *peranakan* identification as Suku Asli for several reasons. The 'real' Suku Asli had a bilateral kinship system and did not distinguish paternal and maternal kin. This means that *peranakan* and Chinese could become their kin through marriage alliance. On the basis of such a kinship system, more importantly, neighborhoods and everyday cooperation appear much more important in their social ties than actual kinship. They regard people who live nearby, cooperate in activities, and share food as *kawan* (friends) (see Chapter 3) and have a strong sense of camaraderie. The *peranakan* and Chinese could share food and everyday cooperation with the Suku Asli, while Muslims could not do so because of Islamic customs. As a result, the 'real' Suku Asli accepted that *peranakan* identify themselves as Suku Asli and regarded them as kinfolk or friends. In addition, the alliance with the Chinese population did not intervene in Suku Asli traditional ancestral worship. As mentioned above, while the paternal descendants of the

Chinese have to follow *peranakan*/Chinese customs in rituals, this rule is not applied to maternal descendants. This means that the 'real' Suku Asli could maintain their traditional rituals. The Suku Asli could accept the *peranakan* without entanglement in their *adat*, which could be very problematic in the alliance with Muslims. Finally, the alliance with the Chinese could be economically beneficial.

As I mention in the next chapter, *touke* and Suku Asli are in a relationship between patron and client. Although the *peranakan* Suku Asli have some boundaries with *touke*, they share the same ancestors with *touke* and are regarded as potential kin. For 'real' Suku Asli, alliance with *peranakan* was desirable, as it may have brought waged labor and advantageous barters in relation to *touke*. These conditions have been created in a situation in which Suku Asli, *peranakan*, and *touke* have shared the same living space of coastal banks. I return to this topic in the next chapter.

Although the 'real' and *peranakan* Suku Asli have shared almost all elements of their everyday life, they have distinguished their ancestral rituals. This is because, as mentioned earlier, maintaining their respective rituals was essential in both cultures, and this is one of the main reasons why they chose each other as alliance partners.

Non-Islamic alliance and state intervention

I would like to suggest that the identity and category of Suku Asli is established on the basis of a non-Islamic alliance. With the expression 'non-Islamic alliance,' I imply that they do not have a single ancestry or single *adat*, but their identity and category is sustained by its boundaries with Muslims. This alliance covers not only Suku Asli and *peranakan*, but also Rawa and Akit. The difference of ancestry and ancestral worship was not problematic for Suku Asli identity inside their communities. As mentioned in Chapter 3 and 4, their social relationship is characterized by the maintenance of personal autonomy, free association, flexible membership, and the lack of a group outside the domestic family, which can be summarized by a concept of 'open aggregation' (Gibson and Sillander 2011). They are connected by kinship and mutual cooperation in everyday life individually, whereby they have maintained their personal autonomy. This differs from how the Siak and Indonesian governments imagined them to be.

It should be emphasized here that Suku Asli have sustained such a loose and flexible social relationship based on their agency. As Benjamin (2002) points out, the formulation of tribal position is sustained by the people's individual choice to be tribal and, as mentioned in Chapter 1, the Utan or Suku Asli have avoided government control in their history. The establishment of the non-Islamic alliance and the maintenance of an 'open aggregation' relationship are some of their ways to resist state intervention (see also Osawa 2017). Rejecting the institutionalized systems that can be a receptacle of state interventions, they have maintained their autonomy.

The situation of the Orang Suku Laut in the Riau-Lingga Archipelago is similar to the Suku Asli. Their settlements dot the scattered inlets and isles of a vast area of the archipelago, and they are divided into a dozen regional *suku* (groups) such as Suku Galang, Riau, and Mantang (Chou 2010: 20–5). However, they have been regarded as the Orang Suku Laut ethnic group by the state since the precolonial era because of their salient cultural feature of living on boats, and, after the 1990s, the government tried to develop their society through sedentarization, education, and Islamization programs (Chou 2010). However, Chou (2020: 224) argues that the Orang Suku Laut have avoided the state's capture of their activity by taking actions summarized by the concept of a 'war machine.' Gilles Deleuze and Félix Guattari (see Chou 2020: 224) argue that the 'war machine' is 'a mode of being or a social state that de-identifies from the state and thus prevents its formulation' by employing 'an assemblage of non-specified strategies.' Instead of the use of institutionalized resistance, the Orang Suku Laut have taken the assemblage of non-specified strategies, in which they adopt Christianity and Confucianism as registered religions (see Chapter 6), do not preserve administrative documents, avoid net fishing that may bring a sedentary way of life, and so forth. The Suku Asli have maintained their personal autonomy in much the same way.

After the 1990s, these strategies gradually became difficult because the Bengkalis regency government has regarded mangrove logging, which was their main labor, as illegal and, with the rise of environmentalism, has tried to restrict and prohibit the export of charcoal (see Chapter 3). After 2000, the government began to directly intervene in their society, providing a development program that included a variety of recognition and support for Suku Asli. In this process, the government provided them with an image of 'how they should be' through the development program, and their indigenous and ethnic identity and position have been destabilized and problematized.

Once the Bengkalis government was concerned with the legitimation of the Suku Asli position as an indigenous ethnic group, it was necessary to prove it 'objectively' for the outsiders. As I mentioned in the introduction and Chapter 1, indigeneity and its Indonesian version of '*adat* community' are critical in the government policies to define people as indigenous, and cultural content is one of the main criteria in distinguishing the peoples. For the government, as well as the activists of the *adat* movement, the concrete image of *adat* in an *adat* community includes a common history of origins, a long-established territory, traditional political and legal institutions, common religious practices and beliefs, shared material cultures, and so on. In the wave of government interventions in local communities and the rise of the *adat* movement in the recent decentralized Indonesia, cultural content became problematic.

From an objective perspective on the *adat* community, Suku Asli identity may partly lack integration of its cultural content. At first, in terms of their non-Islamic religion, the integration of religious practices and beliefs is rather difficult. As mentioned above, in the case of *peranakan*, the non-Islamic alliance has been formed through the maintenance of Chinese ancestry and ancestral worship, as well as the rejection of Islam, while the 'real' Suku Asli also had their own form of ancestral worship. This resulted in the distinction of their ancestry and their ways of ancestral worship within a community; thus, from an outsider's perspective, they appear to have unintegrated religious practices and beliefs that can be a powerful symbol of ethnic integration. In addition, the common economic activities on the riverbanks did not help to prove their integration. They developed their communities along brackish rivers, each of which covered a certain area of the hydrographic basin. Thus their communities are a certain distance from each other. A number of such communities, each of which are next to Malay or Javanese settlements, are scattered like enclaves over the vast area of the Siak estuary. It was quite difficult for them to have an integrated political and legal institution that directly showed their integration or could be a powerful agent to integrate their cultural content. It was also difficult to imagine a bounded and integrated territory. In short, although the Suku Asli had a clear religious boundary and shared common economic activity in the river-coast space, they did not have clear cultural content that could show their integration when interacting with the government.

However, the Suku Asli have tried to create an image of integrated cultural content for the purpose of establishing their position in the decentralized era of Indonesia—although Suku Asli attempts to show integrated cultural content are not completely consistent with the government's image. The Suku Asli have their own view of social relationships based on their history and experience. They employ a cultural logic that draws upon these images and represents their integration both internally and externally. This cultural logic is based on the common and continuous ancestry described in this chapter, and, indeed, they connect this image of common and continuous ancestry with their living space, ethnic organization, traditions, and religion.

The Suku Asli situation reminds us of Barth's (1969) argument about 'ethnic boundary' and the following debates; in his famous book on *Ethnic Groups and Boundaries*, he insists that an ethnic group is defined by self-ascription and ascription by others, and emphasizes the importance of focusing on the formation and maintenance of ethnic boundaries. He calls the cultural content of an ethnic group 'cultural stuff' (norms, values, origin myth, and so on) and points out that it is not really significant for defining an ethnic group because such content is chosen haphazardly (Barth 1969: 9–15). According to Barth (1969: 14):

> although ethnic categories take cultural differences into account, we can assume no simple one-to-one relationship between ethnic units and cultural similarities and differences. The features that are taken into account are not the sum of 'objective' differences, but only those which the actors themselves regard as significant.

However, as a result of his reconsideration of his own work over twenty years, Barth (1994: 16) admits that the choice of cultural content is less haphazard than he argued. Individual experience, the activities of elites, and state policies form certain images of cultural content, and such cultural content supports the ethnic category or group (Barth 1994: 16–29; see also Colombijn 2003b). In Suku Asli society, an ethnic boundary separating them from the Muslims existed almost since the very beginning, and this formed their history and identity without integrated 'cultural stuff.' The government has required them to define themselves more clearly, and they have tried to do so through attempts to integrate their cultural content not only according to the government's image but also according to their own practices and beliefs. It is these transactions between Suku Asli images and those of the government that I explore in the following chapters.

In summary, the Suku Asli have had their non-articulated, unconscious, and subjective identity and category of 'us' and 'others,' and have held a flexible identity—that is to say, *orang asli* identity, which comprises the Suku Ali, Akit, and Rawa. This identity is sustained by their historical moves and their life on riverbanks, and they express this identity in the phrase, 'We have the same ancestors.' However, in examining the difference in the ancestral worship between 'real' and *peranakan* Suku Asli, we can see that their identity is not really sustained by a single ancestry or common practice of ancestral worship. Instead, they have been brought together in a non-Islamic alliance in their history without real integration of ancestry and cultural content. This was their way of resisting state intervention. When the government began to intervene with the notion of an *adat* community, this ambiguity and flexibility became problematic, and they are trying to show their integration based on both the government image and their own.

The flexibility and diversity of Suku Asli identity and category is derived not only from their uncentralized social structure, but also from the difference of ancestral worship among the *peranakan* Suku Asli. Such historical instability of their indigenous and ethnic identity has and will put them at a marginal position. Therefore, in their 'indigenous movement,' while they try to integrate the segmentary social structure by connecting distant communities, they simultaneously try to legitimate the unstable position of the *peranakan* Suku Asli who have relationships with the marginalized Chinese in Indonesian state policies. Indeed, like the fact that Ajui became the headman of IKBBSA, the *peranakan* Suku Asli and their ideas have played important roles in the Suku Asli indigenous movement, and their attempts to maintain their Chinese ancestral worship while grasping a legitimated position have provided the essential motivation for the movement. In this sense, their indigenous movement has an aspect in which the potentially non-indigenous attribution of the *peranakan* Suku Asli drove them to claim and legitimate their position as indigenous by emphasizing Suku Asli commonness of culture and identity.

In such a situation, their identity both in relation to other *orang asli* and the *peranakan* started changing. The main factor behind this change is the fashion in which their attitude to land is also changing. In the next chapter, I explore this particular change.

Chapter 3

Consolidation of People and Place: Foraging, Space, and Historical Continuity

Land and resources form a key concept for understanding the indigenous movement. National and international activists have tried to formulate the concept of indigenous peoples for the purpose of protecting rights to land and resources among those who have lived on a particular land but who have been marginalized; thus, definitions always mention a peoples' priority in terms of access to land and its resources (Dove 2006: 192; Kenrick and Lewis 2004; Niezen 2003; Saugestad 2004). While concrete political actions in this movement vary, those of Indonesia are generally characterized by the quest for the protection of land and resources against the government or government-sponsored corporations, which exploited local land and resources under 'centralized' policies prior to 1998 (Davidson and Henley 2007; Duncan 2004b; Wee 2002). In many cases, the arenas for such struggles are the rainforests, from which local communities have customarily obtained their living. Local rights may often be legitimated by showing historically continuous use of the land, as well as identity that is backed by ancestral cultures in the particular regions. Thus local authorities and activists define such lands as ancestral land that has been utilized under local *adat* (*tanah adat*; *tanah ulayat*) and try to protect locals' rights to it (Acciaioli 2007; Li 2000).

However, for the locals themselves, ancestral or *adat* land has not always been clearly defined. This is not only because the historical and legal boundaries of the land are often vague in peripheral forest regions, but also because their ancestors and *adat* form only one of several ways to represent their attachment to and need for land. The connectedness between people and land can also be represented and explained by logics such as economic activities needed for their survival, the symbolic value of land as a sacred place or an essential part of the world in their cosmology, attachment to the land from their aesthetic perspective, and even the economic and cultural potential in the future. For indigenous people, land constitutes part of their world as a whole, and the connectedness is usually unconscious and subjective, which can be summarized by 'indigeny' (Benjamin 2002, 2016a, 2016b); further, it is framed according to distinct cultural logics in each local community when they need to explain it to others. However, in competition for land, local elites and activists try to objectify the unconscious and subjective connectedness between people and land and summarize such explanations or practices into the concept of ancestral land for the purpose of legitimating their land usage. In this sense, ancestral land can be seen as a perspective, not a substantial thing. The land, to which the locals feel attachment, is something to be objectified and emphasized as ancestral land in and through the problematization of the connectedness and the process of demonstrating the historically continuous use of the land.

As I mentioned in previous chapters, the Suku Asli have lived on riverbanks and depended on the resources obtained around coastal space; their attachment to the space constitutes an important part of their identity. However, if we examine Suku Asli words, most of them have not recognized mangrove swamps, from which they have obtained their livelihood, as their ancestral land. Rather, as they have naturally used the resources in the 'niche' space, their connectedness with mangrove swamps was a subjective and unconscious one in which they did not objectify the riverbank space as ancestral. However, through competition with outsiders and their interactions with the state, some Suku Asli, especially the leaders of IKBBSA, have begun to claim the right to riverbank space in very recent years. In this activity, they define the river-coast space as ancestral land. Their ancestral land emerges through competition with other peoples and the state, as well as through the rise of indigenous movements. In this chapter, I explore Suku Asli recognition of their relationship with their living space and the way it has changed in the state intervention and competition with outsiders through the ethnographic and historical description of the village of Teluk Pambang.

Bengkalis Island and Teluk Pambang

Bengkalis Island is situated at the estuary of the Siak River on the eastern coast of Sumatra (see Map 1 in the introduction). The island has an area of 938 square kilometers and a population of 124,652 people according to the 2018 census (Pemerintah Kabupaten Bengkalis n.d.). The lands are flat and marshy—the highest altitude is only several meters high—and are mostly covered by tropical peat soil (Badan Restorasi Gambut 2018). Bengkalis town (Map 3.1) is the largest town on the island and the capital of Bengkalis regency, which includes part of mainland Sumatra and other islands.

In the precolonial era, the coasts of the Malacca Strait were mostly unpopulated (Barnard, T. 2003: 15; Trocki 1997: 87). Before the twentieth century, the hinterlands were covered by thick tropical peat swamp forests, which people were unable to use as a rigid production base for living and trading (Masuda et al. 2016: 148). In addition, there were several brackish rivers, each of which had numerous tributaries, the coasts were covered by thick mangrove forests, and the water paths looked like labyrinths. Although

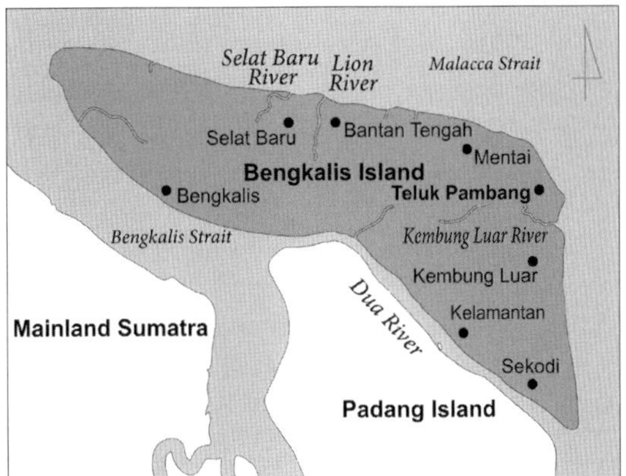

Map 3.1: Bengkalis Island

the Dutch colonial government temporarily put the capital of Eastern Coast Province on the area of present-day Bengkalis town at the end of the nineteenth century, other areas were totally frontier, and small and sparse settlements on the coasts were scattered over the island. In particular, the eastern coast of the island was an unpopulated area, and there were few settlements of the Utan and Malays. In this situation, people exclusively depended on transportation by water and villages were developed along the coasts, as with other villages in eastern Sumatra (Kathirithamby-Wells 1993). First, a proto-hamlet was formed on a sea or river coast, then the hamlet gradually encroached on the hinterlands and became a village. Finally, such villages were connected with roads. On the island, roads were gradually constructed after the independence of Indonesia.

The island has experienced a dramatic increase in population during the past one hundred years. In the late nineteenth century, many ethnic Chinese migrated to the eastern coast of Sumatra to harvest timber. Then, around the beginning of the twentieth century, central Sumatra became a main region for immigration from other areas of Sumatra and Java (Gooszen 1999: 83), and the population of Bengkalis Island also increased as it was the political and economic center of the eastern coast. According to the census conducted by the Dutch colonial government in 1930, the population on Bengkalis Island was 17,035 people (Tideman 1935: 31). Then, about forty years later, the 1971 Indonesian census shows 57,154 people (Kantor Sensus and Statistik Propinsi 1972: 49). As the population in 2018 was about 120,000 people, the population on the island has increased more than seven times over the past ninety years.

As a result of the construction of roads and the increase in the population, almost all the hinterland of the island has been opened and used for gardens and settlements. The lands are used for well-maintained gardens of coconuts and oil palms, rubber, and so on, which can be grown when people open the peat swamp forests and drain and dry the peatland through the construction of ditches. The land is unsuitable for cultivating crops. Almost no forests remain on the island, unlike elsewhere in Indonesia, where the government nominally and legally owns most of the vast forests based on the national forest laws, while local communities have traditionally only used the resources. The forests that remain around the boundaries of the administrative villages cover a few hectares and are owned by individuals or logging groups in each administrative village. Each village is connected by paved roads; the houses stand at intervals of several dozen meters along the roads. While some villages are bounded by rivers, their borderlines are generally vague. On the other hand, most mangroves, which cover the river and sea coasts, still remain. These areas are tidal swamps, and it is impossible to use them as farmland, although the local communities have used the resources.

It is quite important for understanding the local perception of space to know that this region has two landscapes of hinterland and waterline. On maps, the two spaces look to be directly connected, and their boundaries are extremely vague. However, they are separate and different landscapes in reality. When traveling the roads, we cannot perceive the sea and rivers, despite their closeness, because the view is restricted by garden trees and mangroves. It is also impossible to view the hinterland from the sea and rivers, as the coasts are covered by mangroves. In this situation, people have a mind map that is based on the two poles of *laut* (sea or water line) and *darat* (land). The category of *darat* literally indicates land, while that of *laut* includes the sea, rivers, and mangroves. Their boundary is the tidemark line. Local Malays often indicate direction with the two expressions and recognize the cosmological difference between the two spaces.[1] Suku Asli also have the same perception and idioms.

It is in the space just behind the mangroves that Suku Asli have lived. The Malays use '*orang dalam*' or '*pendalam*' (inner people: people living inside the forest) to indicate tribal people living in the forest. Suku Asli are also referred to as *orang dalam*, but their settlements have been not in the thick rainforest around headstreams but along the brackish rivers near the sea and directly connected with the unbounded open world through the waterline. But the mangrove forests form an obstructed view for outsiders. Their space is characterized by the ambivalent qualities of open and closed, where they were able to form their indigenous ethnic identity.

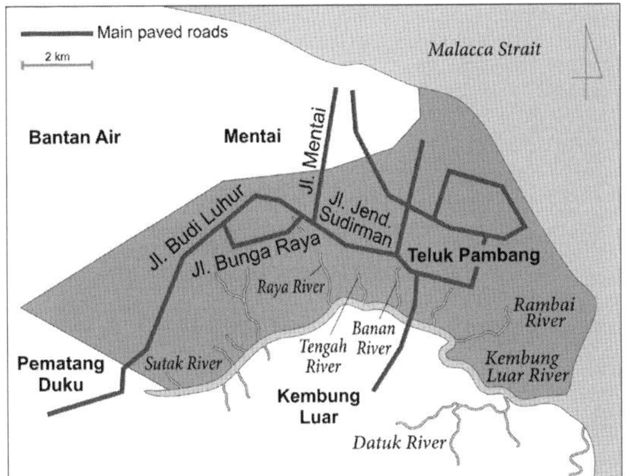

Map 3.2: Village of Teluk Pambang

Teluk Pambang and its history of immigration

The administrative village of Teluk Pambang is situated at the eastern edge of the island, about forty kilometers from Bengkalis town.[2] The village is situated on the northern coast of the Kembung Luar River, and has an area of approximately seventy-five square kilometers and a population of 6050 people. According to the government census in 2010, the population of the Suku Asli in this village was 1769 people (346 households) (Dinas Sosial Kabupaten Bengkalis 2010: 225). The majority of the population was, first, Javanese and, second, Malays and Suku Asli; there were also a few dozen houses of others such as the Minangkabau, Batak, and ethnic Chinese.

According to a map issued by the Ministry of Environment and Forestry in 2019 that designates land category related to the state forest (Kementrian Lingkungan Hidup dan Kehutanan 2019), most of the land in the village is categorized as *Areal Penggunaan Lain* (APL: areas for other purposes; non-forest area), which can be owned by individuals and organizations and used for farming and dwelling. In the western boundary area near the villages of Bantan Air and Pematang Duku, there are small areas of lands categorized as the state forest of *hutan produksi tetap* (production forest) and *hutan produksi yang dapat dikonversi* (convertible production forest). The production forest was lent from the government to a company for thirty-five years. The coastal mangrove forest along mainstream Kembung Luar and its tributaries are categorized as the state forest of both *hutan produksi terbatas* (limited production forest) and *lokasi indikatif perhutanan sosial* (social forestry indicative area), which can legally be used for social forestry with the select cutting of trees, although the use of the area for farming and dwelling is prohibited.

The following village history is based on villagers' oral history. I often visited the houses of elders, not only of Suku Asli but also Javanese and Malays, and listened to portraits of the village landscape and community in the past, and I tried to check facts by asking elders living in other settlements.

The village was developed around the north coast of the Kembung Luar River. In the nineteenth century, there were some small settlements of the Suku Asli and Malays on both banks of the river, and the Dutch colonial government regarded these settlements as the administrative village of Kembung. Then, at the beginning of the twentieth century, the settlements of the northern coast were separated from Kembung, and Teluk Pambang was established. According to the villagers, the first people who lived in this area were the Suku Asli. Then the Malays and Javanese established their settlements in this area.

It is uncertain when the Utan first entered Bengkalis Island, but Suku Asli elders estimated that it was around the turn of the nineteenth century. Given the genealogies of their *batin* headmen, which they remember fragmentarily, it seems to be certain that there was an Utan community on the island at the beginning of the nineteenth century at the latest. According to the elders, the Utan moved to this island from the Rawa region on mainland Sumatra, traveling through the eastern islands of Padang and Merbau, as mentioned in previous chapters. The first settlement was around the present Sekodi village, then some people moved to an area around the mouth of the Kembung Luar River and made up the first settlement around the Rambai River, a tributary of the Kembung Luar River (Map 3.2).

From the very early period of their move to this area, Chinese traders from Melaka and, later, Singapore often visited for trading.[3] Between the late nineteenth and early twentieth centuries, the Chinese population dramatically increased because of the introduction of the *panglong* system. After the number of Javanese migrants increased around the turn of the twentieth century, their main settlement was moved to around the tributaries midstream of the Kembung Luar River, the space between the Banan and Raya rivers.

Just after Suku Asli immigration, the Malays also set up their community on the northeast seashore of present-day Teluk Pambang. They were fishermen who had lived on Rangsang Island and moved to this island to seek new fishing grounds. They conducted fishing in the Malacca Strait. As their settlement was a typical fishing village, it expanded along the sea coasts rather than the hinterland or river coasts.

At the end of the nineteenth century, the first Javanese immigration occurred. These Javanese were those who had migrated from Java to Malaysia in the early colonial period and moved into this region for the purpose of possessing their own gardens.[4] They first settled around Rambai River, bringing their families from Malaysia, and deforested the hinterlands. In 1903, the first administrative *penghulu* (headman) was appointed by the Dutch colonial government, and the village of Teluk Pambang was established. The headman was a Javanese, and his office was situated at the north of the Rambai River, an area that has been the center of the administrative village. Immigration continued intermittently for more than forty years, and people's gardens rapidly extended to the hinterland towards the north and the west. Their interests were mainly in the hinterland because gardens close to rivers or the sea were often damaged by brackish water.

Around the time of Japanese occupation in the 1940s, a log plant was established at the meeting point of the Raya and Kembung Luar rivers, and a canning plant to process fish was also constructed in the Malay settlement. These plants were operated by *touke*. For the purpose of managing the plants, a dozen Chinese households moved to each area from towns on other islands.

After the independence of Indonesia, the regency government tried to open the hinterlands. In the second half of the 1960s, the government carried out a project that deforested the western part of the village, and constructed a path that connects the village with Pematang Duku. In the late 1970s, a path connecting the village with Mentai was also built. These projects were conducted through a process by which the regency government solicited local people to engage in construction and deforestation. The village office granted them land for gardens and residences along the paths. In parallel with construction and deforestation, the second Javanese immigration to this village took place after the 1970s. These Javanese were people who applied for the resettlement program led by the government. By the second half of the 1990s, the paths were gradually paved, and almost all areas of the village were deforested and changed into gardens.

From the village history of Teluk Pambang, we can see the different perspectives on the landscape among the Malays, Javanese, and Suku Asli. The Malays saw the fishing ground in the open sea, and they established their settlement along the seashores and engaged in open-sea fishing. They were not interested in hinterlands and brackish rivers, which were far from the harbors for their boats. The Javanese saw the hinterland forest as potential gardens, and extended their settlements to the hinterlands to create coconuts gardens. They avoided the river and sea banks because of the brackish water. And, as explored below, the Suku Asli saw the mangrove coasts, and lived in the space between the tidal mangrove forest and hinterland rainforest. The open sea and hinterlands were the outside world for them, although they occasionally passed through these spaces for the purposes of transportation and hunting. Thus the Malays oriented their cultural landscape towards the sea, the Javanese towards the hinterlands, and the Suku Asli towards the rivers. Each did not encroach on the different landscapes of the others, as the economic basis of their lives was established in a particular space.

In the early days of the first Javanese migration, there would have been some tensions and negotiations between some Suku Asli and the Javanese. While the details of the conflicts have not been handed down to present-day villagers, according to Suku Asli, some Suku Asli families lived on the banks when the Javanese first arrived. The families moved to the midstream Kembung Luar River, but they maintained their small gardens of coconut and durian trees. However, these gardens were subsumed by the Javanese gardens or settlements without any compensation. Although violence did not occur, some Suku Asli still complained that the Rambai River was their space. However, this would have been an exceptional case in the early days. Because of the difference of their cultural landscapes and low-population density, the living spaces were not really in competition until the 1960s. The Suku Asli have lived in the midstream Kembung Luar River, the Javanese on the banks of Rambai River and the hinterland, and the Malays on the northeastern seashore. Each settlement was separated by thick rainforest, mangrove forest, and rivers or the sea, so they were rarely involved in land conflicts or competition.

It is noteworthy how the government has seen the land in this region. The landscape perception of the post-independence government almost corresponded with that of the Javanese. The second Javanese immigration/resettlement, sponsored by the government, was in areas of government development schemes. The resettlement was, first, programed to fill the space that the government regarded as 'empty.' Second, the government aimed to improve local economies by providing the local population with progressive, diligent, and effective models of sedentary Javanese agriculture (Duncan 2004b: 105; Li 2007b: 80). In short, the government's ideal landscape in this region involved coextensive with the effectively concentrated, well-connected, and harmonious agricultural villages, which are represented in the rice-producing areas of Java (SKEPHI and Kiddell-Monroe 1993: 247; see also Geertz 1963). While similar transmigrations have been conducted elsewhere in Indonesia and often caused serious conflicts between the settlers and the indigenous communities (Duncan 2004b: 104–05), the resettlement to Bengkalis Island had not brought about violence. Almost all hinterlands effectively changed into well-maintained gardens and villages. Also, some of the Malays who depended on fishing obtained gardens in the hinterlands and became farmers. They now often intermarry with the Javanese, and their ethnic boundary is vague at present.

Yet, in the government landscape, the coasts of labyrinthine rivers are peripheral. In the 'blueprint of development' for the Sakai, Akit, and Suku Asli, the Bengkalis regency government repeatedly implies that their poverty is derived from their way of living on riverbanks (Dinas Sosial Kabupaten Bengkalis 2010). The separation of cultural landscapes between the Javanese, Malays, and Suku Asli and the difference in the meaning attached by the government to the spaces reconfigures the Suku Asli's marginal position in terms of space within the state. As I mentioned in Chapter 1, the Suku Asli living place has not been geographically isolated if compared with other tribal populations in Southeast Asia. However, even after independence, they have actually been isolated politically in the narrow but complex space characterized by numerous tributaries and tidal mangrove forests. The government development scheme of landscape centering on hinterland gardens formulated and maintained the marginal position of the Suku Asli.

Suku Asli recognition of the river coastal space

The past way of life and economic dependency on river-coast resources

Let us explore the Suku Asli relationship with the river coasts in detail. During my fieldwork, I often asked Suku Asli elders about their memories of the past. We sat on benches at the front of their houses or took chairs under tents that were prepared for ceremonies in their gardens, and we talked. In most cases, the elders gladly chatted nostalgically about their past foraging ways of life, and taught me a lot of things about their ways of looking for food, building houses, and communicating with people in the coastal area. However, such information was often confusing because the scenes in their stories seemed remote from present village situations. At present, Suku Asli houses in Teluk Pambang are scattered along the paved roads near to rivers, and their transportation depends on the road. Almost all Suku Asli settle in semi-permanent houses made of boards and timbers. Noticing the perplexed look on my face, they stressed, 'The situation was different from now.' Following their words, I erased roads, lanes, gardens, and most of the houses in front of us from my mind, replaced them with forests, and tried to imagine their past ways of life. As a result, their past life, which depended on the waterline, emerged little by little. I formulated the following descriptions from the information given by the elders. Although it is difficult to specify an exact time period for their stories, these ways of life and landscape were generally in existence before the 1960s.

In the past, there were no roads and gardens and fewer people; the lands were covered by forest. There were very few houses in Teluk Pambang, and the Suku Asli lived in settlements with only two or three huts assembled together. A husband, wife, and their children lived in each small hut. Trunks of *bakau*[5] were used for the pillars[6] of the hut. The frames were also *bakau*, and were joined together by string made of bark. The roof was thatched with the leaves of *nipah* (nipa palm) or sago palm. For the floor, the trunks of *nibung* (nibung palm) were arranged on the *bakau* frames, or people simply trod on the soil so as to harden it. The walls were made of bark. The spaces around the huts were cleared, and people made small gardens and planted *ubi* (tubers). They may also have planted durian and coconut palms.

These settlements dotted the spaces behind the mangrove forests along the tributaries of the Kembung Luar River. Between settlements, there were dense mangrove forests, swamps, rainforests, and canals. Although there may have been trails between them in some parts, the people usually used canoes to go back and forth between the settlements. Each settlement was called by the name of the tributary, such as Sungai (River) Raya, Sungai Banan, and Sungai Tengah. At the headstream of the tributary and meeting point of the rivers, they enshrined *datuk* to protect the place by setting up a stand on which they offered food. This place was thought of as *keramat*, and a *dukun* managed each *keramat* by holding annual rituals.

The most important food was sago, in addition to tubers planted around huts. People harvested *meriyah* (sago palms) that grew naturally between mangrove swamps and hinterland rainforests. They extracted the *sagu* (sago) and preserved it in their houses. They often gathered shellfish in mangrove swamps as well. Game—in particular, wild boar (*hisim*; *nagoi*)—was also an important food. However, they rarely went hunting in the rainforest of the hinterland (*dalam utan*; *dalam*). Because wild boars often came down to the edges of the rainforest close to their settlements and the mangrove swamps, they simply hunted them with spears and snares. They ate the sago and tubers together with fish and various shellfish obtained around the rivers. Each household had a *jalor* (dugout canoe) or a *sampan* (boat)[7] by which they conducted fishing and transportation. The canoe, which was handled with two sculling oars, was an essential tool that was used every day.

The Suku Asli traded various forest and coastal products such as *rotan* (rattan), *guta sondek* (wild rubber), screw pine, and fish with *touke*. However, the most important product was the trunks of *bakau*. The manner of trade involved going to the *touke*'s house and arranging to exchange *bakau* trunks for commodities such as iron products, fishing gear, clothes, rice, salt, sugar, tobacco, and money. They promised the *touke* a certain amount of *bakau* by a certain date. During high water, they went into the mangrove forest by canoe and logged the trunks. *Touke* created charcoal from *bakau* in their charcoal huts, and exported it to Singapore and Melaka. According to Suku Asli elders, their fathers and grandfathers had also logged *bakau* and traded with *touke*, and the logging of *bakau* was their main waged labor until 2006.

They often moved around. A household lived in a settlement for as long as a few years then moved to a different settlement or unoccupied land. If they found a *tempat baik* (good place) for living when away from their settlement, they moved to the new place. The move was often within a narrow space; they may have moved to the banks of the next tributary using canoes. The old land was often simply abandoned. However, when the new residence was nearby and they had planted durian or coconut trees in the small garden in the old place, they may have returned to harvest them. People who wanted to move to the old place paid money for the trees and could move there. They occasionally moved to distant places outside the Kembung Luar River or Bengkalis Island, relying on connections with kinfolk and friends, as previously mentioned. There were a number of similar settlements in the region between Rupat Island and Mendol Island. If people moved to a different community, they met the *batin* headman of the new place and reported that they would like to live in the place for a while; they earned their livelihoods by mangrove logging or temporary labor under *touke*. Some may have soon moved again, and some may have lived around the same place throughout their lives.

In the memories of their past life, we see Suku Asli dependency on the resources of the brackish river coasts. Their building materials of *bakau*, *nipah*, and *nibung* grow in a zone between tidal mangrove forest and hinterland rainforest (Giesen et al. 2006). The staple food, sago palm, also grows in this space. In addition, the most important commodity, *bakau*, develops in tidal forests under certain water salinity levels and less so in coastal areas facing the open sea (Giesen et al. 2006: 12–15). However, the mangrove swamp environment itself is very harsh for living due to the difficulty of obtaining fresh water, the undulations of the land surface caused by ebb and flow, and the astonishingly large numbers of mosquitoes, so Suku Asli did not actually live in the tidal forest. Yet hinterlands were inconvenient for transportation and obtaining resources. As a result, their settlements have been concentrated on the space behind the mangrove forests in the midstream and upstream areas of brackish rivers.

Photograph 3.1: A canoe and Raya River

At present, their houses are made of plank walls and tin or sago-leaf roofs, their transportation mostly depends on the roads, and they more frequently eat rice as a staple food. Also, as the empty spaces have almost disappeared, they move to different places less frequently. However, they still fish on the brackish river, hunt wild boars in mangrove swamps, grow sago palms in their gardens, and log mangrove timber by canoe when a *touke* requests it.

Living space and indigeny

The Suku Asli's historical economic dependency on the riverbanks is obvious. In the same way, their emotional attachment to the river-coast space behind the mangrove forest appeared to be firm. They explained that while they obtained gardens in the hinterland between the 1970s and 1990s, and even though the mangrove swamps largely lost their economic value after 2006, they still live around coastal spaces. Furthermore, as I mentioned in Chapter 2, for Suku Asli, living near rivers and coasts and engaging in mangrove logging is one of the most important criteria distinguishing *orang asli* from others. For me, they seemed to have a clear image that Suku Asli lived near rivers to utilize the resources. This seems to mean they have a clear attachment to some of the concrete conditions of the river-coast space.

In the field, I tried at first to confirm and prove this through the voices of the people. I asked some Suku Asli why they had chosen to live near the coast. One said, 'There was an empty space here before'; another said, 'Because my brother's house is close to here'; yet another said, 'Here is distant from other houses and a quiet place.' They gave varied answers and I could find no common voices. I then tried to find a pattern in the present distribution of Suku Asli

Photograph 3.2: A house of the Suku Asli (Raya River)

houses, connecting them with resources, kinship, or religious monuments. They used the resources of the mangrove swamps anywhere they could access them. Some houses were built near their kinfolk but many houses were not. They did not stick to particular distances from ancestral graves and *keramat* places. I could find no obvious patterns or conditions except that they lived on riverbanks where the Malays and Javanese did not live.

Trying to explore their attachment to land, one day I asked Koding what constituted a 'good place' for living in when they had moved frequently. I expected that he would point out the particular conditions of land in the coastal space, along with an explanation to do with the riches of resources, kin, or ancestral relationships with the land, or the ancestral monuments or territory represented by graves and *keramat* places. However, he looked slightly perplexed and thought for a bit before answering, 'It was *yang suka saja*' (just doing as one likes). He continued, 'If we found a "good place" while *jalan-jalan* (walking around), we moved and lived in the place. If we had good friends, we also moved...and lived in the place.' I tried to grasp their preferences for location, and asked, 'How about living in the hinterland forests?' He answered, 'No, it's *jauh dari laut* (far from the river), difficult to live.' I continued, 'How about living on banks facing the open sea?' He said, 'It's okay. But strong winds and waves shake our canoes. It's terrifying. I do not want to live there.' In addition, I asked, 'Do you prefer to live near to the family houses?' He replied, 'If the person wants to do so, it's okay. But it is not necessary to do so.' He concluded that, 'In the past, there were much fewer people around here. People did as they liked.'

Koding stressed the existence of 'friends.' Friendship is established by living together and sharing food, and friends may often be categorized as kin because Suku Asli share a vague notion that they had the same ancestors and may extend this category through the idea of bilateral kin relations. However, emphasizing the word 'friend' did not mean that consanguineous closeness or kin categorizations influenced their choice of where to live. If they establish a good relationship with other people (usually the Rawa, Akit, and ethnic Chinese), they may move nearby. Therefore, their way of life seems to be characterized as 'open aggregation,' in which 'all groups beyond the domestic family are loosely defined, ephemeral, and weakly corporate, and in which membership is fluid, elective and overlapping' (Gibson and Sillander 2011: 1; see also Chapter 4). Therefore, they could live in any coastal areas they wanted without specific social relationships with neighbors. However, even around river coasts, they do not live in the settlements with the Javanese and Malays, with whom it is relatively difficult to share food and intermarry. According to Koding, they feel *takut* (fear) and *malu* (shame) at the prospect of communicating with such outsiders.

Peter Gow (1995) describes how the people of the Bajo Urubamba in Peru see kinship in their lands. Past relations, especially through the production and exchange of food, constitute kinship between people. They recognize the extension of their space beyond the horizon by mentioning kin living in a distant place, although space is separated by forests. They also remember the history of the land and those who occupied it in the past. He concludes that people recognize space by the social relationships within it. The Suku Asli would also see social relationships in the coastal area in quite a similar way.

After talking with Koding, I thought friendship was one of the essential conditions in their preference for land. However, checking my field notes that evening, I found that friendship was only a small part of their non-objectified world. Although friendship was important for them, Koding said, 'It was just doing as one likes.' Clearly, he only mentioned friendship as an example. Even if they do not have a friendship, they still choose a place to live. Indeed, the person who emphasized the quietness of his home lived more than 500 meters from neighboring houses.

I rethought the details of my conversation with Koding. Although he clearly explained the reasons why he thought some places were 'bad,' he was vague about why some living spaces were 'good.' I wondered whether Suku Asli had lived in coastal spaces behind the mangrove forest by a method of elimination. This might be partly true, but it did not explain their attachment to the land. Immediately, I thought this question was nonsense because it might not be easy to evaluate a living place and address it in words. I thought about it from a personal perspective and asked myself how I would explain in words how 'good' my home village in Japan was. Before I left home to continue my education at university, I had been a kind of autochthonous person in rural Japan, where my family had lived for generations. I could not think of how to explain it as 'good,' other than that it was because I was born there. The village was my living place and an essential part of my world as a whole. I was connected with the land in so many ways and this had sustained my life as a whole and in practice. If I compared the village with different places and focused on specific points, I may be able to explain only a part of it in words. I felt that Koding must be in the same situation. While he could compare river coasts with sea coasts and hinterlands, he could not explain his attachment to the riverbank directly in words. Therefore, he used friendship as an example. Through thinking aloud, I was able to understand that connectedness between people and land is unconscious and subjective.

There is a sequel to the conversation with Koding. Some days later, I talked with him about shamanic techniques and he said, 'I remembered that there is an important reason to choose a "good place" for living. The important thing is whether the place is occupied by "people" or not.' 'People' does not refer to actual humans but nonphysical humans—that is, *orang* or *orang bunyian* (people or people of sounds). These people are invisible and walk around the forests, rivers, settlements, and other places. Although they are neither benevolent nor malevolent to human beings, if houses are built on their paths, they get angry and cause illness and misfortune to the family. *Dukun*, supported by the local *datuk*, can communicate and negotiate with the *orang bunyian*. Ordinary people can also communicate with such *orang bunyian* in their dreams. If they found that a new place was occupied by *orang bunyian*, they moved to another place. These *orang bunyian* are not fixed in particular places and move around the same way as the people in the past.

This cosmological explanation and description seem to symbolically represent their traditional relationship with space. Both people and spirits moved around, and sacred places and graves were also transient in the past. However, this is also only a part of their connectedness with the land. In our conversation, our topic was about shamanic techniques and the relationship between spirit and land, and Koding objectified and exemplified a spirit's connectedness with the land.

In the Suku Asli way of choosing a living space, we can see their indigeny in the river-coast space (i.e. unconscious and subjective attachment to space). However, the Suku Asli case seems to be slightly different from Benjamin's (2002: 15; 2012) definition that emphasizes linkages between people and a concrete place. For them, space is not comparted as places but extends continuously, and their linkage is not limited to a concrete place but to the river-coast environment itself. Chou (2013) points out the recognition of space among sea nomads, including the Orang Suku Laut. For them, 'space has always been conceptualized as a continuous expanse for them that is defined by movement, perception, behaviour or activity' (Chou 2013: 64). Similarly, Suku Asli have moved around coastal areas to obtain resources, and the river-coast space constitutes an essential part of their world.

In the conversation, connectedness between people and land is partly objectified in specific contexts. Some anthropological studies of indigenous peoples emphasize their strong attachment to their lands in their cosmologies. Lye Tuck-Po (2005) points out that the Batek, hunter-gatherers in the Malay Peninsula, are 'looking after' the forest. In their cosmology, the Batek are the essential agents in the care of the forest and play the 'guardianship' role; if the people left the forest, the world would collapse. She concludes by seeing the forest as necessarily implicated in social existence. Tenas Effendy (2002) explains the cosmology of the Petalangan, swidden cultivators in inland Riau, in a similar manner. For them, a tree, which is the essential component of the forest, and the human body are entwined in a mutually metaphorical relationship, and so they take great care to protect the forest environment. Chou (2010: 90–5) also points out a similar cosmology among the Orang Suku Laut in the Riau-Lingga Archipelago. While their cosmological connectedness between people and land must be a truth, it is only an aspect of their connectedness as a whole. The anthropologists or the peoples themselves objectify their unconscious and subjective connectedness into a cosmological human–nature relationship.

The reason for the focus on cosmological connectedness seems to be primarily because anthropologists or peoples themselves try to show the historical and cultural use of the lands. Describing the cosmological and ancestral connectedness between peoples and their territories underlines their priority of land occupation in time and cultural distinctiveness in the international definitions of indigenous peoples. This may result in supporting people who do have written records or legal legitimations of their territories and who have been marginalized. All people described in the ethnographies mentioned above were in predicaments caused by outsider encroachment on their territories. Their connectedness is objectified in competition for lands.

However, Suku Asli in Teluk Pambang have not clearly shown their connectedness with or attachment to the coastal space around their houses. This is, first and foremost, because the space was less competitive. However, they objectified their attachment to the land first in the hinterland and then in mangrove forests around brackish rivers when these spaces became competitive with the Javanese.

Connecting land and people

Participation in the deforestation of hinterland

The Suku Asli did not depend on the resources of the hinterland forests. They only used the land when they passed through it or for occasional hunting. However, it was the hinterland rainforest that became the first kind of place/space that the Suku Asli objectified and to which they demonstrated their connectedness with land. Through outsider images on the linkage between people and land, they started to manifest attachment to the hinterland space earlier and more clearly than to the coastal space.

After the 1940s, the population around the Raya River increased dramatically. When the log plant was established on its banks, many Suku Asli engaged in the logging and transportation of timbers under the management of ethnic Chinese. At the end of the 1960s, the land on the shores of the Raya River became insufficient. Some Suku Asli began opening the hinterlands to the west of the river. Some moved to the upper reaches of the Kembung Luar River. In government deforestation and construction projects in the 1960s, Suku Asli joined together with the Javanese. They opened the forest and the village headman recognized their land right in the northern area along the present Jl. Budi Luhur (see Map 3.2).[8] The details of this land opening are unclear because most of the people concerned had passed away when I was in the village.

In 1979, Suku Asli established an agricultural group, the Pondak Condong, and asked the Javanese administrative headman to allow them to open the western hinterland of Jl. Budi Luhur in order to create gardens. At this time, 115 Suku Asli households joined the group and cleared about 300 hectares of the forest, and each household received the right of land use to about two-and-a-half hectares. After the implementation of the Basic Forestry Law of 1967, the region of Teluk Pambang was categorized as *kawasan hutan* (the forest zone) and the ownership of the zone was attributed to the state. (At present, most of the region of Suka Maju village is categorized as the APL or non-forest area.) Therefore, the Suku Asli at first obtained an *izin tebas tebang* (slashing permit) issued by the village and subdistrict offices, which certified the right of land use to the opened forest. During the 1980s, the slashing permit was gradually replaced by the *Surat Keterangan Tanah* (SKT; land letter) in Riau (Mujiburohman et al. 2014). A set of the SKT and *Surat Keterangan Ganti Rugi* (SKGR; compensation letter), which is issued by village and subdistrict offices, enable the holders to transfer the right of land use to others. While the detailed legal standings of the SKT and SKGR in relation to the national laws are vague and controversial, lands are broadly transferred through these letters in Riau (Dethia et al. 2020: 427–9).

In the late 1990s, a new Suku Asli organization called *Organisasi Pemuda Suku Asli* (OPSA; Suku Asli Youth Organization) was established by Ajui. OPSA cleared 200 hectares of the hinterland forest adjacent to the gardens opened by the Pondak Condong, the village boundary with Bantan Air. At this time, 120 Suku Asli households joined the project and each received two hectares. In this land opening, OPSA members no longer obtained slashing permits, but could apply for the SKT and SKGR.

The Suku Asli obtained gardens as a result of these hinterland deforestations. However, the gardens have not become the main sources of their livelihood. According to the Suku Asli, they wanted to gain their livelihood from the gardens, and at first they planted seedlings of coconuts and rubber. Yet it took several years until they were able to harvest them. Therefore, they did not move to the gardens from their houses near the rivers, where they had historically gained their livelihood, but went to the gardens several kilometers distant from their houses to work on a daily basis. It gradually became more difficult to go every day, and they eventually sold the gardens to outsiders. This process had significance in terms of the national law. Although the Basic Agrarian Law of 1960 set out the right of individual land possession, the right was legitimized for dwelling space, gardens, and fields that were well maintained. If the land returned to forest, the state could claim its ownership (Acciaioli 2007: 312). Based on such a legal aspect, the Javanese village headman would have required the Suku Asli to maintain the land as gardens. Therefore, the Suku Asli had only two choices: either they cultivated and maintained the gardens continuously with tremendous effort or they sold the land.

Almost all land opened in the regency government project in the 1960s was sold to the Javanese who came to the village in the second wave of immigration just after the project. The deforestation led by the Pondak Condong in 1979 was a relatively complex situation. According to the administrative village headman at the time, he permitted the deforestation presupposing the Basic Agrarian Law of 1960, which partly recognized the customary land rights of the *adat* law community. He allowed each agricultural group in a customary community to open the forest only for the purpose of making gardens and homesteads. He also required that people opening the land should not sell the opened land outside the community, and land transactions were permitted only within their community when all members of the group agreed. An agricultural group was established in the Javanese community and applied for the land right to the hinterland forest. The Suku Asli established the Pondak Condong, consisting of

Suku Asli members, and accepted the two conditions from the village headman, and the group's right to the opened land was recognized. However, eventually, most parts of the land were sold. In most cases, the land right was sold to ethnic Chinese living in Bengkalis town who wanted more gardens. The Suku Asli regarded the ethnic Chinese as the same ethnic group in these dealings, based on their kin network with ethnic Chinese, and they persuaded the village headman, as well as the group members, to allow the sales.[9]

In 2012, the lands sold to Chinese city dwellers began to be used as oil palm gardens. Suku Asli were employed by the city dwellers to cut down the coconut palms and rubber trees that had been planted, and to plant the oil palm seedlings. This was in accordance with the explosive expansion of oil palm plantations and its industry in Riau, which had begun in the 1990s (Masuda et al. 2016: 176–8). However, oil palms did not suit the peat soil with its brackish water. In 2019, I often found small oil palms that had yellow leaves and had stopped growing. According to villagers, even when they bore nuts, the productivity was extremely low.

On the other hand, in 2012, most lands opened by OPSA in the late 1990s were still owned by Suku Asli. While some well-off Suku Asli have bought land from other Suku Asli to extend their gardens, these involved dealings between members. By the second half of the 1990s, the roads were almost all paved, many people had obtained motorbikes to travel to the gardens from their coastal settlement, and their access to the land had become much easier. However, the majority of land has not been used in productive ways as gardens. Although people sometimes attended to the land, maintained the ditches as boundaries, and killed the weeds, quite a few landholders did not harvest the rubber and oil palms. The land thus did not return to forest but became bush. They derided such lands and ashamedly called them *hutan buatan* (manufactured forest), which implies an ambivalent situation for the landholder; although one has opened the land for growing coconuts or rubber with much effort and government permission, one appears only to grow bush on the land.

In 2015, Indonesia had record-breaking low rainfall and large-scale forest fires broke out across the archipelago. The peatland opened by OPSA also suffered a fire, and the gardens and *hutan buatan* were lost. After this fire, the lands were almost abandoned for some years. In 2017, a Buddhist organization, *Majelis Pandita Buddha Maitreya Indonesia* (Maitreya Great Tao), suggested an effective use for this land and has been supplying Suku Asli with areca nut seedlings, fertilizer, herbicide, and wages for everyday cultivation, and the Suku Asli have worked their own parcels of land. The organization receives 70 percent of the products, of which 10 percent of the proceeds are used for the

Photograph 3.3: Manufactured forest in Teluk Pambang

maintenance of the Buddhist temple in the village. The fund is sustained by donations from Chinese or *peranakan* Buddhist communities in cities, who have kin relations with *peranakan* Suku Asli on Bengkalis Island. In 2019, areca nuts had not yet been harvested, but thirty-one Suku Asli households with eighty hectares of land had joined the project. According to a project manager dispatched from the Buddhist organization, 'This is a challenge. We wish we will be able to mitigate the poverty of this village through this project.'

According to Graeme MacRae (2003: 159), land can be a commodity under legal registration. He points out that the legal title to land changes inalienable land into a commodity, for the title casts off customary restraints on alienation. Furthermore, for the Suku Asli, the new gardens were not customary lands. Therefore, Suku Asli appear to be dealing with the forest as a commodity. However, Nicolas Long (2009: 80–1) points out that, even if legal rights are fixed, lands can neither wholly become a capitalist commodity nor become free from 'the webs of social relationships and cultural logics.' Indeed, the gardens that were sold were involved in the webs of social relations and the cultural logics of Suku Asli.

Lands as kinship: 'for children and grandchildren'

One day, sitting on benches in front of his house as usual, I again talked with Koding about the history of the village. I asked him, as one of three leaders of the Pondak Condong, the reason why he organized the agricultural group and led the deforestation of the hinterland. For me, it was slightly strange that they opened gardens that were not always necessary for them and, indeed, were then sold. He told me that the deforestation was *untuk anak cucu* (for their children and grandchildren): 'People increased, and it was necessary to make sure of the lands where our children and grandchildren would live.' I questioned him: 'Why were such lands sold to others?' He also sold most of the land he had opened in the government project through the activity of Pondak Condong. His face, with a genial look until then, hardened, and he stated, 'The lands were sold not for money for cigarettes (*uang rokok*)...The lands were sold for preparing money for our children's education, building houses, and buying motorbikes and medicine for children. Everyone is the same.' Our topic of conversation then returned to the history of the village. However, after a momentary pause, he suddenly stressed again, 'The lands were sold for our children and grandchildren. For preparing money for our children's education and to buy their medicine, we sold the land,' he said with a somewhat sorrowful look on his face.

Opening forest 'for children and grandchildren' is not Koding's improvised expression. The phrase was used to negotiate with the Javanese headman in the 1960s, and, indeed, many Suku Asli registered the newly opened lands with the names of children and grandchildren. The Javanese village headman who allowed the Pondak Condong to open the hinterlands remembered the words: 'As they told me that they wanted to open the land for their children and grandchildren, I allowed them to do it.' For the village headman, the words 'for children and grandchildren' fitted with the legal regulations that recognized the customary rights to land, as well as his feeling as a Javanese about the land and its importance. As lands had not been inherited in the foraging way of life among Suku Asli, this idea of 'for children and grandchildren' appears to be molded in a hegemonic relationship between Suku Asli and the Javanese or the government.

However, the idea is not just an imposed one—it also fitted with the Suku Asli idea of children and grandchildren, and was used for integrating the members of the Pondak Condong. For Suku Asli, descendants, including children and grandchildren, are not only those who are loved and cared for but also those who will take care of them in the future through rituals. The Suku Asli are obligated to offer food to their ancestral spirits in periodic rituals (see Chapter 2). At the same time, it is an obligation to have and guard descendants who will feed them in the future, and to ensure their livelihoods. Although every Suku Asli more or less shares this feeling, it is much stronger among the *peranakan* Suku Asli than 'real' Suku Asli. The *peranakan* Suku Asli have maintained their strong relationship with their ancestors and descendants through their relatively frequent (almost monthly) practices of ancestral rituals in 'Chinese' ways. It is not an accident that the three leaders of the Pondak Condong, including Koding, were all *peranakan*.

Despite the descendants and newly opened lands being deeply related, why did the Suku Asli sell the land? It was for the same reason, 'for children and grandchildren,' according to Koding. Based on this reason, people chose either to sell or preserve cleared lands. A Suku Asli who kept a manufactured forest, a *hutan buatan*, told me that if his two sons, then living together, marry in the village, they would build houses and gardens in the *hutan buatan*; however, if they left the village, he would sell the land to someone else. Indeed, he had sold part of the land to an ethnic Chinese living in Bengkalis town when his daughter had married and left the village. His thoughts consistently fit the cultural logic of Suku Asli, who did not open the lands to sell them as a commodity.

Nor is the productivity of the land for their children and grandchildren necessarily brought about by the land itself. Selling land and buying medicine or sending children to school is also productive. This is more obvious if the land is hard to access. Long (2009) describes a similar case in the arbitration of a land conflict matter between the Malays and the Batak in the Riau Archipelago. A Malay wife, whose husband had the ancestral legal right to an orchard very far from their house, wanted to sell the land to a Batak because 'the sale of the land at a time of economic hardship would facilitate her in becoming the mother and grandmother she wanted to be, enabling her to better provide for her family' (Long 2009: 73–4). This shows the importance placed on the value of taking care of one's kin in Malay kinship. Long (2009: 74) concludes, 'The "commodification" of the land was thus not in tension with "customary" Malay practices and values but an alternative means of their actualisation.' For the Suku Asli, selling land was also an 'alternative means of actualisation' of care for their children and grandchildren consistent with their cultural logic. Lands were opened and sold not as simple commodities but as a reflection of their culture and identity.

It is a dilemma that although they have an ideal picture of the cleared land as constituting the livelihood of the descendants, they cannot accomplish their aim. Therefore, selling land involves some emotional turmoil. Koding's restless attitude in our conversation surely represents this, and their cynical attitude to the manufactured forest can also be understood in the same context. Identity and land are deeply connected in their world. The fact that they sold their land to the ethnic Chinese can also be understood not only as an expedient for negotiating with the group members or the village headman, but also as a feeble attempt to preserve their social identity, which is attached to the land. By selling the land to the ethnic Chinese, who may be regarded as their kin, they try to keep open the possibility that the social identity attached to the land is maintained. They sell the land for their children and grandchildren to ethnic Chinese who are potential kin. Selling the land, which is rather an individual action, can become morally positive and accepted by the society so long as it involves the possibility of maintaining or reproducing their social identity (Bloch and Parry 1989).

The image of land, which emerges in Koding's comments and responses, provides us with quite a different impression from the stories about their past life. According to these stories, they moved around freely without attachment to specific land. When they moved, they abandoned the land or sold only the trees on the land to others. In particular, lands in the hinterland forest were outside their world. However, in his comments about the opened land, the land seems to be something emotional and concerned with identity. It is connected with their future children and grandchildren. Now, land and people are mutually implicated. Suku Asli landscape has changed.

As a result of Javanese immigration, land shortage, and government interventions, they extended their world to the hinterlands and represented the feelings 'for children and grandchildren' by attaching them to the land. Although their past relation to landscape ignored the land itself, their landscape is now characterized by mutual implications between people and land, as well as by the temporary continuity from the past to the future. Suku Asli see kinship in the opened land. In the opened hinterlands they see their children and grandchildren who will feed them in the future. Therefore, their relation with the hinterland has changed and this change came about through their relation with outsiders and the state after the 1960s. In other words, their relationship with hinterland was problematized in the competition for land and the government development program, and they objectified their total connectedness with the land as descendants' lands.

Movements in coastal space: mangrove swamps and ancestors

Although the hinterlands were connected with their descendants and then sold after the 1960s, the change of coastal space where the Suku Asli lived was relatively undramatic. After the first Javanese migration, they began opening the hinterland and did not encroach on the western tributaries from the Banan River to the west of the Raya River. Historically, some Javanese households had bought land in this space from the Suku Asli or had moved to empty land; however, they have since moved to the hinterlands. This is because this space was generally less suitable for harvesting coconut or rubber. When they cultivate these plants, they need to dig ditches to drain the swampy peatland, but the brackish water from the tributaries runs into the gardens through the ditches and the soil often becomes damaged. In addition, it would have been uncomfortable for the Javanese to live on land surrounded by non-Islamic people. Even today, Suku Asli populations are concentrated on the coastal space between the Banan River and west of the Raya River.

The Suku Asli did not explicitly connect with their ancestors and the lands in this space. They have lived in this space from the past to the present. They obtained their main livelihood from the river and mangrove forest, logging mangrove trunks, fishing in the river, cultivating tubers and coconuts in small gardens, and gathering sago and shellfish. They rarely sold the lands in this space, and the lands were, indeed, less involved in competition and conflict. For them, this space was naturally their own. However, this space began to be actively connected with their ancestors in very recent years in a totally different process from that in the hinterlands. The trigger was not the land where they have lived, but the tidal mangrove forest, where they gained their main livelihood, in combination with the progress of environmentalism as a fundamental part of the recent political agenda.

The encroachment on the riverbank and the inflow of brackish water in this space became problematic in Teluk Pambang after the second half of the 1990s. Even before this, the riverbanks were gradually washed out, and brackish water flowed into gardens near rivers or the sea at high tide, but the frequency of the inflow has gradually increased in recent years and its harmful influence on the productivity of the gardens has become more and more serious. In particular, the gardens around the mouth of the Kembung Luar River, including the banks of the Rambai River, have suffered from the serious effects of floods. The Javanese living around the Rambai River attribute the main cause to the decrease of mangrove forests in this area. Indeed, the mangrove forest forms an important natural bank protection (Giesen et al. 2006: 34–5). The Javanese began trying to protect and regenerate the mangrove forest by planting *bakau* seedlings and restricting the logging of mangrove forests. This attempt was also related to their livelihoods, as the mature *bakau* trunks can be sold as charcoal and building materials. However, for the Javanese, one of the major obstacles to carrying out this project was logging of *bakau* by Suku Asli.

Although the hinterlands of the tidal mangrove forest had been divided among and legally used by individuals, the mangrove swamps, into which brackish water flows everyday, are state forest categorized as 'limited production forest' under the national law. In practice, its resources were customarily used by local communities. Suku Asli conducted the logging of *bakau* in this space freely, and went back and forth along the Kembung Luar River by canoe. If they found good trunks, they often entered the Rambai River and conducted logging. In order to stop their logging, the Javanese began applying for the usufruct right

Photograph 3.4: A washed-out swamp and mangrove seedlings (Rambai River)

of the mangrove swamps along the Rambai River by organizing a logging group. They applied for *hutan kemasyarakatan* (community forest), in which the community obtains 'the permission for timber production from the plantations created through the scheme' for thirty-five years and part of the profit is shared with the government (Ota 2011: 123). Their applications were accepted by the village headman and the regency offices and the right was given to the logging groups. They stretched ropes around the swamps, put signs at riverbanks indicating the group's management, and built sentry huts in places where there was good *bakau* forest. Suku Asli were excluded from these swamps. At the beginning, Suku Asli did not take counter actions, but there were some minor conflicts between them and the Javanese because some Suku Asli entered the swamps to log. However, they always ran away when they met the Javanese in the forest and no collective action was taken.

In 2003, OPSA applied for the land title to thirty hectares of coastal space along the Raya River, in the same way that it had applied for the hinterland of the 'non-forest area.' Although part of the land had been state tidal mangrove forest, it was vaguely accepted by the village headman as the boundary between the 'non-forest area' and the 'limited production forest.' According to Ajui (the head of OPSA), using the same logic as OPSA had when opening hinterland, the application was for the right to build houses or gardens for members. They dug ditches on the land and distributed the land to the members, and some obtained from the village office SKTs on which their children and grandchildren were registered as the owners. However, the mangrove lands were not used for houses and gardens at all, and were left as they had been, since brackish water often flowed through them. I asked Ajui the reason why he had distributed the land, even though he must have known it was quite difficult to use tidal land for

Photograph 3.5:
A signboard showing the management of a mangrove forest by the Javanese group Makmur Bersama (Rambai River)

houses. At about this point, his answers became vague. It seems that the move had been intended as a counter action against the Javanese—because OPSA felt strongly about the encroachment of swamp by the Javanese, they had tried to resist. They also seemed to have an agenda to ensure their logging space in the future. However, this agenda ended in failure.

After the late 1990s, quite a few domestic and foreign researchers visited the island for the purpose of investigating the rich and unique mangrove forests. According to regency officials in Bengkalis town, the central government ordered the regency government to protect the mangrove environment on the island following reports submitted by such researchers. In 2006, the regency government stopped renewing the export licenses of charcoal huts on the island.[10] Although the government still issued licenses for charcoal huts to supply products to local communities, this was desperately unprofitable for *touke* who ran large-scale huts and exported the products to Singapore and Malaysia. Although some *touke* and Suku Asli leaders protested to the government, their complaints were not accepted. Eventually, several charcoal huts along the Kembung Luar River were closed and Suku Asli villagers lost their main livelihood.

During my fieldwork in 2012, Suku Asli seemed to depend less on coastal resources than in the past. Some people had boats and engaged in net fishing and in logging mangrove timbers for building materials, and people also went occasionally to the mangrove swamps and gathered shellfish. However, waged labor in gardens owned by the ethnic Chinese and the Javanese provided them with their main livelihood. Part of these gardens was the land that they had sold in the past. Temporary labor to construct roads and buildings was also important. On the basis of such labor, they made an income from their own small gardens in which coconuts, rubber, and areca nuts were planted. In any case, their transportation was totally dependent on the roads and lanes and the motorbikes that every household uses. As for food, although they planted sago palms in the corners of gardens, they more frequently ate rice that was provided by the government[11] or bought with their wages.

In addition to closing the charcoal huts, the government continued to facilitate the environmental movement to protect the mangrove swamps. During my fieldwork in 2012, the government offered many subsidies to a Javanese logging group in Teluk Pambang and encouraged it to plant *bakau* seedlings. The government also held occasional seminars for logging groups. I attended one such seminar in the village of Bantan Air. In the seminar, an official with knowledge of the coastal environment spoke about how important the mangrove trees were for maintaining the coastal environment and how important the coastal environment was for sustaining fishing and agriculture. Some Suku Asli loggers from Selat Baru also attended that meeting.

One day Ajui told me about a plan to apply to the government for the right of use of mangrove swamps around the Raya River as a 'community forest'. In his plan, a few hundred hectares of mangroves, which cover most swamps of the Raya River, would be registered for the exclusive use of OPSA, which would build sentry huts in the forest, and protect the land and the mangroves. I found this plan strange because I knew that the land that had been divided in 2003 had not been used for houses or gardens. It also seemed to be difficult to negotiate with the central government about reopening the charcoal exporting huts. I therefore asked him why he would want to do this. His answer struck me: 'It is because the mangrove forest is our land. From ancestors, we have possessed it. We have to *jaga* (look after) the land.' It was the first and only time that I heard a clear claim made in terms of their ancestral land. As mentioned above, ordinary Suku Asli did not always regard the tidal mangrove swamps as such. However, Ajui knew that the post-Suharto government might recognize the usufruct right of mangrove swamps if people demonstrated their ancestral use of the land.

This application to register the mangrove forest as 'community forest' was accepted by the regency government in 2013. Seventy Suku Asli households joined the activity, in which they planted 10,000 *bakau* seedlings on 120 hectares of swampy land in 2014. The seedlings were supplied by the regency branch of the Ministry of Environment and Forestry. According to Ajui, the mangrove timber will be logged and sold around 2022, and the profits will be distributed between the households who joined the activity and partly used as OPSA funds.

The area east of the community forest was Suku Asli gardens and mangrove swamps. As the gardens were frequently damaged by brackish water, many Suku Asli abandoned the gardens and, in 2016, a company bought the abandoned gardens from the Suku Asli owners and obtained the usufruct right of the mangrove forest from the government. In 2017, a shrimp-breeding farm, established by a Chinese owner living in Pekanbaru, commenced operations on the land and a dozen Suku Asli worked the farm. This was in accordance with a regency policy to promote the construction of shrimp-breeding farms. According to staff of the company, the regency government promoted the shrimp-breeding program to prevent the encroachment of coastal banks caused by canal construction for oil palm plantations (cf. Suryadi 2019). The government issued permission to use the mangrove swamps, and the company took on the responsibility of planting mangrove seedlings around the farm to prevent the encroachment. Indeed, the company planted 50,000 mangrove seedlings around the farm as its corporate social responsibility. In the process of the construction of the farm, Suku Asli did not protest because, according to Ajui, 'The company legally obtained the land right outside our "ancestral forest". Furthermore, the owner is a *peranakan* [Chinese], and Suku Asli work in the farm. That's no problem for us.'

Although the Suku Asli have had an attachment to the coastal space, it was a small-scale connection and was unconscious and subjective. However, after the mangrove swamps became difficult to access due to Javanese activities, they began trying to designate boundaries in the coastal space and to connect the space with their ancestors. Porath (2000) describes a Sakai case in mainland Sumatra in which the burial mound of a historical Sakai hero was 're-appreciated' as ancestral space after they had lost much of their space due to an oil company's encroachment on their forest. While the Suku Asli also have 're-appreciated' their mangrove swamps, I would like to suggest that this process can be seen as the objectification or embodiment of a new way of relating to land in their world. They have objectified the space as ancestral land by emphasizing *adat* community and using it in the competition for space and their interaction with government interventions. It is also remarkable that the 'community forest' right is only a usufruct right for thirty-five years, so it was difficult to adopt the 'for children and grandchildren' logic. As a result, ancestral land as a form of space has emerged in a Suku Asli perspective. Their unconscious and subjective attachment to the coastal space, which can be summarized by the term 'indigeny,' has transformed into a conscious and objective linkage between the people and the land on which the outsiders' image is reflected—that is, the emergence of indigeneity in their society. Again, the linkage between people and land is endorsed by their imagined kinship or ethnicity. Therefore, the encroachment of mangrove forest by ethnic Chinese was accepted.

Space: from transient individuals to enduring social order

As Ajui stated, the Suku Asli obtained the community forest rights not to sell the land or obtain money but to 'look after' the mangrove forest. This means that mangrove swamps became something inalienable, which was inherited from their ancestors. As Karl Marx (see Bloch and Parry 1989: 4–6) pointed out, the relationship between people is symbolically embodied in the relationship between persons and things. The relationship between persons and spaces can be included in this context. Chou (2010: 76–8) sees the territories of the Orang Suku Laut in the Riau-Lingga Archipelago as the 'inalienable gifts' from their ancestors. Maintaining ancestral territories, including not only land but also sea routes, is deeply rooted in their social identity, and through its maintenance they reconfigure and reproduce the relationship with their ancestors, as well as their future descendants. In so doing, they are demonstrating their territorial rights against recent government infrastructure and building projects along the shore. However, the case of the Suku Asli shows a more dynamic aspect of the relationship between persons and things.

The transformation of the relationship between people and land among the Suku Asli can be seen as a process to establish an enduring, long-term social order transcending individual relationships with land. The Suku Asli connection with a place in the past can be characterized by a short-term transient and individual quality. They moved from place to place relatively freely and obtained only the resources they needed from the space, which was not concerned with the moral social order. However, their present-day connection with a place is characterized by a long-term constancy and collectivity. In the process of their participation in the deforestation of the hinterland, they connected lands with their descendants, and the lands were gradually involved in their moral order. Even though the newly opened lands were sold, this was justified in relation to the moral sphere as a practice that assured the livelihood of their descendants. In addition, mangrove marshland became an inalienable space unconcerned with any individual transient profits. Here, the land is something that was inherited from ancestors and will be inherited by descendants as an 'inalienable gift.' In this context, space is clearly characterized by a transcendental quality that is deeply connected with the reproduction of their social order and morality.

In this transformation, it is remarkable that two agents have played essential roles. The first one was the Javanese. Their interventions in the Suku Asli landscape in the form of encroachment on hinterlands and the development projects have encouraged the Suku Asli to change their perception of space to a long-term one. Second, the roles of the *peranakan* Suku Asli are also important. Compared with 'real' Suku Asli, they have the stronger ideology for maintaining the symbolic relationships with their ancestors and descendants. This ideology was embodied in the idea of assuring descendants' livelihoods through the newly opened gardens. In other words, the *peranakan* Suku Asli have had much greater potentiality to accept the longer-term circle of lands. As a result of the stimulation from these two agents, the connection between persons and space became natural and inevitable, and the marshland came to be regarded as an inalienable gift.

The Suku Asli have changed their perception of space through competition with and the intervention of outsiders, which is something characterized by exogeny and seems to be shared in common with many forest-dwelling indigenous people. In many cases, their social system in terms of their connection to land was not obvious, and they were individually related to the land in a small-scale and family-level fashion. Then, through competition with outsiders and interventions by state development programs, they started to establish a social order that transcended individual relations to land. Again, it is remarkable that the process can be seen as one where the current people are reconfiguring historically continuous relationships with their ancestors and descendants through their acquisition of lands. In other words, they have obtained a collective identity that has spatial and temporary continuities through the transformation of their perception of and relation to space. The solidarity of their *adat* community is reinforced by emphasis on their connections via their possession and usufruct right of land.

Again, connectedness between people and land is unconscious and subjective. However, when it is problematized in a particular context, people objectify the uncounted significance of land for living and embody specific forms of land. In the Suku Asli case, their connectedness was problematized in and through land competition and government intervention, and they have objectified and embodied the hinterland as their descendants' land and the mangrove forests as ancestral land. In this process, they have obtained something to be regarded as a collective identity, in which the people, mediated by land, are connected from their ancestors to descendants.

It is noteworthy that the consolidation of Suku Asli identity in interaction with the government has its roots in the negotiation of land. The Pondak Condong was the first organization formed by the Suku Asli on Bengkalis Island. After its success in obtaining a variety of rights, many Suku Asli agricultural, fishing, and logging groups have been organized in other villages on the island. OPSA, which supports the life of Suku Asli villagers through negotiations with the government, was established in the late 1990s by Ajui under the advice of his father, Koding, who was one of three leaders of the Pondak Condong. On the basis of OPSA, IKBBSA was established in 2005, and Suku Asli interaction with the government has dramatically increased. However, the reason they established an ethnic organization was not because they wished to protect their land and resources, nor was the protection of traditional land and resources the main purpose of their recent manifestation of indigeneity; furthermore, they seem to have no specific economic or political purposes in having done so. Instead, rather than economic reasons, the reason they established IKBBSA and manifested their indigeneity is much more related to political power, in which the state and local agents are entangled. I would like to explore this in the next chapter.

It is also remarkable that, as a result of their configuration of descendants and ancestral lands, the distinction between the Suku Asli and Akit has become more obvious. This is because, after they began recognizing their descendants and ancestral land, territory became more important in relation to identity. In terms of this problem, the establishment of the ethnic organization also played an important role. I will reconsider this topic in the next chapter.

Thus, through their changing relation to the land, the Suku Asli have the beginnings of a 'proper' identity—in other words, by emphasizing their connection to a particular land, they can start to differentiate themselves from other *orang asli* (i.e. other lands) and to unite the 'real' and *peranakan* Suku Asli into a single society. Of course, this change is further reinforced by a number of other changes—like the establishment of an ethnic organization, the unification of their ritual practices into a single *adat*, and their acceptance of Buddhism as their ancestral religion. Beginning with their ethnic organization, the next three chapters will discuss these changes.

Chapter 4

Establishment of an Organization: Leadership, Power, and Government Intervention

In the era of decentralization in Indonesia, the authority and power of *adat* have dramatically increased, and the wishes of the local *adat* community are more or less reflected by the policies implemented by government institutions. In this process, local *adat* institutions conduct counterpart negotiations with government institutions. For example, in Bali, the local *adat* assemblies called *krama desa* or *krama banjar* are the counterpart to government *dinas* (local branch) institutions (Warren 2007). In West Sumatra, the local and traditional institution of *nagari,* a conglomeration of villages or settlements, has been revived and implements local policies based on Minangkabau *adat,* although it was once deconstructed during Suharto's era (Biezeveld 2007). These *adat* institutions are organized based on the clearly defined *adat* and *adat* community. In contrast, in the regions where *adat* and *adat* community are not clearly defined (in many cases, these people are in a tribal or marginal position), NGOs such as AMAN have supported people as the counterpart of government institutions or have established local *adat* institutions in communities (cf. Acciaioli 2007: 302).

In Suku Asli society, the main counterpart of government institutions is the ethnic organization of IKBBSA. This organization is a network of *batin* headmen who are appointed in each administrative village and cover all Suku Asli villages in the Bengkalis and Meranti Islands regencies. In each administrative village, there is a *batin desa* (village *batin*) at the top and other incumbents, such as *sekretaris* (secretary) and *kepala adat* (*adat* manager). Beyond the village *batin,* there are two *batin kabupaten* (regency *batin*). According to IKBBSA incumbents, all ordinary Suku Asli—most of whom have not participated in IKBBSA activities—are members of the organization. The organization is regarded as representative of Suku Asli communities and is the main agent that claims their indigeneity and position as an *adat* community. However, IKBBSA is not an organization that has been established based on a clearly defined *adat,* nor was its establishment supported by AMAN. Instead, it is a collaboration between a small number of Suku Asli elites and the regency government.

IKBBSA was established based on the government image of an *adat* community, in which people are related with clear *adat,* and was designed with modern bureaucratic-like systems to implement certain policies within the community. However, instead of a clearly defined *adat* or *adat* community, IKBBSA seems to have been established and maintained based on traditional *batin* leadership in Suku Asli everyday life—that is, the recognition of power and authority related to their indigeny. If this is the case, what role did past *batin* headmanship play, and how are the Suku Asli experiencing leadership in their everyday lives? As mentioned in Chapter 2, Suku Asli society can be characterized by their 'open aggregation' (Gibson and Sillander 2011), in which the people had no institutionalized corporate groups outside the domestic family, freely associated with each other, frequently shifted their membership, and had inclusive policy (Macdonald 2011: 18). Through these practices, they commit themselves to 'solidarity while simultaneously defending an extensive degree of personal autonomy' (Gibson and Sillander 2011: 1). In this situation, the role of the *batin* headman is limited to specific tasks, and leadership in everyday life is situational and flexible. Nevertheless, the Suku Asli have a particular form of recognition of power and authority. In such a situation, IKBBSA has tried to manifest their indigeneity and has had a considerable impact on indigenous and ethnic identity among them.

Headmanship, leadership, and power

I distinguish 'headmanship' and 'leadership' following Benjamin's (1968: 1) definition: while the former refers to the position that is legitimized in relation to outside authority or the government, the latter is one that the people recognize themselves internally. In this section, let me begin with descriptions of situational and flexible characters in *batin* headmanship and leadership in everyday life in Suku Asli society. I would then like to explore Suku Asli recognition of power and authority by emphasizing a particular point of their leadership.

Batin headmanship in Teluk Pambang

'*Batin*' is a title of the traditional headman and is broadly found among tribal or indigenous people and some Malays not only on the eastern coast of Sumatra, but also in the Malay Peninsula (Skeat and Blagden 1966 [1906]: 494; Andaya 2008: 202–25).[1] Although its origin is unclear, given the fact that it prevails over a broad area along the Malacca Strait, the title might have existed among tribal people before they were subsumed under the control of the precolonial Malay state, and the role was then absorbed into the state polity as the local authority or as headman. Under the Siak kingdom, *batin* was one of the official titles that the kingdom legitimized. According to the *Bab Al-Qawa'id*, published by the colonial Siak government at the beginning of the twentieth century, forty-seven *batin* were recognized as headmen on a regional basis (see Junus 2002: 68–76).

According to historical records by van Anrooij (1885: 352), there were two *batin* in Utan communities on Bengkalis Island, *Batin Kembung* and *Batin Bantan*. The oral history of present-day Suku Asli supports this record. According to Suku Asli in Teluk Pambang, while the former was the representative of communities in the eastern part of the island, including the present villages of Kembung Luar and Teluk Pambang, the latter represented those on the northern coast, such as the present villages of Bantan Air and Selat Baru. In addition, according to U. U. Hamidy (1991: 136–8), a local anthropologist in Riau, there were three roles (*antan*, *tongkat*, and *monti*[2]) in assisting *batin* under the polity of the Siak kingdom. Although my friends knew that there had been such positions, they did not know the details.

According to colonial history, the situation of Bengkalis Island was slightly different to that of other areas in the Siak kingdom, as the island was ceded to the Dutch colonial government (see Chapter 1). However, the interest of the Dutch government lay mainly in ensuring the safety of its political center, Bengkalis town, and obtaining customs duties from the ships passing through the channels, so it would have established little control over lands and populations on the island (van Anrooij 1885: 307–10). Therefore, the relationship between the Utan and the Siak kingdom would not have changed immediately after Bengkalis Island was ceded to the Netherlands.

The change in *batin* headmanship in Teluk Pambang began due to the increase in Javanese immigrants and their power. At the end of the nineteenth century, the Javanese immigrated to the eastern part of Bengkalis Island known as Kembung village at that time. The Javanese regarded the *Batin Kembung* as having much authority and legitimacy in the region. Therefore, according to Javanese elders in the village, when the Javanese first arrived in the area, they visited the *batin*'s house and asked for permission to open the lands. After their population increased, the Javanese applied to the colonial government for recognition of their own headman. The government separated the area north of the Kembung Luar River from Kembung village, established the new village of Teluk Pambang, and recognized a Javanese administrative headman or *penghulu* in 1903. After the independence of Indonesia, the post-independence government reappointed a Javanese *penghulu* as the official administrative village headman.

The Suku Asli who lived on both sides of the Kembung Luar River at first had minimal contact with the Javanese, although the people living in the realm of Teluk Pambang gradually recognized the authority of the Javanese *penghulu* and, by the 1970s, had negotiated with him to open the hinterlands (as described in Chapter 3). The *Batin Kembung*, who still lived in Kembung Luar village in the 1960s, was not at all concerned with this movement to open land in Teluk Pambang, according to Koding, who participated in the land opening.

When Teluk Pambang was separated as a new village, Kembung Luar village was established on the south coast of the river. Just after independence, the *Batin Kembung* was appointed *penghulu* of the village of Kembung Luar. However, after a few years the regency government replaced his role with a Javanese *penghulu*. Also, the *Batin Bantan*, who lived in present-day Selat Baru, did not become *penghulu*, as the Malays and Javanese were dominant in the village. The last *Batin Kembung* and *Batin Bantan* died in the 1970s and the 1980s, respectively. Suku Asli did not appoint new *batin*. The two *batin* titles were abolished and their authority disappeared.

The position of *penghulu* was replaced with *kepala desa* (village head) in the second half of 1960s when the central government implemented a national law (No. 19/1965 on Village Government) to integrate village administrative systems across Indonesia. In the 1980s, elections were introduced to local administrative villages. In both Teluk Pambang and Kembung Luar, Javanese headmen continuously held the roles until 2017, when a Suku Asli was elected as the village headman of Kembung Baru, which was the new village established in the western part of Kembung Luar at the end of 2012.

Interestingly, the abolishment of the title of *batin* on Bengkalis Island can be contrasted with the Akit situation. In Rupat, two *batin* titles, *Batin Akit-Hatas Titi Akar* and *Batin Akit Selat Morong*, were maintained even after the independence of Indonesia. This is because the post-independence regency government reappointed the two *batin* as *penghulu* in the new administrative villages of Titi Akar and Hutan Panjang, and they continued in their roles. When elections were introduced to the villages, the regency government required them to separate the posts of *batin* and *kepala desa* because, according to an Akit, while the *batin* is the head of the Akit, the *kepala desa* is the head of the administrative village where Javanese and Malays also live. The community selected new *batin* titles, and the titles continue to be maintained.

The general Suku Asli attitude toward *batin*, *penghulu*, and *kepala desa* is plainly summarized in a comment by Odang: 'We have *ikut* (followed) *batin* in the past, then *penghulu* and now *kepala desa*.' Through experiencing the pivotal role of the *penghulu* in actual political affairs in post-independence Indonesia, Suku Asli in Teluk Pambang seem to recognize the authority and power of *penghulu* and *kepala desa*. When the *batin* role lost recognition by the government, the *batin* lost their authority and the title was finally abolished. The deprivation of legitimacy by the government reduced the opportunity to maintain *batin* within their community. The title of *batin* headmanship in Suku Asli appears largely to have been sustained by government politics and authority.

However, it is also certain that *batin* had tasks that were necessary for the Suku Asli community and not limited within the realm of an official appointed by the government. As the two *batin*, *Batin Kembung* and *Batin Bantan*, lived until the 1970s and 1980s, some Suku Asli elders remembered various tasks they performed. According to them, the tasks of *batin* in their community were, first, to mediate disagreements between Suku Asli. When disagreements emerged, the *batin* called both sides to a meeting in his house and mediated between them. Second, when Suku Asli moved to a different community, the *batin* of the new community gave permission for them to live there. Third, when they held weddings or funerals, they invited the *batin* to manage the ceremony. Finally, they always asked the *batin* for help when they needed to negotiate with outsiders. I could not correctly specify their manner of leadership within the Suku Asli community in more detail than this. Nevertheless, it seems to be certain that the final point—communication with outsiders—was an essential part of their leadership. Before exploring this topic, I would like to describe leadership and cooperation in everyday life.

Leadership and cooperation in everyday life

'Leadership' is a term that I am using as an analytic term as I defined it above; it is not the word the Suku Asli use in everyday life. Although they often use synonyms of 'leader' (e.g. *kepala*, *penghulu*, *peminpin*, and *ketua*), these terms seem to be used only for those who have a title or post as headman, such as the present *batin* and *adat* manager, and for the *Ketua Rukun Tetangga/ Rukun Warga* (*Ketua RT/RW*; heads of neighborhood association/community association), which is the headman of the neighborhood community appointed by the administrative village headman, regardless of one's leadership within the community.

At first, leadership based on kinship is not clear within their households. A household is usually composed of a nuclear family whose members live together in a house. I have never seen Suku Asli parents try to control the behavior of their children except to protect small children from dangerous actions. Also, parents do not intervene in the choice of their children's spouses. One night, I was talking with Kiat as usual. We were chatting before sleep and the topic was about the marriage of his eldest son. While I was enjoying the gossip about the son, I asked, 'Have you ever advised him about the choice of girls?' He was laughing and answered, 'Never. If my children get a *jodoh* (mate or suitor), they should just marry, as it is their matter.' Suku Asli youngsters were actually going from place to place looking for a *jodoh*. I have never seen a case in which parents decided children's marriages. In the same way, after marriage, parents do not intervene in the affairs of the children's households. They do not have a clear system of paternal or maternal leadership in the family.

In terms of economic activities, their leadership also appears vague. For example, until 2006, their main livelihood was mangrove logging. When they wanted to earn money, they promised a *touke* the amount of timber they would deliver, then went into the mangrove swamps with a small canoe and logged the timber (see Chapter 3). According to Kiat, this was an individual labor. Today, while waged labor is an important source of income, it is also rather individual work. During my stay at his house, Kiat occasionally stayed away and worked in road construction. One day, he decided to work and stay at a construction site for some weeks in order to buy a new motorcycle. He went to a *touke*'s house in the village and was dispatched to the site in a neighboring village. Several days later, I visited him there. It was lunch time and he was relaxing in a hut. Among the workers who were also resting, I found that there were no Suku Asli acquaintances. I asked, 'Aren't you working together with the people around your house?' He answered, 'No. This is my business. I don't come to work calling out my friends.' Of course, this does not mean he always worked alone. He often worked together with his wife and sons to process coconuts to make copra and cooking oil. Once or twice a month, he worked together with neighbors to provide the labor to maintain roads in *gotong royong* (mutual cooperation), a social service organized by *Ketua RT/RW*. However, he rarely worked together with neighbors beyond his household in economic activity.

One exceptional case involved hunting. During my stay, Kiat went hunting several times with a man living in the neighborhood. They walked around coconut gardens and mangrove forests all through the night, and caught two wild boars. The tools of hunting, snares and spears, were owned by the other man, but, according to Kiat, the game was equally divided. Also, Odang often called out his neighbors to collect shellfish in mangrove swamps. But this was individual work; one retained the amount one collected. Their labor appears to be characterized by individuality and equality. In this situation, leadership is not clearly manifested.

However, this does not mean that their society is characterized by a lack of communication and cooperation. When they hold rituals for weddings, funerals, anniversaries of the dead, and shamanic séances, people gather together at a house and together set up the site and prepare food. In such rituals, they erect temporary tents next to the house, and often more than a hundred people may visit. The visitors chat and play card games under the tents. Several neighborhood seniors or kinfolk lead youths in the preparation and clearance of the site and food. In particular, specific elders who have knowledge of the rituals eagerly give directions to the host family and manage the procedures—they clearly appear to take the role of leader. However, it does not mean that they have power and authority to control the people, and their leadership seems to be exercised only during the ritual process. In other spheres of everyday life, I have not seen that people have a special reputation due to knowledge of ritual or that they exercised authority and power toward others.

In the same way, even in kin relationships and economic activities where someone must take the role of leader (such as deciding to begin cooperating or when something goes wrong), no one appears to control the behavior of others outside an individual context. In this sense, I can say that the Suku Asli leadership is generally situational and flexible. One night, when confirming with Kiat the names of incumbents of the IKBBSA in other villages, he suddenly began criticizing the village *batin*. According to him, 'Many people do not like him. He frequently gets angry and scolds people. Who wants to follow such a person?' It seems to be common sense among Suku Asli to detest a person who tries to control other people's behavior.

Again, their society seems characterized by open aggregation, in which the members strongly commit to 'solidarity while simultaneously defending an extensive degree of personal autonomy' (Gibson and Sillander 2011: 1). While they cooperate with each other, they do not constitute a group, and, as such, they have tried to maintain personal autonomy by rejecting established institutions and fixed leadership. This kind of society does not have traditional hierarchical systems and is characterized by egalitarianism. Society is sustained by egalitarian ideas and it is difficult to institutionalize fixed power, authority, and leadership (Lee 2005: 19–20). In the past they were foragers who moved from place to place and obtained resources through hunting and gathering. This character remains to a certain extent today, and it is hard to fix Suku Asli leadership and authority in their everyday life; even if a person leads a specific activity, it seems they cannot exercise power and authority over others in a different sphere of life.

Internal leadership within the Suku Asli community appears situational and flexible, and their social relationship is far from hierarchical. In this situation, they did not develop an *adat* committee or institution that can organize people and exert influence on people, which can be a counterpart to government institutions. However, IKBBSA actually has its basis in a particular form of leadership—that is, political communication with outsiders or the state which is inevitably necessary for Suku Asli.

Communication with the state

Let me return to the topic of *batin* headmanship in the past and analyze such leadership. According to van Anrooij (1885: 285–310), the *batin* of the Siak kingdom had both rights and obligations in terms of control of lands, resources, and population in their territories. *Batin* had rights to impose taxes or labor obligations on their subjects, to receive fines from criminals, and to control resources. On the other hand, they had obligations to pay tax to, and organize their subjects to engage in labor for, the kingdom. These rights and obligations would have been relatively strictly imposed on the people subjugated by the state. However, the situation for *batin* among the Utan, Akit, Rawa, and Sakai would have been slightly different. Their rights and obligations were much weaker since they lived on the peripheries of the kingdom. Furthermore, their *batin* seem to have communicated with the state based on their voluntary motivation to fulfill the necessities of their communities.

I could not gather concrete and clear information on past *batin* in Teluk Pambang. However, there is a well-known heroic anecdote of past *batin* among the Akit on Rupat Island. Moi, the *batin* headman of the Akit in the village of Hutan Panjang, remembered some of the patterns of interaction between their *batin* and the Siak kingdom before the independence of Indonesia. According to him, *batin* occasionally went to the capital of the Siak kingdom, Siak Sri Indrapura, some hundred kilometers from Rupat, and met the sultan. They used small sculling canoes and brought *hadiah* (gifts) of forest products such as sago, rattan, and beeswax. Usually, the *batin* collected the products individually, and he and a few followers carried them by canoe. Such gifts were carried to the sultan not on fixed dates or even annually, but *sekali-sekali saja* (only on rare occasions).

Moi's memory shows some characteristic features of the *orang asli batin* in relation to the state. First, he indicated that the forest products that *batin* carried were gifts, not *pajak* (taxes), and *batin* brought the products only on rare occasions. This indicates that the *batin*'s obligation to pay tax was weak, and a *batin* himself decided when to bring gifts to the sultan. Van Anrooij (1885: 303–05, 349) also recorded that the kingdom was able to receive the forest products only when the Rawa and Sakai brought them. Second, a *batin* did not obtain the forest products from his subjects. He and probably a few of his kinsmen or friends collected the products and brought them to the sultan.

Therefore, the *batin* did not implement taxation on his people. I have never heard of *batin* imposing taxes on the people of Bengkalis and Rupat islands. *Batin* headmanship was not sustained by rights and obligations imposed by the state system; rather, the *batin*'s autonomous agency was much more important in this relationship.

If this is the case, why did they bring gifts to the sultan? The answer clearly relates to the quest for both individual and community authority. In the Malay kingdoms, the sultan gave titles in return for gifts—that is, the tributary system (Andaya 2008: 216). The title legitimized not only the individual status of the *batin* but also the position of his community in the state. In addition, it is important that the title was obtained by his heroic adventures and individual gifts. When I occasionally heard anecdotes of *batin* in Rupat, they were mentioned with some respect due to their great accomplishments. By bringing gifts to the sultan, they not only obtained the legitimacy of their role and the position of their community in the state, but also demonstrated their authority and power as leaders in their community. Bringing gifts was an exchange of forest products for political power, and *batin* conducted the exchange for the purposes of obtaining power. A *batin* was able to receive or maintain his title through the gifts.

According to historians, this was not only related to the exchange of materials but also to the exchange of supernatural powers in Malay kingdoms, including the Siak kingdom. In the precolonial and early colonial eras, the legitimacy of rulers was backed not only by titles and the use of force, but also with their strong supernatural power, called *daulat* (Andaya 2008: 63, 109; Barnard, T. 2003: 27–28, 128–30). *Daulat* was 'the supernatural power that guaranteed the wealth and prosperity of the entire population' (Barnard, T. 2003: 27). This power was strongly associated with *orang asli* groups living in the forest who were believed to have strong supernatural powers, and the sultan could absorb this power by receiving gifts from them (Barnard, T. 2003: 26–8). *Orang asli* received the titles with great pride and reverence as an example of the king's munificence. For the *orang asli* recipients, the titles not only assured their practical status and prestige, but also gave them the opportunity to absorb the potent supernatural power of the rulers themselves (Andaya 2008: 216). Although the Suku Asli do not presently use the term '*daulat*,' supernatural power is actually related to leadership, as I explain below.

The anecdote of past Akit *batin* shows that *batin* headmanship and leadership are two sides of the same coin. The authority and power of *batin* were obtained through tributary services to the state, thus the *batin* headmanship appears to be sustained by state authority. However, *batin* went on a voyage to the capital on the basis of voluntary motivation, obtained the legitimacy of their community, and simultaneously established reputations. The reputation has been handed down in the form of the anecdote. A *batin* must have leadership or authority and power to a certain extent within his community because his travel was necessary for the community.

Although this was the case on Rupat Island, Suku Asli leadership must have been maintained in similar ways, as they were in the same position under the Siak kingdom. While it is unknown whether they carried gifts to the capital, the community often faces the necessity of communicating with Malays and Javanese on various occasions. However, as per Koding's comment about 'fear' and 'shame' in Suku Asli communication with the Javanese (see Chapter 3), it is generally difficult for ordinary Suku Asli to negotiate with outsiders. In such situation, *batin* take the role of deputy or representative of the relevant Suku Asli. Indeed, as I mentioned above, Suku Asli elders pointed out communication with outsiders as one of the main tasks of the past *batin*. Through this activity, *batin* could establish and maintain their reputation and honor in the community, and obtain power and authority over the people to a certain extent.

Communication with spirits

Another position that is related to communication with outsiders is that of the shaman or *dukun*. In Teluk Pambang, séances are often held for the purpose of healing diseases and asking for peace in the community. When people fall sick, *dukun* are asked to hold healing rituals. Some of them also hold annual rituals to guard the people and the territory from the intervention of evil spirits. Before the séance, people prepare offerings such as tobacco, *sirih*, areca nuts, eggs, turmeric rice, and *bebuang* (small model shrines made of trunks of sago). During the séance, *dukun* fall into a trance, negotiate with benevolent spirits or *datuk*, and, in exchange for the offerings, settle the problems caused by malevolent spirits such as *orang bunyian* and *setan*. Using the shamanic technique, *dukun* care for ordinary people's troubles and anxieties.

Odang is a famous *dukun* in Teluk Pambang. When I visited his house, I often heard shamanic techniques and cosmologies from him. According to him, by using mantras and resin incense, a *dukun*'s *semangat* (soul) can fly to a different world. This different world has a seven-layered structure, and *dukun* can ask for the support of *datuk* living at each stratum in exchange for gifts (i.e. offerings). The higher the stratum, the stronger the *datuk* and the more danger the *dukun*'s soul is in. Odang can reach the third stratum, but he cannot reach higher. In the past, *dukun* had stronger *ilmu* (shamanic techniques), and they were sometimes able to reach the seventh stratum and ask for the support of the strongest *datuk*.

Shamanic séance is not political communication with outsiders. However, shamanic technique and cosmology seem to be analogous in the significance to the anecdote of *batin* on Rupat Island. They leave home to ask a powerful existence to settle problems. The goal is distant and dangerous, and in exchange for gifts, they can obtain the solution and bring it back home. It is not for their individual benefit but for that of the community.

While the above is my interpretation, Suku Asli also seem to understand the worlds of spirits and the government in an analogous way. Koding is also a famous *dukun* in Teluk Pambang. When I asked him the difference between *datuk* and other spirits, he used a metaphor about the hierarchical structure in government. According to Koding:

> *Datuk* is, in short, a *bupati* (regent) who can control people and an area. On the other hand, others (*orang bunyian, setan,* and so on) are ordinary people living in or passing through the area. If getting angry, they may do evil to us, and it brings problems. *Datuk* can soothe and scold them, and usually they follow the *datuk*. However, if they do not follow, the *dukun* look for and meet a greater *datuk* like *gubernur* (governor) living in a higher place, and ask for control.

In addition, while each *datuk* has an individual name, it may include titles in past Malay kingdoms. For example, '*hulubalang*' and '*panglima*' were the titles of commanding officers in Malay kingdoms, and these are the popular individual names of *datuk*. In their world, the order of spirits and government is mutually analogous; therefore, they communicate with spirits and government in similar ways.

Dukun seem to have relatively strong leadership in their communities. People come to their houses and ask for advice when they see something peculiar in a dream or have a plan in the near future, such as moving to a different settlement. This means that *dukun* have influence on people's behavior even outside the context of ritual. By supporting villagers, they can obtain a reputation that is sustained by their communication skills with spirits—that is, powerful outsiders with whom ordinary people find communication difficult. However, it should be noted that such leadership is exercised only when they are requested to do so. I have never seen *dukun* advise other Suku Asli or intervene without people's requests.

Ajui's experience and the essence of leadership

Ajui is one of the founders of IKBBSA and the regency *batin*. Before the Meranti Islands regency was separated from Bengkalis regency in 2010, he was the only regency *batin* of IKBBSA, and his effort enormously contributed to its establishment. He was known even in Suku Asli villages distant from Teluk Pambang and was the main counterpart of negotiation for the government. Not only Suku Asli but also Javanese from the village frequently visited his house to ask him to support various kinds of documents submitted to the government and hear his advice. His position seems to have been established through his experiences of having communicated with various people.

Ajui was born in Teluk Pambang, the first son of Koding, in 1966. He graduated from primary school in the village and junior high school in a neighboring village. As most Suku Asli of his generation dropped out of elementary school education, graduating from junior high school was quite an achievement. More importantly, according to him, he was a very good football player in his school days, and established excellent friendships with Javanese boys in neighboring villages. He learned Javanese during these days. After graduation, he worked in the village for about ten years in mangrove logging. In 1991, he was employed by a *touke* and worked for an oil corporation in the Rawa region for several years, and learned about things beyond the village. After he returned to the village in the mid-1990s, he organized OPSA.

According to Ajui, OPSA was first organized by some of his friends for the purpose of obtaining subsidies from the regency government for sport and leisure activities. As his Javanese friends in the village had obtained subsidies, he planned and applied in the same way. The result was that OPSA obtained funds and bought several footballs and volleyballs. Then, at the end of the 1990s, he applied to the village headman to open the hinterland forest at the border area of the village in the name of OPSA (see Chapter 3). At this time, around a hundred households joined the application, and they cleaned up the forest. At the beginning of the 2000s, he again applied for subsidies from the government for the purpose of distributing rainwater tanks and plastic chairs and tables to Suku Asli households. He obtained these materials and distributed them to the Suku Asli households in Teluk Pambang.

His leadership seems to have been exercised in successful political communications with outsiders, especially with the government. Based on his experiences in junior high school and with an oil corporation, he organized OPSA and negotiated with the government. Through these negotiation, he has contributed to the Suku Asli community. This is the basis of his reputation as the political leader of Suku Asli.

It should be noted here that he rarely intervenes in the everyday lives of ordinary people in other spheres, and his leadership outside the sphere of communicating with the government is quite vague. In addition, Ajui 'became' a *dukun* in the latter half of the 2000s. According to him, the *datuk* of his father, Koding, emerged in his dreams several years ago, and he mastered the way of controlling these *datuk* under the tuition of his father. He held an annual shamanic séance together with Koding to pray for the peace of the village.

Here, Ajui's leadership is linked with the past *batin* headmanship. The authority of the past *batin* was legitimated by the state in their tributary relationship, and this relationship was established by the *batin*'s approach to the state. In the same way, Ajui obtained his leadership through an approach to the government and through his success in obtaining the subsidies and recognition of their land possession and usufruct right. In short, political communication with outsiders is one of the few spheres in which leadership appears to be clearly manifested in their lives. Even though Suku Asli society is characterized by open aggregation (Gibson and Sillander 2011), people can acquire reputation and honor through communication with outsiders. As the state is the most powerful outsider, people who can access state power are respected. The people I am referring to as the informal leaders in this chapter are those who can take care of communication with the government as representatives of the community. When government intervention increased, leadership, along with such a quality, became more necessary and the leaders' power increased.

As I discussed in Chapter 1, the Indonesian government has tried to intervene in the communities categorized as KAT. Its policies include governmentality, in which the government provides opportunities of support and recognition for people to accomplish their aspirations and desires. This means that opportunities or contexts to manifest leadership have been increasing in Suku Asli society. The government supported the establishment of IKBBSA in one such intervention, and some Suku Asli have tried to establish their leadership through communication with the regency government. Ajui's attempt to collaborate with the government was sustained by such motivations.

The tributary actions by the *batin* to sultans and their roles within the community, shamanic power and its cosmology, and Ajui's career draw out a picture of leadership in Suku Asli society. First, leaders can communicate with outsiders who have power and may intervene in the Suku Asli community. The communication is risky because it includes travel and negotiation with counterparts, both of which are potentially dangerous. Leaders have courage, skill, and knowledge to overcome such adventures and communications. Second, leaders can bring benefit to their communities in and through communication.

In this process, they fix and improve the relationship with the outsider's strong power that may intervene in a community, and construct harmony and order within the community. The *batin* title and the legitimacy of the Utan community provided by sultans, the support to heal patients and keep the peace of a settlement, and the subsidies and recognition of land possession/usufruct right can be understood in this context. Finally, however, leaders rarely intervene in the community. The internal controlling or ruling of everyday life and behavior does not sustain their leadership. In short, the power and authority of leaders is dictated by their communication skills oriented toward the outside world.

Again, Suku Asli non-articulated and unconscious leadership can be characterized by communication with outsiders. It is quite significant to point out here that the outsiders with whom leaders try to communicate are those who can be regarded as having exogenous quality and strong power. It can be said that exogenous quality and strong power are mutually associated, and leadership in the Suku Asli community is endorsed with exogenous power. It is in this process and schema that indigeneity has been introduced to their community by leaders as the main agent. A leader's purpose is ultimately to bring harmony and social order to the community and obtain reputation and power in the community. Leaders try to adopt the government idea and system as long as the policies do not contradict their customs and ways of life on the basis of their indigeny. The ethnic organization of IKBBSA, which can be seen as the embodiment of their indigeneity, was established in the context of the collision between their indigeny and the state system, and we see that leadership tries to mediate between the two. As a result, unstable power is partly institutionalized in a bureaucratic organization.

Establishment of IKBBSA and its influences

I could not confirm the very first agent who suggested the establishment of the ethnic organization of Suku Asli. Ajui said that he had asked the government to entrust a new organization with an administrative procedure; however, government officials said that the government had needed to implement the administrative procedure among the Suku Asli and thus had established the organization. Either way, it is certain that the administrative procedure of issuing marriage letters and birth certificates was the main trigger for the establishment of IKBBSA.

Project to issue marriage letters

In Indonesia, legal matters of marriage are administrated by the Ministry of Religious Affairs. Muslims can obtain the necessary letter at a local office of the Ministry of Religious Affairs, while Buddhists, Christians, and Hindus need to apply to the specific religious body to which they belong. A religious body authorized by the government issues a *surat pernikahan* (marriage letter) for a couple only when they hold their marriage ceremony under its management. This letter is also used to obtain an *akta kelahiran* (birth certificate), which is an essential official document when children want to enter higher educational institutions or obtain a passport. Although it is possible to obtain the birth certificate without a marriage letter, this is an exception generally meant for a child of a single mother; applicants for this form of certificate have to complete cumbersome office procedures in the regency capital and pay relatively expensive charges.

Before 2005, almost all Suku Asli lacked letters or birth certificates because they did not belong to any religious body; even those who did, rarely held a marriage ceremony under its management. They preferred to hold ceremonies within their community in the traditional Suku Asli or *peranakan* way. Although it was possible to hold the ceremony twice, both in administrative and traditional ways, this was economically difficult. It was also extremely difficult for them to obtain the birth certificate without the marriage letter because of the cumbersome procedures and the expensive charges. The lack of documents was not so problematic at first, as family registers were kept in administrative village offices and their basic citizenship was assured. However, according to Ajui, problems have arisen in recent years:

> It was very difficult to get marriage letters for us in the past. So, everyone did not have the birth certificate. It was unequal and often inconvenient. When we want to send children to high schools or professional schools and get a passport, we had to complete troublesome chores at regency offices. The charge was also expensive...Therefore, we asked the government to issue the letter via IKBBSA.

For them, obtaining the letter was largely concerned with access to education, which has become important for the future of the Suku Asli. They also wanted to change the situation of having to pay considerable amounts of money to obtain the letter and to be able to obtain a passport. Therefore, changing the system was an issue that was related to their disadvantaged and marginalized situation. According to him, it was Ajui who had asked the government to issue the letter more easily and cheaply.

From the government's perspective, however, it was judicially necessary that the Suku Asli obtained such basic official documents. Therefore, the officials needed to begin negotiations with Suku Asli leaders to encourage them to obtain the documents. As mentioned later, Ajui's points about sending their children to high school and obtaining passports would not have concerned ordinary people's aspirations. Therefore, it is probable that his emphasis was a result of the government approach during previous communications with him, in which the officials had emphasized the Suku Asli's marginal position and stimulated his desire to be like ordinary Indonesians in terms of their legal obligations.

The project to provide the letter and certificate for Suku Asli began, and the government enabled the Suku Asli to issue the *surat perkawinan* (marriage letter) by themselves.[3] At first, it was necessary to have a body that recognized and ensured the marriages in their community on behalf of the religious bodies. Therefore, IKBBSA, which was first established with the name *Ikatan Keluarga Besar Batin Akit Jaya* (IKBBSAJ; Akit Jaya Headman's League), was the body that certified marriages, and people were appointed in each administrative village to issue the letters. These people were given the traditional title of *batin* in the organization. Finally, the government allowed a subdistrict office, which is slightly nearer to Suku Asli villages than the regency office, to issue birth certificates with less expensive charges based on the letters issued by the *batin*.

In this system, which started in 2005, *batin* are not formal officials. They do not receive a salary or have roles in the government. Their task is to issue marriage, divorce, and death letters in return for a small charge. In addition, they began issuing the letter of descent, first *Surat Keterangan Suku Akit Jaya* (the certificate of Suku Akit Jaya) and then *Surat Keterangan Suku Asli* (SKSA; the certificate of Suku Asli), which endorses one's membership of a community and the validity of the letters. These letters are valid only when written by *batin* of the ethnic organization at each village, and are required to be submitted in the course of various procedures at government offices at village and subdistrict levels. It was announced that obtaining the letters was essential for Suku Asli, and almost all Suku Asli households obtained them within several years after 2005. Therefore, in practice, the *batin*'s role is backed by the government legitimation, and the government recognizes them as representatives of Suku Asli.

In designing this system, the government and Suku Asli leaders would have consulted the model case of the Akit. In Rupat, *batin* began to issue marriage letters in the late 1990s. Among the Akit, as the role of the two *batin* had been maintained, the government could simply delegate the task to them and the transformation was not dramatic. However, in the Suku Asli case, it was necessary to appoint new *batin* first, a process that brought about the new leadership of some people and the consolidation of their power.

The selection of *batin* and establishment of IKBBSAJ/IKBBSA

When the project to entrust Suku Asli with issuing the letters began, the government and Suku Asli informal leaders, who had taken the role of communication with outsiders, held repeated meetings. The main negotiators for the government were officials of Bengkalis regency. The main negotiator for the Suku Asli was Ajui, and he was strongly supported by Kimdi, who was another essential agent in establishing the *batin* organization. He was a 'pure' ethnic Chinese and a *touke* in Teluk Pambang. He was born in the village of Selat Baru, but had moved to Teluk Pambang when he married a *peranakan* wife there. He had a master's degree in political economy from a university in Jakarta, and was elected as a *Dewan Perwakilan Rakyat Daerah* (DPRD; regency assembly member) of Bengkalis regency in 2005. He was much respected by the villagers, as he made donations to maintain graves, shrines, and roads in the village. Also, many Suku Asli worked in his coconut farms and boat slip, which exported the coconuts. The houses of Ajui and Kimdi were very close and they would often come and go from each other's house. In terms of the start of the project, Kimdi's contribution would have been substantial, as he had considerable knowledge of the law in terms of issuing the letters and strong connections with government officials. He often advised Ajui in the ways of negotiation. Also, as a regency assembly member, he approached the government officials to smooth the approval of the project.

After the negotiation between Ajui and the regency officials, Ajui was in charge of selecting new *batin* at each administrative village on Bengkalis and Padang islands. Ajui actively went back and forth between each administrative village and met his friends and village leaders. He asked them to be the new *batin* or to recommend someone appropriate to take on the role. The essential qualification was good literacy because the new *batin*'s main task was to write the letters. In some villages, the informal leaders became *batin*; in other villages, young and educated men were appointed as *batin*, as they were more literate than the leaders, who were often aged.

At the establishment of IKBBSAJ, the leaders adopted the government image of an ethnic organization to a large extent. First, the organization has a bureaucratic order involving hierarchical and regional organizations. The role of regency *batin* is at the top of the hierarchy. Then there are the roles of the subdistrict *batin* and village *batin*. Under the village *batin*, there are the *adat* manager and secretaries. The first regency *batin* of Bengkalis regency was Ajui. The eastern islands of Padang, Rangsang, Tebing Tinggi, and Merbau, separated from Bengkalis regency in 2010, became the new Meranti Islands regency. At this time, in 2005, a leader who engaged in the selection of *batin* on these islands became the new Meranti Islands regency *batin*. With the support of Ajui, who had a strong connection with the Rawa region, a similar organization was established among the people who had been called the Rawa who lived in Siak regency. Second, the organization had an election system, in which the *batin* was appointed by voting within the committee. According to Ajui, this system was introduced because the government required them to adopt a 'democratic way.' The first vote was conducted in 2005. At this time, all committee members who had been recommended by Ajui were appointed as *batin*. In 2010, a second vote was held. At this vote, some *batin* were rejected because, according to Ajui, 'they did not carry out their responsibility.' These systems are totally new ones created through cooperation between the government and the Suku Asli leaders.[4]

Identification and certification

The establishment of IKBBSAJ brought about a change in terms of Suku Asli identification and certification. This change began with the creation of their ethnic name, which was adopted in parallel with the organization's establishment. Before 2005, the government had, since the colonial era, continuously used the term '*Orang/Suku Utan*' to refer to them. Indeed, all government documents and books written before 2005 referred to the people in this way. But some people also used '*Suku Asli*'—an article at the end of the 1980s mentions the people as the '*Suku Hutan atau Asli*' (Utan or Asli) (Hamidy 1991: 134), and the people themselves would have used names depending on the context and situation.

The term most frequently used within their community was '*Orang Asli*.' As I mentioned at the beginning of the introduction and in Chapter 2, this term most closely fitted their identity. Even during my fieldwork, many people used this term when they referred to themselves in conversation. However, this term is vague, as '*orang asli*' is generally used to indicate people at an indigenous/tribal position—'*Orang Akit*,' '*Orang Sakai*,' and '*Orang Rawa*' all identify themselves as '*orang asli*.' Even if they identify themselves as '*Orang Asli*' in conversation with an outsider, the outsider would ask an additional question in order to specify the group, such as, '*Dan, sukunya apa*?' (And, what is your *suku*?). In this context, they used '*Suku Asli*.' '*Orang Akit*' was also used by many people who had kinsmen or ancestors related to the Akit in Rupat. However, some would probably have used '*Orang Utan*' as well before 2005, at least in their interactions with the government, because it was the ethnic name legitimized by the Siak kingdom and recognized by post-independence governments.

At the establishment of the organization of the Suku Asli, it became necessary to integrate the various and vague names. This process involved tough negotiations between the government and the people, and they considered a number of different options. For example, '*Orang Asli*' was entertained because the people had used it. However, this name was rejected by the government because it was not a proper name but a shared one. The government suggested the name '*Suku Melayu Utan*' (the Forest Malays). However, Suku Asli leaders strongly rejected this name as they were neither Malays nor living in the forest. In addition, '*Suku Akit*' and '*Suku Rawa*' were options and the leaders considered these in their discussions. They could not decide between them, because those who regarded themselves as having close kinship with the Akit in Rupat approved the former, but those who believed that they had been derived from the Rawa region were in favor of the latter.

Eventually, the government decided on a completely new ethnic name, '*Suku Akit Jaya*' (the Prosperous Akit), overriding objections from the leaders. Using the words '*Suku Akit Jaya*' in 2005, the first organization was established with the name of IKBBSAJ and the government called them that. However, this name was completely new and remote from their own identification, so the people did not accept it. Therefore, in 2006, the leaders requested the government change the name to '*Suku Asli*,' which they had been used to calling themselves. This name involved a similar problem as '*Orang Asli*' and the government was hesitant to recognize it. However, as a result of the leaders' negotiations, the name '*Suku Asli*' was officially recognized by the regency officials. Following this, the organization name became *Ikatan Keluarga Besar Batin Suku Asli* (IKBBSA).

The Suku Asli name was fixed, which had meant not only accomplishing an agreement with the government but also clarifying their identity. This clarification of identity was reinforced by the documents. All documents that are issued by *batin* use the IKBBSA letterhead, which includes the name 'Suku Asli.' In addition, the marriage letter was issued in a set with the SKSA, which certifies the holder as a member of the Suku Asli community. This can be seen as a landmark event in terms of the certification of their identity. They have had choices of identification based on their individual history of moves, complex kinship networks, ancestral connections, and the community in which they lived, as I described in Chapter 2. However, the documents simplified the issues and clearly designated them as belonging to one ethnic group, the Suku Asli. Although their identity does not always coincide with the addresses on documents, this certifies them as Suku Asli and becomes the main basis of their identification in relation to government administrative procedures. According to Ajui, all Suku Asli who obtained the letter from IKBBSA are members of IKBBSA, and they are Suku Asli.

Many *peranakan*—the *peranakan* Chinese, who had less intimate ancestral relationships with the Suku Asli, spoke the Chinese language, and lived in Chinese communities—asked the *batin* to issue their letters too. At the establishment of IKBBSA, the role of *batin* was important not only in the administrative villages where many Suku Asli lived, but also in those villages where most of the population were *peranakan* Chinese. This would have been a concern of Kimdi's, in which he tried to support the *peranakan* Chinese and enable them to acquire the right letters, especially for obtaining passports. Until 2007, when the ethnic Chinese wanted to obtain passports and register in order to vote they had to apply for a *Surat Bukti Kewarganegaraan Republik Indonesia* (SBKRI; Certificate for Indonesian Citizenship) at regency offices; this was an official certification to show that the person was an Indonesian citizen. The charge was very expensive and was an economic burden for non-wealthy *peranakan*. However, the SBKRI could be replaced by the SKSA letter from the *batin*. Therefore, *peranakan* Chinese, including those who were working outside Bengkalis Island, actively applied for the letter. According to Ajui, 'At present, more and more *peranakan* [Chinese] *masuk* (become) the Suku Asli.' Many people who may have been regarded as ethnic Chinese 'became' Suku Asli, at least on the document. On the other hand, through the change of ethnic name and the documentation of the letters, the boundary with the Akit is becoming clearer than in the past.

During my short trip to Rupat, an Akit village headman showed his skeptical attitude to the change of the ethnic name of the Utan. According to him, 'They say "We are the Suku Asli," but *suku asli siapa* (which *suku asli* are they)? They were the Akit or Utan, but I don't know who the Suku Asli are.' His opinion was the same as that of the government officials—that is, the name '*Suku Asli*' is ambiguous—but for the Akit, it seems the Utan are people who share the same ancestors with them. Therefore, his opinion involved some discomfort in terms of the Suku Asli's apparent disregard of their common history. After IKBBSA was established, Suku Asli leaders repeatedly invited Akit leaders to their meetings and festivals, but the Akit leaders did not attend. In addition, the documents with the new name can be a potential criterion in distinguishing the Suku Asli from the Akit.

By 2018, the regency government announced that the subdistrict offices on Bengkalis Island essentially should no longer accept the marriage letters issued by *batin* as formal referencing material to provide the birth certificate. This is because entrusting IKBBSA to issue marriage letters was a temporary arrangement to encourage the Akit and Utan, who often lived remote from a religious body, to obtain birth certificates. During the decade following 2005, several Buddhist temples were established even in the distant villages, and the government determined that the Akit and Suku Asli also should obtain the letters from a religious body. Nevertheless, according to the manager of a Buddhist temple, this announcement is still nominal. A letter issued by a *batin* may be accepted if a leader, like Ajui, negotiates with the officials, as the letter is just one of various reference materials. Indeed, as of 2019, IKBBSA still issued marriage letters and SKSA. According to Ajui, 'New couples have to obtain a marriage letter from IKBBSA if they have a ceremony using *adat*, the same as that under the management of a Buddhist temple.' *Adat* here indicates either Suku Asli or the *peranakan* way of ritual. While the marriage letter has lost endorsement by the government authority, obtaining the letter and SKSA seems to have become something customary in Suku Asli communities.

Through the fixing of their ethnic name and the official certificates, Suku Asli identity, which involved vagueness and diversity characterized mostly by the 'non-Islamic alliance' until recently, has started obtaining coherent and distinctive substantiality. Scott (1998: 1–83) points out that the government has attempted to reduce complex local knowledge and backgrounds through the simplified identification in order to control them more easily and effectively. In addition, as Hirtz (2003: 910) points out, when one tries to legitimate 'tradition-based' social institutions, one is 'forced to make use of [the] rational form of organization and institution-building' that the national or international authorities legitimate. It could be argued that the government accomplished this in the Suku Asli case through the establishment of the organization. In particular, documentation of their ethnicity is one of the most powerful and rational ways to fix, simplify, and embody their fluid identity in the modern nation state. This is the real change in their society.

Leadership and the maintenance of personal autonomy

The establishment of IKBBSA brought about changes not only in identification and certification, but also in terms of the leaders' power. First, IKBBSA created political networks between leaders living in distant communities. Before its establishment, they did not generally communicate and, if they did, it was individually. Leadership was recognized by a local community and connected with the relatively small place where a leader lived. However, after the establishment of IKBBSA, the leaders held meetings, inviting all the incumbents to come together at certain times of the year. In these meetings, they discussed the problems and issues of each village, and decided the direction of IKBBSA as the representative of a local community. They recognized each other as leaders under an integrated organization and the community members under them as Suku Asli. Now it was possible to imagine the Suku Asli as an ethnic group beyond the small-scale and unconscious connections with a place. Their identity, which was rather fragmented and vague in the past, was integrated at least at the level of the leaders.

Second, IKBBSA enabled the leaders to behave as representatives of the Suku Asli in their engagement with the government. The government had to deal with the leaders' petitions in the same way they had to deal with those from the ethnic organizations of the Javanese or Malays. This dramatically raised the possibility that the Suku Asli could receive support and recognition from the government as 'Suku Asli.' The leaders built an IKBBSA *balai pertemuan* (community center) in Teluk Pambang using government subsidies. They began holding annual festivals and periodic meetings, which received government support. IKBBSA is a new channel to enable them to negotiate with the government collectively as Suku Asli. The relationship between leaders and the government became closer, and they were able to acquire government support as one of the *adat* communities in the region.

The reputation of some leaders was dramatically strengthened. This was related to the accumulation of knowledge about negotiating with the government. During my fieldwork, I saw that many people who were leaders around Teluk Pambang gathered in Ajui's house every day. Their purpose was to think about new ways to petition the government, and they created various documents, such as SKT and SKGR applications, and petitions to obtain subsidies for fishing and agricultural groups. Ajui had a computer and kept copies of the documents he submitted to the government. People wrote the documents in his house, took them back to their communities, and applied for government support or recognition. This raised Ajui's and the leaders' reputations in their communities.

Although the establishment of IKBBSA dramatically increased leaders' power in society, the ordinary people's situation does not appear to have changed dramatically. After the new *batin* began issuing the letters, almost all people obtained the letters and certificates from the new *batin*. However, they have simply kept them in their houses and not used them for the purpose that Ajui specified. This is natural because although a few well-off Suku Asli and many *peranakan* Chinese wanted to obtain the documents easily and cheaply for the purpose of sending their children to higher education institutions or obtaining passports, ordinary Suku Asli seem to have no such desires. For them, it is often difficult to send their children even to junior high school in the village. Also, I have never heard of any Suku Asli, including the leaders, obtaining passports using the letters, though some *peranakan* Chinese will have done so. For ordinary Suku Asli, obtaining the letter appears to have been no more than a new obligation imposed by the government. They have obtained no clear benefits from the documents, at least not yet.

In addition, they have not been involved with the selection of *batin*. The choice of *batin* was exclusively conducted by Ajui and other leaders. The organization has been maintained by the voting system conducted within the *batin* committee. Furthermore, because *batin* were appointed by the administrative village, the leaders of some small distant settlements were not selected as *batin* or other functionaries. I met some Suku Asli villagers living on the periphery of an administrative village who did not know who the village *batin* was and confused the village *batin* with the informal leader of their small community. This resulted from the fact that although people obtained their letters and certificates following the advice of the government or the new *batin*, they appear not to have understood that they were also involved as members of IKBBSA.

Also, while the boundary between the Suku Asli and Akit has been shown on the ethnic certificate, it has not influenced communication among ordinary Suku Asli. The Akit are also regarded as an ethnic group as a result of government intervention around the late 1990s. However, as I mentioned in Chapter 2, Odang commented that he 'may well become an Akit' if he moved to Rupat. This shows that although ordinary Suku Asli did not readily recognize the importance of the way in which their identity was being addressed on the document, it is possible that it will gain more importance than an identity based on the region in the future.

In short, IKBBSA has been organized and operated neither to reflect the aspirations nor the participation of ordinary Suku Asli. Rather, it is an embodiment of the aspirations of elite (leaders and *peranakan* Chinese) and government administrators. On the one hand, the organization has enabled the elites to accomplish their aspirations, and then increase their economic and political power through their communications with the government. On the other hand, the government has managed to force the people to obtain the administrative certificates that all Indonesian citizens are required to hold, and identify them more clearly within the administrative procedures. Although '*orang asli*' is still generally used within their community, it is also true that ordinary people began using their own ethnic name, '*Suku Asli*,' and have received indirect benefits through the operation of IKBBSA. However, these are simply the results of their leaders' quest for economic and political power, and ordinary people are not really involved in these activities.

The relatively superficial application of the institutionalized system of IKBBSA demonstrates a separation between an ethnic organization and the actual ethnic group. Ethnic organizations and ethnic groups are not equal. As Rogers Brubaker (2004: 15) points out, 'organizations cannot be equated with ethnic groups...Although common sense and participants' rhetoric attribute discrete existence, boundedness, coherence, identity, interest, and agency to ethnic groups, these attributes are in fact characteristics of organizations.'

IKBBSA is at the center of how identity, boundedness, and coherence are demonstrated, and embody Suku Asli identity, but it does not always reflect the feelings of ordinary people. However, it also demonstrates Suku Asli attitude towards power in a tribal position. While the ordinary Suku Asli have not taken institutionalized actions of resistance, they have minimized the influence on their lives by putting the documents away, ignoring the IKBBSA events, and employing their traditional category of people. These can be understood with the concept of 'war machine' to prevent state intervention in their lives by an assemblage of non-specified strategies (Chou 2020: 224; see Chapter 2) and maintain their personal autonomy in the 'open-aggregation' relationship.

A new relationship between the people and the state

In the recent political engagement between the Suku Asli and the regency government, we can see a specific way of creating a new relationship between people in a tribal position and the state. The state's readiness to recognize local and traditional authorities has not been a new governing method; the government has always looked for informal leaders, who are outside of state politics, in order to exert control over rural areas effectively (Ufford 1987). For example, in the period of 'ethical policy' (1905–30; see Chapter 5), the colonial government looked for *volkshoofden*, or informal leaders, and legitimized them through voting in order to drive 'modernization' in rural areas (Ufford 1987: 146–8). After independence, *kijaji*, local Muslim teachers in Java, were transformed into 'cultural brokers' who mediated between the national and local levels under government pressure to implement religious policies in rural areas (Geertz 1960). Philip van Ufford (1987: 146) analyzes the government attitudes as follows:

> Any government which declares that modernization is important must find tools for implementing its views. It is in this context that the government may look for people's representatives...informal leaders. The quest for change requires not only 'tradition,' but also a view which makes change manageable. The government, incapable of knowing the myriad of local differentiations, is also faced with its incapability to deal with all of them, and must find people who are able to do so effectively. The concept of the local leader, representing all those 'bound by tradition,' provides this need.

However, the government seems to have taken this approach only in its encounters with relatively 'civilized' populations, like the Javanese, and did not apply it to tribal societies. During the Sukarno and Suharto eras, the government almost ignored such societies or tried to directly reform and restrict their behavior and ways of life. The people were regarded as the subjects of development projects that were supposed to make 'backward' and 'primitive' people 'civilized.' In this scheme, recognizing leaders' positions was contradictory with the government scheme of 'development' or changing the traditional society and, indeed, the government replaced their traditional headmen with administrators from the civilized outsiders (Effendy 1997: 633–4).

In the post-Suharto era, these policies have changed, and in this change we can see the emergence of governmentality in the manner of government intervention in the lives of 'tribal people.' The government has recognized their traditional but informal leaders and political institutions and engaged with them. Through these policies, they try to educate the leaders and ultimately to configure habits, aspirations, and beliefs among the people as a whole. In other words, the government has tried to shape their 'conduct of conduct' (Li 2007b: 5). The desire, aspirations, and habits that the government wants to introduce into tribal communities can be summarized as 'becoming *adat* community,' a government image of an ideal and harmonious rural community, a specific form of 'indigenous people.' Therefore, in the process of these policies, the government requires the leaders to show their concurrence with the government image and criteria, and the people show it in 'modern' ways that the government accepts. In the Suku Asli case, they introduced the bureaucratic and 'democratic' ethnic organization and the documentation of identity. In other words, the government has tried to introduce indigeneity to tribal communities by effecting an ethos of governmentality. In this sense, indigeneity can be a tool to bring the people to the modern nation state, which is framed in terms of how the people are or, perhaps, ought to be as, first and foremost, indigenous.

Thus governmentality is limited. This limitation emerged because of the cultural logics among the people themselves. In the Suku Asli case, the leaders pursued their reputation and honor in communication with the government, but they were not really interested in controlling or ruling the ordinary people, which the government had expected. However, the ordinary people did not want strong leadership except in the context of communication with the government. As a result, while Suku Asli identity has been obtaining coherent and distinctive substantiality for the government and Suku Asli participate in the organization, there are many people who are outside this consolidation.

Therefore, it is necessary for the organization to demonstrate a distinctive and coherent position in relation to ordinary people. Indeed, IKBBSA has tried to integrate ordinary people through performances that demonstrate the Suku Asli as an *adat* community. I explore the way in which IKBBSA tries to involve ordinary people in this way in the next chapter.

Chapter 5

Manifestation of Tradition: *Adat*, Performance, and Integration

'*Adat*' is a key word for understanding cultural diversity and national integration in Indonesia, but its meaning is quite complicated. The word derives from Arabic and is often translated as 'tradition,' 'custom,' and 'customary law.' In more detail, Franz von Benda-Beckmann (1979: 429) translated the word in his glossary as 'tradition,' 'custom,' 'law,' 'morality,' 'political system,' and 'legal system.' Clifford Geertz (1983: 210) added 'ritual' and 'etiquette.' In short, '*adat*' can be seen as a whole set of enduring practices or ideologies that have been inherited from the ancestors in a society. It is said that *adat* has certainly existed in each rural community since the precolonial era, and there are myriad communities that have their own *adat*—that is, '*adat* communities'—in Indonesia. As *adat* involves the local legal system that may be different from national laws, there have been continuous communications between the locals and the state in terms of and about *adat*. In the colonial era, the government recognized the significance of *adat* as local law in each '*adat* law community' as a subpart of the national laws. After independence, while *adat* lost its legal legitimacy in the implementation of integrated national laws, *adat* communities were seen as the essential components of post-independence Indonesia. In recent years of decentralization, '*adat*' and '*adat* community' have been a banner of the Indonesian indigenous movement. They are the basis on which the local populations claim land rights that were ignored during the Suharto regime. This means that the concept of *adat* community is the Indonesian version of the international concept of indigenous people. *Adat* emerges at the interface between locals and the state in the history of the Indonesian state once again, and national activists and local authorities have tried to regain the authority of *adat* in recent years.

However, the relationship between *adat* and state policies cannot be reduced to a simple and fixed arrangement of historically continuous local traditions versus newly imposed national regulation. Reflecting the debates on 'the invention of tradition' (Hobsbawm and Ranger 1992), the concept of *adat* in each local community has been influenced by state policies since the Dutch colonial era (e.g. Burns 1989; Henley and Davidson 2007; Josselin de Jong 1948). While some locals had unique terms to indicate their 'tradition,' 'custom,' or 'customary law'—such as '*dresta*' in Bali, '*aluk*' in Tana Toraja, and '*adat*' in western Sumatra—these have been transformed into the pan-Indonesian concept of *adat* by policies regarded as acceptable by the state (Acciaioli

1985). In addition, the forces of 'tradition' or 'custom' within a community differ from region to region. Although some local populations, such as the Balinese and Minangkabau, have had strong traditions or customs, there were communities where traditions or customs were more flexible and diffuse (Li 1999: 10; 2000: 159). In the latter case, people have conceptualized their *adat* in communications with the government as relatively flexible and situational, and this process continues today.

The Suku Asli are among the peoples who have had a flexible and diffuse *adat*. As I mentioned in Chapter 2, their collective identity does not necessarily depend on a single *adat*, and they have used the term '*adat*' in the very limited sphere of ancestral worship. Rather, their *adat* has been something conceptualized and objectified in historical interactions with the state instead of implying a whole set of socially enduring systems or ideologies. However, in recent interactions with the government through IKBBSA, they have begun using the term more frequently and with slightly different meaning from their traditional usage—that is, as 'art' represented performatively. By describing the national concept of *adat*, the meaning of *adat* in Suku Asli communities, and their recent manifestation of *adat* in art, I would like to explore the Suku Asli way of manifesting indigeneity in this chapter.

Conceptualization in political communication

The state definition of *adat* began to be formulated in the early days of the late colonial era in the process of the government trying to effect national laws over the archipelago. In the early colonial era of the eighteenth century, the main interest of the VOC was in the exploration of resources and products obtained from the archipelago, rather than in ruling the native population. The distinction between Europeans, Dutch subjects, and native populations was not so strict in the legal system of this era, and local legal systems were outside the VOC control. For example, Christians and city dwellers who engaged in the miscellaneous activities of Dutch trade were regarded as the subjects of Dutch national laws, but the rural populations were regarded as the subjects of their traditional customary laws. The VOC government flexibly applied this legal system to the population (Fasseur 1994; Li 2007b: 44). However, after the Dutch government set about reinforcing direct rule over the archipelago at the beginning of the nineteenth century, the government tried to classify the population based on 'racial' difference between Europeans and *inlanders* or *bumiputera* ('Natives') (Moniaga 2007: 277). In the government regulations for the Netherlands Indies of 1854, for example, it was codified that, while Europeans were subject to

Dutch national law, 'Natives,' including city dwellers and Christians, were to be the subjects of 'their own religious law, institutions, and customs' (Fasseur 2007: 50; see also Li 2007b: 44). The court system was also divided into two: one for Europeans and one for 'non-Europeans' (Fasseur 2007: 50). In this legal pluralism, local law systems held a fully legitimized position, even though the laws played only a minor role under Dutch national laws. In this system, land ownership by the local customary communities was fully recognized, and although the uncultivated land was leased out to Europeans and Chinese, they could not possess the land permanently (Henley and Davidson 2007: 20).

However, this legal pluralism gradually became difficult to sustain at the turn of the twentieth century when some Europeans and officials began insisting on the necessity of effecting an integrated national law (Fasseur 2007: 50). The ownership of uncultivated lands became problematic outside Java following the expansion of private plantations, and Europeans began requiring the government to apply a European system of land ownership, which allowed Europeans and Chinese to permanently possess the uncultivated lands (Henley and Davidson 2007: 19–20). In response to this movement, some scholars and officials required the government to protect the rights of the local communities based on their 'ethnic' nature because the severe economic policies, best represented by the 'Culture System' imposed on Java, brought about serious poverty among the locals (Li 2007b: 40–1).[1] Between the two factions, a debate was sparked at the beginning of the twentieth century on whether a single legal system should be established or not. At the center of the latter stance was the Leiden School of *adat* law studies in the Netherlands, where Cornelis van Vollenhoven and his colleagues began to abstract, elaborate, and generalize the concept of *adat* in order to oppose the application of the Dutch national laws in the Netherlands East Indies.

Van Vollenhoven claimed the recognition and protection of the *hak ulayat* (right of allocation; right of avail)[2] enjoyed by an *adatrechtsgemeenschap* (*adat* law community); he defined the right of allocation as recognizing the free use of uncultivated land within a territory by the '*adat* law community' and its members, and restricting alienation and an outsider's use of the lands (Burns 1989: 9–10, 2007: 74). In parallel with this claim, he and his colleagues elaborated the concepts of '*adat*' and '*adat* community.' Peter Burns (1989: 56–7) argues that Leiden scholars regarded *adat* as a total worldview. For them, *adat* community was an organic whole in which people were related to each other and were also connected with the natural world through supernatural beliefs; the role of '*adat* law' (*adatrecht*; *hukum adat*) was to restore and maintain the balances and harmonies in the world (see also Li 2007b: 48). As this idea was totally different from the European legal system, the Leiden scholars insisted that the population of the Netherlands East Indies should be governed by their own legal principles (Henley and Davidson 2007: 21). In order to develop their argument, the scholars carried out research on *adat* and rural communities. They categorized the legal-cultural areas of nineteen *adatrechtskringen* (*adat* law areas) in the Indonesian archipelago, each of which involved numerous but similar *adat* communities. This categorization almost corresponded with the map of major Indonesian languages and cultures (Burns 2007: 73).

It is remarkable that the Leiden scholars' discourses saw the cultural independence of each local community as the main source of the legal right to land. As local communities maintained their cultural independence, in which the locals harmoniously and 'naturally' adapted to a region and environment, they held priority over access to the land. By emphasizing the position of a historically coherent culture that continued from the past to the future, the Leiden scholars tried to strengthen the argument that local communities' land rights should be protected. As Li (2000: 159) points out, 'The Dutch concept of the *adat* law community...assumed, as it simultaneously attempted to engineer, named, bounded, and organized groups' across the archipelago. The government adopted this idea and reflected it in policies to control the archipelago. A series of government policies that actively intervened in rural lives with the intent of reforms based on this idea was called 'ethical policy' and continued from 1905 to 1930 (Li 2007b: 32, 41–51). Through these policies, the *adat* community began to be considered the basic rural component of the colonial state polity.

Some scholars point out that the Leiden School was the main agent in constructing the images of *adat* and *adat* community. For example, around the era of Indonesia's independence, J. P. B. Josselin de Jong (1948) questioned the validity of the concept of *adat* law, referring to it as 'confusing fiction.' He points out that the government and Dutch scholars' emphasis on *adat* was based on European-centered perspectives on law and custom, and ignored the complexity of *adat* at local levels. Burns (1989) also suggests that the concept of *adat* is a 'myth,' which was constructed by Dutch scholars and embedded in the polity of post-independence Indonesia as an 'axiom' of the state ideology. He stated, 'the difficulty I have with the myth...is that once it is offered as an explanatory device, it is not susceptible to empirical correction' (Burns 1989: 93). It worked as a too-persuasive and powerful conceptual framework and rejected deviations. The deviations were interpreted as breakdowns or polluted repertoires of as pristine an *adat* as ever existed (Burns 1989: 78–9, 94–7). The images of *adat* and *adat* community—that is, a historically continuous and harmonious rural community—were articulated in the interactions between locals and the state for administrative and economic reasons before the independence of Indonesia.

Transformation of the state concept

The Leiden scholars promoted an ideal, balanced, and harmonious image of *adat* and *adat* community, and this image was inherited by the post-independence government. The 1945 Constitution of the Republic of Indonesia included this ideal image of *adat.* It was accomplished by the contribution of Supomo, a graduate of the Leiden School and a principle author of the constitution. However, '*adat*' in the constitution was not the same as that of the colonial era, and the value of rural communities was more emphasized. During the Japanese occupation, the Japanese colonial government deployed propaganda that Asian people share common values completely different from those of Europeans, especially the Dutch. In this propaganda, *adat* was regarded as the basic value among Indonesians (Bourchier 2007: 116–17; Henley and Davidson 2007: 21). As a result, the concept of *adat* was abstracted and embedded in the constitution as a pan-Indonesian value. Li (2007b: 51–2) expresses this abstraction: 'the *adat* of the constitution was *adat* in the abstract, *adat* as the embodiment of the zeitgeist, repository of the authentic Indonesian spirit, not the functioning customary practices of rural communities.' *Adat* became something related to the Indonesian nation and nationalism, to which everyone who lived in Indonesia was or should be related. Because of this idealization, both elites and peasants accepted the concept of *adat* community, but it was embedded in the political structure of postcolonial Indonesia as a political tool.

The new national concept of *adat* community had two remarkable points. First, the legal legitimacy and autonomy that had been enshrined in the past concept of *adat* community was dramatically disempowered. In the Sukarno regime, for example, the Basic Agrarian Law of 1960 referred to the term '*adat* law community,' but it specified that when customary land rights and national law contradicted each other, it was *adat* that had to be amended. In the beginning, this law had provisions on behalf of local communities in order to 'recognize customary land rights, redistribute former plantations leased to Europeans, and distribute private land held by individuals in excess'; however, as the bureaucracy was limited when it came to exerting state authority, the government failed to implement the reforms (Li 2007b: 52–3). In addition, in the early Suharto regime, the Basic Forestry Law of 1967 also involved the term '*adat* law community.' However, this law was generally interpreted as ensuring the priority of the state's right over the *adat* communities (Henley and Davidson

2007: 11). By this minimization of the legal aspects of *adat*, the government tried to defuse not only obstacles based on *adat* that might prevent the state from having free access to the resources in a territory, but also the potential risk that *adat* might bring about particularism and even secession from the state.

Second, the linkage between culture and *adat* was maintained or even celebrated. 'Culture' here refers to traditional practices with a '"thing-like" quality' such as dances, songs, music, architecture, handicrafts, and so on (Yang 2011). This was partly because the government tried to facilitate tourism, in which culture became the important resource to attract foreign travelers. Indeed, Bali and Tana Toraja became the center of mass tourism, emphasizing their 'culture' after the 1980s (Acciaioli 1985: 158–9). However, more importantly, it was because the government tried to control local populations through the culturalization of *adat*. By defining local *adat* as culture, the government was able to reduce the legal and political influence of local *adat* without strong resistance. By simplifying local cultures in terms of *adat*, the government was also able to catalogue them and make them 'a constituent of an alleged national culture' (Colombijn 2003b: 337). I will return to this topic at a later part of this chapter.

After the fall of Suharto in 1998, the autonomy and self-determination of local communities was reconsidered under the banner of *reformasi*. A series of laws, which suppressed local rights, were amended. Under this government framework, the connection between *adat* and the law has been reconstructed by NGOs and local authorities. The most influential NGO, AMAN, includes the term '*adat* community' in its very name, and adopted '*adat* community' as the translation of the transnational concept 'indigenous peoples.' It is trying to recover local land rights in the areas where the government and corporations have exploited land and its resources, and emphasizes the importance of protecting the rights of local people in terms of *adat*. AMAN advocated for the term '*adat* community,' not '*adat* law community,' which was recognized by the Dutch colonial government, because adopting the latter term risks 'suggesting that the indigenous peoples are only those who own a systematised, measurable law practice' (Arizona and Cahyadi 2013: 54), and might ignore the reality of tribal indigenous peoples who hold unsystematized practices and values as *adat*. After several meetings among the members, AMAN formulated the *Rancangan Undang-Undang Pengakuan dan Perlindungan Hak Masyarakat Hukum Adat* (Draft Law on the Recognition and Protection of the Rights of Indigenous People) and suggested it to the central government. The term '*adat* law community' in this draft was a compromise; by using the term in the 1945 constitution, they tried to allow legislative process to continue (Arizona and

Cahyadi 2013: 52–5).[3] In addition to such activists, the local elites also have begun to claim their customary land rights against the government's encroachment. They also emphasize the value of their *adat* and *adat* community and have tried to negotiate with the government (Henley and Davidson 2007: 1–5). This means that a legal character has been attached to *adat* once again in the recent indigenous movement in Indonesia.

In recent years, the focal point of the concept of *adat* community has been the transfer of the rights of the state forest—which the government has claimed based on past laws but which local communities customarily have used for their livelihood—from the central government to local communities. A 2012 Constitutional Court Decision (No. 35/PUU-X/2012) raised the legal status of *adat* forest in relation to the state forest (Arizona and Cahyadi 2013: 53; Warman 2014). Following the suggestion of AMAN, the Indonesian parliament discussed the definition of '*adat* law community' (Hauser-Schäublin 2013: 10), and the definition was reflected in several national policies concerning village autonomy, land use, and forest conservation (Warman 2014: 6).

After his election as Indonesian president in 2014, Joko Widodo announced a social forestry program between 2015 and 2019, in which the government formally legitimatized the use of resources by local communities within the area of the state forest. This scheme targets 12.7 million hectares of state forest, and the Ministry of Environment and Forestry plans that 6.3 million hectares of this will be recognized as *hutan adat* (*adat* forest) (Bisnis.com 2019). In the social forestry program, the category of '*adat* forest' differs from other categories such as 'community forest,' which was mentioned in Chapter 3; while the former recognizes the permanent customary use of forest products so long as people do not change the function of the forest, the latter assures usufruct right for thirty-five years (Regulation of the Minister of Environment and Forestry No. P.83/MENLHK/SETJEN/KUM.1/10/2016 on Social Forestry). However, the approval process of *adat* forest has been slow and limited. Until March 2019, the government had recognized only 28,286 hectares of *adat* forest across Indonesia (Arumingtyas 2019). In Riau, the central government recognized the first *adat* forest in Kampar regency in February 2020. Although the regency government had applied for the recognition of 10,318 hectares of forests (Riauonline 2019), only 407 hectares were recognized (Antaranews 2020). It is still necessary for local communities to demonstrate their status as an *adat* community or *adat* law community to the central, province, and regency governments to assure their land rights.

Impact of the state concept on local communities

The state concepts of *adat* and *adat* community were formulated after the late colonial era, and their implications have been changing in accordance with the implementation of government administrative and economic policies. However, at the level of local communities, local authorities have employed their own *adat* when mediating negotiations and disputes within their communities (Acciaioli 1985: 150; Li 2000: 159). Therefore, the locals have been confronted with the necessity to adjust the implications and operations of their *adat*, which were inherited from their ancestors as practices, in accord with the change in implications created by the state concept.

The impact of the state conceptualization of *adat* on the local *adat* can be seen as a process related to its reduction or 'erosion' (Acciaioli 1985: 152). Greg Acciaioli (1985) describes such a process among the Da'a Toraja. Suggesting that '*adat* has provided the primary frame of reality' for the local communities, he argues that 'the penetration of national organizational forms has operated to relativize *adat*, to situate it as but one plan for living among a host of others' (Acciaioli 1985: 151–2): 'No longer a matter of practice, following *adat* has become a matter of consciously adhering to prescribed ceremonial, of performing ritual and acting in accord with an etiquette deemed valuable though not exclusive in its claims to adherence.'

Adat was an unconscious and exclusive frame of reality for the local communities. However, in the process of the state's penetration into local life, *adat* was eroded and became an alternative to the national law and reduced to a ceremonial one. Yet, in contrast, state policies also encouraged the locals to codify and elaborate their *adat*. Franz von Benda-Beckmann and Keevet von Benda-Beckmann (2011) argue that the Minangkabau elites elaborated and codified their *adat* in terms of land rights in the judicial pluralism that existed under Dutch colonial rule. Analyzing the records of local government and courts in western Sumatra, they note that in the colonial government policies that forced the Minangkabau to cultivate cash crops for exportation, Minangkabau elites conceptualized the right of allocation as *adat* in the latter half of the nineteenth century, and this has been maintained by the locals until today. They emphasize the role of local agency and, in this sense, *adat* became a counterclaim of the locals against the national policies. Either way, ancestral practices, which have been unconsciously inherited from the ancestors, have been objectified and fixed in each local community under the influences of the state policies regarding *adat*.

However, the transformation of the local *adat* did not happen simultaneously in every community across the archipelago; rather, the process has been gradual. As the trigger was the Dutch colonial or post-independence government politics, the transformations have been brought about in accordance with the increase of engagement with the government. Li (2000) points out that tradition or *adat* was formed as a result of state interventions rather than inherited from ancestors, and the process is not homogeneous over the archipelago:

> it corresponded better to the formations that arose as [a] *result* of colonial interventions (including the *adat* codification process itself) than it did to those that existed prior to Dutch control. In regions of little interest to the Dutch, the process of traditionalization did not occur or was incomplete, and identities, practices, and authority in matters of custom remained—and in some cases still remain—flexible and diffuse. (Li 2000: 159; see also Benda-Beckmann 1979; Benda-Beckmann and Banda-Beckmann 2011; Li 1999: 10)

The communities that experienced the transformation of *adat* were only those in areas in which the colonial government was interested and had strong influence, such as West Sumatra and Bali (see Benda-Beckmann 1979: 120–5). However, there were many areas in which the colonial government was less interested, in which the local authorities did not work adequately, and in which the possession of uncultivated land was not competitive. In such communities, *adat* has remained flexible and diffuse, and the transformation of *adat* is something continuous, even today. The Suku Asli are clearly some of those who have not been influenced by state policies until very recently and have had flexible and diffuse customs.

Meaning of *adat* in the Suku Asli community

While some societies have unique terms to indicate their ancestral practices, such as '*dresta*' in Bali and '*aluk*' in Tana Toraja, the Suku Asli do not; they use '*adat*.' Given the fact that the term was derived from Arabic, Suku Asli initially adopted the concept through their communication with dominant Malays and Minangkabau after they were subsumed under the polity of the Siak kingdom in the eighteenth century. It is unknown how they used the term *adat* in the eighteenth and nineteenth centuries. However, present-day Suku Asli use the term in a very limited sphere of everyday life, and the meaning appears to be vague.

During my fieldwork, the word '*adat*' mostly puzzled me. I had known of the term and thought that it must be a keyword to explore the main research topic of indigeneity. However, on commencing my fieldwork, I found that it was an enormously difficult task because everyone knew the word but no one could clearly explain its meaning to me. Additionally, the word was used infrequently in everyday life. For example, one night, Kiat and I were comparing the marriage rules of the Akit and Suku Asli. When he explained Suku Asli rules, he concluded, 'This is the Suku Asli *adat*.' I had rarely heard *adat* used in this context so I asked him if there were other kinds of *adat*. He considered this for a moment and then answered, 'It's everything from our ancestors, such as *acara* (rituals), dances, and clothes…There are many things, but I cannot explain it. Ask Odang.' Similarly, other people could give me examples, but could not explain the concept or its complexity. In fact, Odang did not categorize dance and dress as *adat*. Although rituals related to ancestral worship were often classed as *adat* (see Chapter 2), not all of them were, and dances and clothes have been included more recently.

I found it difficult to understand the situation, and I racked my brain over the question of *adat* in the field. I had initially assumed that while ordinary people could not explain it, some people must know about it, but there were no traditional committees or institutions that dealt with matters concerning *adat*. Odang was the *adat* manager of IKBBSA and while he gave me some important clues, they did not give me total understanding. Then I assumed that *adat* was a political concept that was adopted by the Suku Asli in relatively recent years. This seemed to be partly true, but it was also true that it was deeply associated with their indigenous and ethnic identity as *orang asli* (see Chapter 2). At the least, *adat* could not be seen as the primary framework of their reality or as a summary of their life as a whole.

In each situation, instead of directly questioning the meaning of the term, I observed the context in which it was used and asked questions related to that context. Using this method, I tried to grasp things that could be categorized as *adat*. The following description and analysis are based on these efforts.

At first, Suku Asli did not use the term '*adat*' in terms of land rights and resources. When they talked about the historical transformation of their hinterland garden and coastal space (see Chapter 3), they never referred to *adat* to demonstrate their legitimacy in opening up or using the lands. They just followed the national law or the agreement with the Javanese village headman. Each household usually registered the land use of their homestead and gardens at the village office, and they bought and sold the right based on the market rate and their negotiating skills. When they inherited land, they divided it equally between their children and did not state *adat* rules; the people concerned seemed to naturally accept it. Neither did they mention *adat* in regards to the mangroves, to which the right of allocation might be applied. As mentioned in

Chapter 3, the most important source of livelihood was mangrove logging in the swamps, where people used small canoes to freely log the timbers in the basin of the Kembung Luar River. There was no priority of use; therefore, the Javanese and Malays also logged mangrove timbers. Only after the Javanese began to claim exclusive maintenance of mangrove forests in the late 1990s did the Suku Asli begin to claim their 'ancestral land,' but they did not use the term '*adat*' for this purpose.[4]

In addition, the moral rules or prescriptions of individual behaviors were not referred to as *adat*. For example, Koding rejected the idea that a rule related to mutual aid should be expressed as *adat*. One day, during our chat, his tobacco ran out and he asked me for a cigarette. He used the phrase, '*Minta satu*' (Please give me one). Smoking the cigarette, he began talking about a rule or moral in past Suku Asli society called '*satu*.' '*Satu*' literally means 'one' in Indonesian, as well as in their dialect, but it was often used when a person asked someone to give part of their personal belongings, as seen in his use of the phrase. In the past, according to Koding, the person with the cigarette was unable to reject the request without a plausible reason. If rejected, he might not have received cooperation from others. This rule was applied not only to tobacco and food, but also to cooperation in economic activities in general. Even though this is still the case if one always rejects requests from others, the constraint in the past was much stronger than it is today. Hearing Koding's explanation, I asked, '*Satu* was a kind of *adat*, right?' He looked slightly pensive and answered, 'No, it's not *adat*. It's a *macam peraturan* (kind of rule); it's just a *salah dia* (wrong behavior of the person).' It is very common that they refer to a prescribed behavior as a *peraturan* (rule) and individual deviations from the rule or prescription as *salah* (wrong). However, they did not explain the prescription using the term '*adat*,' and I have never encountered a scene where one tried to negotiate with others using the term in the sense of a whole set of rules prescribing their behavior or moral conduct.

However, Suku Asli certainly used the term '*adat*' to indicate part of their practices within their community—that is, in the context of rituals related to ancestral worship. As I mentioned in Chapter 2, the basic rituals that are related to their ancestral worship are weddings, funerals, the anniversary of the dead, and the *tujuh likur* (New Year) feast, and these rituals are characterized by communication with ancestral spirits. In the wedding ceremony, they call their ancestral spirits by burning incense and informing them of the marriage of a descendant. The parents of the bride treat the attendants to *sirih*, tobacco, areca nuts, gambier, and so forth, which are contained in a sacred *sirih* box inherited from the ancestors. Dances, music, and *silat* are performed as an essential part of the ceremony. At funerals, they inform the ancestral spirits of the death. While the funeral ceremony does not include dances, they perform *silat* when they carry the coffin out of the house. The feast of *tujuh likur* (which means 'twenty-seven'; the New Year's feast held based on the Islamic calendar) is said to be the largest annual festival, and it is held on the 27th day of Ramadan of the Islamic calendar. The Suku Asli set seven bowls of rice as offerings to their ancestral spirits at the front and back entrances of each house. Seven is a sacred number in Malay culture (Skeat 1900: 508–09), and the number emerges in many scenes of every Suku Asli ritual. Dance and music are performed through the night. All these ceremonies include a ritual to offer meals to their ancestors and to communicate with them. They prepare bowls of food in the living room and burn resin incense at the entrance to the house. The head of the family confirms the ancestors' arrival by dropping two coins (which are usually used by 'real' Suku Asli) or wooden tags (usually used by *peranakan* Suku Asli) on the floor. The combination of heads or tails shows the ancestors' will in terms of 'yes' or 'no.' After several minutes, the head of the family drops the coins or tags again to confirm that the ancestors have finished eating the meals. All these rituals are called *adat*. More correctly, the term indicates not only the ritual itself, but also all procedures, conventional actions, properties, and rules that emerge in the ceremonies. For example, they describe the *sirih* box itself as *adat*. Dance, music, and *silat* are also expressed as *adat*.

In the same way, marriage rules were also often referred to as *adat*. In Suku Asli *adat*, the marriage between bilateral kin is regarded as incest. If two kinfolk want to marry, the marriage is regarded as an immoral marriage violating their *adat* (see Chapter 2). The reason that these marriages are prohibited is because, according to Kiat, 'We cannot inform the ancestors of such marriages.' In the past, a couple who violated this *adat* was confined to a large fish trap made of thorny plants and sunk in the river. At present, if such a marriage is conducted, the couple cannot receive any support or celebrations from their parents and ancestors, and have to leave the community. In short, for Suku Asli, everything that is related to their ancestral worship is *adat*.

Interestingly, other rituals were not referred to as *adat*. First, they often conduct shamanic rituals for the purpose of healing the sick or protecting a hamlet. This kind of ritual was not referred to as *adat*. It was explained as a kind of encounter between a shaman's individual power and spiritual existences, and described as *ilmu batin* (inner technique or headman's technique; see note 5 in Chapter 6). In this ritual, while they often offer food to *datuk*, there are no procedures that imply connections with their ancestors (see Chapter 6). Second, and more importantly, no rituals held in the *peranakan* or Chinese way are referred to as *adat*. As I mentioned in Chapter 2, the *peranakan* or Chinese way also involves ancestral worship and such rituals are held periodically; however, this kind of ritual is just called '*acara*' and its procedures and instruments are not described as *adat*. The rituals, procedures, and instruments that may be described as *adat* are all related to those that are 'real' Suku Asli. Therefore, *adat* is something related to 'real' Suku Asli ancestral worship.

However, there was another dimension to the use of the term '*adat*' with a more comprehensive and abstract meaning, which emerges in the context of their relations with outsiders. One day, I talked with Koding about the people living in Teluk Pambang and focused especially on the history of the relationship between the Malays and Suku Asli. After we had talked about the topic for a while, he concluded, 'But today, there are various Suku Asli in this village. There are people of the ethnic Chinese, the *orang Batak* (Batak), and *orang Kalimantan* (people from Kalimantan) and *orang Flores* (people from Flores).' Indeed, in the western part of Teluk Pambang where I conducted the survey, there are three households in which *peranakan* Suku Asli men married Batak women, and there was a household in which a man from Kalimantan married a Suku Asli woman. A bachelor from Flores also worked in Ajui's house. I asked Koding, 'Are they Suku Asli as well?' He answered, 'Sure. They married here and are *ikut adat kami* (following our *adat*).' In the same sense, they sometimes claimed that those who converted to Islam and Christianity (see Chapter 6) or violated the marriage rule 'are *tidak ikut adat* (not following *adat*).' In these contexts, the term '*adat*' is obviously used to indicate not only 'real' Suku Asli ancestral worship but also *peranakan* or Chinese worship. Furthermore, *adat* in these contexts can be seen as their everyday life in their community. Either way, *adat* can work as a criterion to distinguish 'us' and 'others.'

In short, the term '*adat*' is primarily used to indicate the practices and instruments that are related to 'real' Suku Asli ancestral worship, and occasionally used as a criterion of differentiation between 'us' and 'others,' including *peranakan*/Chinese ancestral worship. However, the term is not used to indicate other rules and morals. Throughout my fieldwork, I encountered no situations in which *adat* was used in this way.

Adat as an embodiment of resistance

In studies of Indonesia, *adat* has often been seen as the total worldview of a local community. Leiden scholars saw *adat* in this way. Acciaioli (1985: 152) also sees *adat* as having similar implications and states that, in the past, '*adat* provided the cosmological order, the primary, perhaps sometimes the only, explanation that rendered the world intelligible and informed one as to how to act in it.' For him, and probably among the Da'a Toraja, *adat* involves a macrocosm that shows how people should be and what the world is. *Adat* was seen as a primary and comprehensive explanation of the cosmos and a norm for behavior. In a similar way, Renske Biezeveld (2007: 204) explains *adat* among the Minangkabau:

> *adat* can mean either local custom or a society's fundamental structural system, of which local custom is only a component. In this latter sense *adat* forms the basis of all ethical and legal judgements and the source of social expectations. In short, it represents the ideal pattern of behavior.

However, the Suku Asli do not explain their moral prescriptions, rules of land right, social values, and cosmological order with the term '*adat*.' Rather, *adat* emerged only in the contexts of ancestral worship. This does not seem to be simply a result of the reduction or simplification of *adat* caused by state intervention. Why have they used this term only in these contexts?

Although I cannot comment specifically about why they do not use '*adat*' in the sense of a total cosmos or as an ideal pattern of behavior, these issues seem to be related to the historical process of forming their ethnic identity. As I argued in previous chapters, they were coastal foragers who individually moved around a vast coastal area. In this way of life, they communicated and lived with people who had, more or less, different norms, rules, and practices. More importantly, after the mid-nineteenth century, many ethnic Chinese and some of their customs and beliefs, which were not expressed or understood as *adat*, were accepted by the Utan communities. Through these processes, their *adat*, which might have been an exclusive framework of their actions and reality in the past, was relativized as one of a number of frameworks. Indeed, as I mentioned in Chapter 2, there are two ways of understanding ancestral souls in Teluk Pambang, and both are acceptable. The Suku Asli do not summarize the whole body of their customs or ancestral practices through the symbolic term '*adat*' because of the historically continuous communications they have had with other *orang asli* communities and the ethnic Chinese even before state intervention in the concept became obvious in post-independence Indonesia.

Here, I suppose that *adat* in Suku Asli society is not a total cosmological order or an ideal pattern of behavior inherited from the ancestors. Rather, it is part of their whole tradition, which has been objectified in and through communications with the state, and especially with Muslims. In Suku Asli society, ancestral worship and their criterion for distinguishing 'us' from 'others' are strongly related. They have *orang asli* identity based on the image of having common ancestors, in which their non-Islamic ancestral religious practices have been the main criteria for belonging. However, on the eastern coast of Sumatra, the dominant majorities have been the Malays, Minangkabau, and Javanese, and their religion is exclusively Islam. The Suku Asli have been discriminated against and marginalized because of their relatively weak association with *agama* legitimized by the state. In this situation, the Suku Asli have continuously confronted the necessity to demonstrate the legitimacy of an ancestral worship that does not include the ideology or doctrine of *agama* (see also Chapter 6). In this process, they adopted the term '*adat*' and tried to explain its legitimacy. This term legally enabled them to differentiate their thoughts and beliefs from the dominant ideology and maintain their traditional way of life in the binary schema of *adat* versus state control. The Malays and Javanese could accept this as the term involves the legitimation and justification of local customs in the state image. Therefore, the term '*adat*' in the Suku Asli community comprehensively indicates their traditional ancestral worship, and it also emerges in the context of distinguishing themselves from outsiders.

Yet, other spheres of Suku Asli life were not involved in contradictions or competition with others, and such practices and beliefs are not referred to as *adat*. First, they were not involved in the competition for living space with the Malays and Javanese until very recent years. Before the late 1990s, their livelihoods depended exclusively on the mangrove swamps, and they accessed the resources freely. Therefore, they did not need to objectify and claim traditional land usage and rule as *adat*. Second, the Malays and Javanese had not intervened in or tried to change their moral prescriptions and the codes of individual behavior, as they regarded the Suku Asli as 'backward' and 'primitive' people who do not have *agama* (see Chapter 6). Therefore, the Suku Asli did not objectify such practices and values as *adat*. Third, the Malays and Javanese in this region have not intervened in the shamanic practices of the Suku Asli. Although the Javanese and Malays are Muslims, they also have traditions of shamanic techniques. Finally, in terms of the *peranakan* or Chinese way of rituals, the situation seems to be more complex. The form of rituals obviously derives from China, and Chinese cultures have been always 'foreign' and, since the 1960s, have been oppressed in Indonesian policies. Given such restrictions, it would have been difficult to claim Chinese rituals as Suku Asli tradition in communication with Muslims. Therefore, they do not refer to the rituals as *adat*, although the rituals may be included in the comprehensive and abstract meaning of their *adat*.

In short, *adat* can be seen as part of the whole local tradition that was objectified in competitions, contradictions, and conflicts with state interventions and other outsiders in order to claim the legitimacy of local practices. Moreover, this is the case, or partly the case, elsewhere in Indonesia, where the concept of *adat* has been much more developed and elaborated than in Suku Asli communities. For example, as mentioned above, the Minangkabau objectified and elaborated their traditional rules and rights of land as *adat* when the competition with the Dutch colonial government for land possession became serious in the mid-nineteenth century (Benda-Beckmann and Benda-Beckmann 2011: 178–9). Also, their matrilineal system has been strongly associated with *adat*, as it involves contradictions with Islamic law, which is characterized by a patrilineal system. Their traditional headmanship, the *panghulu* system, has also been strongly related with *adat*, as it does not always conform to the state bureaucratic administrative headmanship (Kahn 1993: 31–50, 119–20, 160–5). While Li (2007a: 338) recognizes that *adat* institutes orderly rule and promotes harmony, she also points out that it may be deployed to challenge the state authority. *Adat* always involves contradictions with the central power or ideology, which the state has exerted on local communities. By claiming *adat*, the local communities may have legitimated their traditional local customs, implying the difference of local particularity and national universality.

In this sense, *adat* can be seen as an embodiment of resistance among the locals against interventions by the state. Indeed, the concept of *adat* has been constructed by the state through the late colonial-era policies and inherited by post-independence Indonesia, as Burns (1989) and others have pointed out. However, in the constructed framework, the locals have protected and maintained their customary practices by objectifying and defining them as *adat*. In particular, this was the only way to claim local rights, self-determination, and autonomy during Suharto's era, in which the government strongly implemented the exploitation of local lands and resources under the banner of 'development.' Using terms such as 'rights,' 'self-determination,' and 'autonomy' was dangerous in an oppressive polity. If the local communities had any conflicts with the government, they used the term '*adat* law' to negotiate. This choice of the term 'was a safer, although not necessarily more successful, way of defending rights than expressing them in overtly political terms' (Benda-Beckmann and Benda-Beckmann 2011: 183). *Adat* is an objectification of local traditions in the struggle with the state, where it is utilized as a tool to claim legitimacy in a form that the state might accept.

I do not intend to insist that all *adat* in Indonesia are manifested in the context of relationships with the state. It is actually the case that *adat* has taken the role of customary laws, a cosmological order, moral prescriptions, and the rules of land usage in contexts that do not display resistance against the government. In addition, the government has constructed *adat* for the purpose of controlling the population. However, *adat* involves a qualification that has been formed and objectified in the resistance of the locals against the central power. This qualification is very obvious in Suku Asli communities. For them, *adat* has not been a whole tradition or a simple inheritance from ancestors nor constructed by the government, but an embodiment of resistance that was objectified in their engagement with the state.

Adat as performance

As I have already suggested, for the Suku Asli the term '*adat*,' first and foremost, indicates ancestral worship and the procedures surrounding it, and has been formed in communication with Muslims. Although this has been the case until now, the meaning of the word has been changing. They are increasingly using the term to indicate a specific part of rituals—that is, music, dance, and songs. This change of emphasis is related to the government's intervention in their life. However, this change is not a form of their resistance, but an adoption of the government idea, and one which brings about the integration of their communities as an *adat* community.

The use of '*adat*' that I first encountered in Teluk Pambang emphasized dance and music in ritual. On the very day of my first visit to the village, a wedding ceremony was held at a house, and I was able to join the feast. Atang, who was a village *batin* at Selat Baru, led me around the site. When four girls wearing matching green clothes began dancing together to music played by a band consisting of a clarinet, a viola, a gong, and two drums, Atang said to me, '*Inilah adat Suku Aslinya*' (This is the Suku Asli *adat*), indicating their dance. After that, I sometimes heard the word '*adat*' in other contexts—such as funeral rituals and weddings, which they called *adat* or *acara adat* (*adat* ceremony)—but most frequently they used it to indicate dances, music with a traditional band, *silat*, or clothes and objects like a *sirih* box used in rituals. The word seemed to be equivocal and ambiguous, but conventional, as in the phrase, 'This is the *adat*.'

Margaret Kartomi (2019: 94) describes how the king's music ensemble or *nobat*, which was the hallmark of the king's legitimacy and power, held a concert for the installation of a prince following the regulations of *adat-istiadat* (customs and traditions) in the Riau-Lingga kingdom. Van Anrooij (1885: 322–3) also describes a ceremony held by a *nobat* in the Siak kingdom together with a series of ceremonial regulations of procedures and dresses. On the eastern coast of Sumatra, music is deeply associated with *adat*, and it seems to be natural to regard dance, music, and clothes as *adat*. However, Odang, an IKBBSA *kepala adat* (*adat* manager), disputes this. One day, I said, 'People use *adat* in the sense of dances, music, clothes, and so on. Is the meaning of *adat* like that?' He answered:

> No, it's different from *adat*. Dances, music, and clothes are *seni* (art), not *adat*. Art is *sebagian adat* (part of *adat*)...There are various *adat*. Ceremonies like funeral and wedding are also *adat*. *Adat* is whole ways from our ancestors and for respecting them...But I know people often use '*adat*' in the meaning of art. This is because officials in the Department of Culture and Tourism say *adat* is like that.

Dances, music, clothes, and songs may be important components of their *adat* or ancestral worship; however, these are not the whole of *adat*. Nevertheless, the reason Suku Asli often refer to these as '*adat*' appears to be because the officials at the Department of Culture and Tourism used it as such.

Their emphasis on art in the usage of '*adat*' relates to their recent communications with the government. The Department of Culture and Tourism is a department in the regency government and is in charge of promoting *kebudayaan* (culture) and *pariwisata* (tourism). Although the Suku Asli appear to have had no relationship with this department in the past, after IKBBSA was established, they began working together when IKBBSA held ethnic festivals and meetings. The department subsidized these events. According to Ajui, the department budgeted for the instruments of their *adat*, such as clothes, a gong, a viola, drums, and other decorations used in rituals, and encouraged them to perform the dances and music at the festivals and meetings. Although I saw no actual communications between the officials of the department and Suku Asli leaders, the government officials must have tried to educate the leaders in how important the manifestation of this form of *adat* was for the Suku Asli in state policies and how it was important to configure their attachment to this form of *adat* when they negotiated the subsidies.

This form of *adat* is most fruitfully performed at the ethnic festival held by IKBBSA. It was first held in 2010 at Penyengat, a village of the Rawa or Suku Asli Anak Rawa in the Siak regency. In 2011, it was held at the village of Sesap of Tebing Tinggi Island in Meranti Islands regency. Although IKBBSA planned to hold the festival at Teluk Pambang in 2012, it was cancelled because they could not obtain subsidies from the Bengkalis government. The festival has since

Photograph 5.1: Marriage ceremony and *tari gendong* (dance) of the Suku Asli (Teluk Pambang)

been held annually at various Suku Asli villages. Although I could not attend the festival in 2012, I heard about it from Ajui and watched scenes that had been recorded at the 2010 festival, in which hundreds of Penyengat villagers, all the *batin* headmen of IKBBSA of the three regencies, and a dozen followers of each *batin* participated. In addition, a dozen officials were invited as guests of honor. During the festival, several officials and *batin* headmen made speeches in which they spoke about the necessity of *pembinaan* (development) and *maju* (progress) for Suku Asli communities as a KAT group. In front of the officials, Suku Asli attendants performed dances, music, and *silat* wearing Malay-like ethnic clothes, which had been prepared for this festival. According to Ajui, representatives of each administrative village took part in a dance competition of *tari gendong*, which is a group dance performed at wedding ceremonies in Suku Asli communities. The dancers of each village practiced dances and music for the events. In their training, according to Odang, the performances were termed '*adat*' following the officials' expressions of the 'art' as *adat*. As a result, many ordinary people began describing dances and music as *adat*, although it was only part of their rituals.

Odang's role as *adat* manager is also related to art rather than ancestral worship. As I mentioned in Chapter 4, some roles were newly created when IKBBSA was established in 2005 in accordance with government guidance. In this process, the role of *adat* manager was also created. Other ethnic organizations, such as *Lembaga Adat Melayu Riau* (LAMR; Riau Malay Adat Organization) and *Ikatan Keluarga Jawa Riau* (IKJR; Javanese Family Association in Riau), already had this role to manage matters of their own *adat*, and IKBBSA adopted it. Odang had adequate knowledge of ancestral worship and its procedures, but he rarely engaged in such work because the ancestral rituals were usually held by the kinfolk and neighbors of the household. Instead, his main role was to provide instruction about dances, music, and songs to the girls who performed them at wedding ceremonies and periodical meetings of IKBBSA, and, because of this, he was recognized as the *adat* manager of Teluk Pambang.

Again, this usage of *adat* seems to be applied only to the dances and music that emerge in the rituals of 'real' Suku Asli. Procedures and instruments that emerge in the rituals of the *peranakan* or Chinese way, such as paper money, incense sticks, and red symbols, are not referred to as *adat*. Also, although Suku Asli use the dedicated drums and gongs in the rituals held by Chinese spirit mediums, I have never heard them refer to the instruments and rhythms as *adat*. In festivals and meetings, while the *adat* that are performed in front of the officials are those of 'real' Suku Asli, the Chinese performances and symbols never make an appearance.

The term '*adat*' seems to be increasingly used to indicate a part of Suku Asli ancestral worship—that is, dances and music—among ordinary Suku Asli. This is a result of the government constitution of art as *adat*, and this usage has been accepted by ordinary Suku Asli through the activities of IKBBSA. It is very important that a number of ordinary Suku Asli actively engage in this kind of *adat* (i.e. dance and music), recognizing that these are their traditional activities, although, as I argued in Chapter 4, they do not really appear to be concerned with the political activities of IKBBSA. In other words, as a result of their emphasis on art, ordinary Suku Asli have been involved in the activities of IKBBSA.

Performance as erosion or participation

The state attempt to redefine local traditions as art is also found in other regions and is associated with the reinforcement of state control over local populations. First, it is concerned with reducing local tradition in the process of strengthening national laws, norms, and morals, as I mentioned in the first part of this chapter. In the study of the Da'a Toraja, Acciaioli (1985) finds the state attempt to identify song, dances, and death rituals as *adat* separates it from their total cosmology and religious beliefs—that is, *aluk*. By doing so, the state can relativize and reduce the values of laws, morals, and norms in tradition without the local resistance that might emerge if the state completely rejected local tradition as a whole. 'Regional diversity is valued, honoured, even apotheosized, but only as long as it remains at the level of display, not belief, performance, not enactment' (Acciaioli 1985: 161–2); as a result, the belief and enactment of the local tradition is eroded. Second, it is related to the efficacy of reinforcing the political and economic dependency between locals and the state. Through the description of the Bunun, an Austronesian-speaking people of Taiwan, Shu-Yuan Yang (2011) suggests that 'music, art, dance, ritual, ethnic attire, and handcraft,' which are a part of the local tradition actively supported by the state, contain a 'thing-like' attribution. This 'thing-like' tradition is vulnerable to appropriation by the state, in comparison to their beliefs, norms, and morals, and the state can control the people and their tradition through the appropriation. Yang (2011: 327) concludes, 'The politicization of culture has the potential to draw the Bunun into the bureaucratized discourse of tradition which would result in their greater dependence on the state and a commodity logic that can further marginalize them.'

This analysis is also true in the case of the Suku Asli. The traditional usage of the term '*adat*' was an embodiment of their resistance, with which the Suku Asli were able to contrapose their ancestral ways with the state ideology and justify its legitimacy. In this meaning, *adat* was something existing outside or in opposition to state control. Yet *adat* as art is something visible, aesthetic, and performative, and it can be placed under the government's cultural policies. That is to say, this *adat* is domesticated and has lost its contraposition to the state ideology. In addition, it is also the case that this *adat* is vulnerable to appropriation by the government. Subsidies from the government are obviously an incentive for the leaders of IKBBSA to hold ethnic meetings and festivals. In order to obtain the subsidies, they follow the government guidance of the way of *adat* and emphasize dances, music, and songs, which are only part of their ancestral rituals, as *adat*. Now, *adat* as an embodiment of the spirit of resistance belonging exclusively to the Suku Asli community appears to be declining. Instead, it is becoming part of the diversity of Indonesian 'culture,' which the state admits and can control through appropriation.

However, simultaneously, *adat* also offers a new conceptualization of the meaning and consolidation of Suku Asli identity beyond various distinctions within their community. First, as a result of *adat* connected with dance and song, *adat* becomes related to more people in everyday life. For example, in Teluk Pambang, the dancers at weddings are young girls. While they may essentially be unconcerned with the *adat* of ancestral worship, they become the bearers of Suku Asli *adat* through their participation in music and dance. For the audiences, whereas music and dance were once simply performances undertaken at wedding ceremonies, now they are seen as their own *adat* inherited from their ancestors, and this brings about a confirmation of their identity as the Suku Asli. Second, the new emphasis on *adat* enables them to fill the gap in identities derived from distinct descent. *Peranakan* Suku Asli conduct their ancestral rituals in the *peranakan*/Chinese way, and these are difficult to express as *adat* because they clearly belong to foreign Chinese culture. However, in terms of *adat* as music and dance, the *peranakan* can actually participate in *adat* through their mutual cooperation with 'real' Suku Asli, and they can insist that they actually have Suku Asli *adat* in their communication with outsiders. By participating in dance and music as *adat*, they can consolidate their identity as Suku Asli and leave aside their ambiguous and ambivalent identity as *peranakan*, which is potentially somewhat risky in Indonesian politics. Finally, through their participation in *adat*, ordinary Suku Asli are involved in the political activities of IKBBSA. Although they may not really be involved in the political activity of IKBBSA, they actively join in dance and music, thus reinforcing the organization. Although some leaders monopolize the political and economic activities in IKBBSA, all members of the community can equally share the aesthetic activities as either performers or audiences. This quality contributes to the consolidation of Suku Asli identity beyond the social distinctions of generation, gender, descent, and political power. Suku Asli leaders appear to actively adopt this definition, and *adat* that is abstracted and embodied in art comes to be a symbol of their identification as Suku Asli.

The culturalization of *adat*, however, has disempowered local legal systems and transformed *adat* into harmless culture. This clearly seems to be the case among the Suku Asli; *adat* that would have been the embodiment of their boundary with Muslims has transformed into art. But it also has the power to connect people and consolidate diverse identities among the locals through participation in the manifestation of culture. Because culturalization involves the latter aspect, even though local communities experienced the disempowerment of *adat* between the colonial and Suharto eras, *adat* in local communities has been revived as a symbol of local solidarity and self-determination in the post-Suharto era. In particular, people who have segmentary and decentralized social structures and flexible and diffuse *adat* can be consolidated by culturalization.

This process is not necessarily seen as construction or invention of their tradition because they actually have these constituents of their *adat*—dance and music—in their practice of ancestral worship. Therefore, their way of conceptualizing *adat* can be seen as a process of objectification and abstraction of their flexible and diffuse traditional practices in the government framework of *adat*. By doing so, they are integrating their diverse traditional practices and reinforcing their identity as Suku Asli in relation to the state.

Again, *adat* is the basic component of the Indonesian version of an indigenous movement—that is, the quest for *adat* communities. Although activists and local authorities may emphasize the 'revival' of *adat*—that is, local tradition and authenticity—it is framed in engagement with historical government policies. Indigeneity emerges in such engagement, and the local community indigenizes itself in relation to the image of being indigenous that is held by the state.

In a similar way to *adat,* the Suku Asli have tried to objectify and abstract their religious practices in relation to state religious policies in Indonesia. In the next chapter, I explore the process of adoption, objectification, abstraction, and integration of their *agama*—that is, religion recognized by the state—in Suku Asli society.

Chapter 6

Creation of Homogeneity: *Agama*, Buddhism, and Abstraction

In the previous chapters, I described the processes whereby the Suku Asli conceptualized and embodied their ancestral space, political organization, and the concept of *adat* in accordance with the state image of how they should be. In addition, religion or *agama*[1] has increasingly been an important factor in constituting their ethnic identity as Suku Asli in recent years. This has occurred through the implementation of the government's religious policies.

In Indonesia, identifying one's *agama* is very important in civil life. In the Pancasila, the five philosophical foundations of Indonesia, the state has a national principle of *Ketuhanan yang Maha Esa* (Belief in one God). Until 2017, people were obliged to register their chosen religion as one of six *agama*—Islam, Catholicism (*Katolik*; *Kristen*), Protestantism (*Protestan*), Hinduism, Buddhism, and Confucianism.[2] *Agama* is stated on various official documents such as *Kartu Tanda Penduduk* (KTP; identification cards) and marriage certificates, and constitutes an essential part of one's citizenship. Also, in school curricula, *agama* is a compulsory subject, and children learn the history and doctrine of the *agama* that they choose. These policies have been developed under the initiatives of Muslims (and some Christians), who have been the overwhelming majority and are dominant in post-independence Indonesia.

People who converted to Islam and Christianity before independence could identify their own *agama* relatively easily. However, people who were neither Muslim nor Christian and followed traditional religious practices (i.e. *adat*) were confronted with the necessity to show their *agama* in response to Pancasila politics. Two powerful ethnic groups, the Balinese and ethnic Chinese, succeeded in having their traditional religions (Hinduism and Confucianism/Buddhism) recognized as *agama* just after independence (Brown 1987; Picard 2011; Tsuda 2012). Some people have tried to legitimatize their *adat* as *agama* by fitting their *adat* into the state image of *agama*. For example, after the 1970s, *adat* among the Ngaju Dayak in central Kalimantan and the Wana in Sulawesi were reformulated as having monotheistic doctrines and were recognized as versions of Hinduism (Atkinson 1983; Schiller 1996). On the other hand, some people adopted one of the established faiths. For instance, the Sakai have been involved in a wave of Islamization and many Sakai identify themselves as Muslim (Porath 2003: 217–218), while the Forest Tobelo in central Halmahera converted to Christianity in the 1980s and accepted the American-based New Tribal Mission (Duncan 2003).

In any case, the *adat* of each local community has confronted the necessity to transform itself because of the implementation of religious policies, as *agama* often intervenes in religious practices and beliefs based on *adat* (Schiller 1996; Kipp and Rodgers 1987). The Suku Asli also confronted the serious necessity to adjust the relationship between *adat* and national *agama* after IKBBSA was established. In the process of claiming their position as Suku Asli, the leaders have had more opportunities to explain to government officials what Suku Asli *agama* is. However, this has been very difficult because they have two forms of religious practices based on 'real' and *peranakan* traditions. In this situation, Suku Asli have tried to integrate their *agama* into Buddhism by redefining the concepts of *agama* and other religious practices based on their cultural logic in order to show its legitimacy in relation to the national law. How have they conceptualized and embodied *agama* and what kind of social change does this bring about? This is the question that I try to answer in this chapter.

Most of the ethnographic facts in this chapter were obtained at my main site, Teluk Pambang, where almost all Suku Asli identify their *agama* as Buddhism. Although I do not have much data on the Christian point of view, I try to describe it based on an interview with a one-time Christian.

Identifying *agama*

The Indonesian word '*agama*' derives from Sanskrit, and was introduced to the Indonesian archipelago sometime during the early centuries of the previous millennium when it became an important trading hub between China, India, and the Near East (Atkinson 1983: 686). The term originally meant "'a traditional precept, doctrine, body of precepts, collection of such doctrines"; in short, "anything handed down fixed by tradition"' (Gonda 1973: 499). Therefore, in its original sense, *agama* is not so different from *adat* (Schiller 1996: 40). The elites in the precolonial kingdoms actively accepted the word because they used the Sanskrit language as a sign of their spiritual and political power, though it was not really related to ordinary people and their lives (Kipp and Rogers 1987: 15).

However, the meaning of *agama* was changed and politicized after the nineteenth century when the state tried to control local religious practices and beliefs (Atkinson 1983: 686–9). Religious policies in the colonial era emerged in the system of interactions between Christianity and Islam. In the latter half of the nineteenth century, when the Dutch colonial government attempted to tighten its control over the archipelago, Islam was considered as a main source of resistance. Therefore, the government permitted and encouraged missionaries in non-Muslim areas for the purpose of establishing Christian enclaves or 'buffers' (Kipp and Rodgers 1987: 16). Then, during the Japanese occupation in the 1940s, the Japanese colonial government supported *Masyumi* (an Islamic organization) because they regarded Muslims as nationalists who resisted the Dutch Christian authority. Islamic organizations continued as major political parties after independence (Tsing 1987: 196). Through these colonial policies, *agama* gradually became something related to state independence and the lives of local populations.

After independence, the importance of *agama* dramatically increased. The Pancasila was first declared in a speech by Sukarno in 1945.[3] The Pancasila included five principles—Belief in One God, Nationalism, Humanism, Democracy, and Social Justice (Kipp and Rodgers 1987: 17). The belief in one *agama* was also addressed in the statements of the constitution. Through these processes, *agama* became a foundation of the new nation state and was associated with social order and citizenship. In parallel with the process of codifying the importance of *agama* in the Pancasila and constitution, the bureaucracy elaborated the meaning of *agama*. The main agent was the Department of Religious Affairs, which was established under the initiative of Muslim leaders in 1946. In 1952, this department designated the meaning of *agama*—'the prerequisite elements [are] a prophet, a holy book, and international recognition' (Tsing 1987: 197). Then, in 1959, the department put forward the definition involving belief in one God as a unified principle of life (Kim 1998: 363). These definitions clearly reflected the monotheism of Islam and Christianity. Michael Picard (2011: 483) summarizes its main elements as follows:

> While the word *agama* in Indonesia is commonly translated as 'religion,' it is a peculiar combination of a Christian view of what counts as a world religion with an Islamic understanding of what defines a proper religion—divine revelation recorded by a prophet in a holy book, a system of law for the community of believers, congregational worship, and a belief in the One and Only God.

Between the 1940s and the 1950s, the government encouraged people who did not belong to one of the two main *agamas* to demonstrate the legitimacy of their religious practices and beliefs. In response to this political atmosphere, the Balinese claimed their traditional religious practices and beliefs as Hinduism by constructing an image of being monotheistic (having a prophet, a holy book, and a codified system of law) and gaining international recognition and believers outside Bali (Geertz 1973; Picard 2011: 497). The ethnic Chinese also approached the government to recognize their faiths as *agama*. On the one hand, some ethnic Chinese who followed Buddhism sent their leaders to Burma to learn Buddhism and established a religious body elaborating their doctrine as a 'world religion' (Brown 1987). On the other hand, the practitioners of Chinese folk religions based on Chinese *klenteng* (temples) were integrated as Confucianism under a particular religious body. Although such temples enshrined the various deities of Confucianism, Daoism, and Buddhism, the religious body designated *Tiang Gong* as the supreme God (Tsuda 2012). After numerous controversies in terms of the definition of *agama*, a Sukarno-era presidential decree (No. 1/1965 on the Prevention of Abuse and/or Disrespect of Religion) recognized six legitimate *agama* in Indonesia—that is, Islam, Catholicism, Protestantism, Hinduism, Buddhism, and Confucianism (Salim 2007:116).

While the importance of *agama* arose in the government politics of the new nation state, discrimination and marginalization against those who did not or could not register their *agama* gradually formed in the state atmosphere. In post-independence Indonesia, such people were regarded as 'people who do not yet have *agama* (*orang belum beragama*)' (Kipp and Rodgers 1987: 21–5) or 'people who believe in "animism" (*animisme*)' (Atkinson 1983: 691); the expression 'not yet' in the first phrase involves the implications of 'an inevitability about the future of these people' (Kipp and Rodgers 1987: 21). In other words, 'animism,' which as a notion would have been introduced to the Indonesian archipelago in the late Dutch colonial era, is associated with Edward Tylor's classic definition of 'animism' (see Tsintjilonis 2004: 427), with an emphasis on anthropomorphism and the implication that 'all natural phenomena have souls'; it also encompasses the implications of Western evolutionism. In particular, in the context of Indonesia, this term is used as an antonym of monotheisms that are legitimated by the state. Thus the people who were labeled as 'animists' were regarded as not believing in one God, and should come to believe in an *agama* in accordance with their progress and civilization. Either way, the people who maintained their traditional forms of religious practices and beliefs without the identification of one *agama* were connected with the image of being 'backward' and 'primitive.'

In addition to this negative image, the marginalization of and discrimination against people who did not claim an *agama* dramatically increased in the rise of the anti-communist movement in the 1960s. The communists were regarded as having a strong connection with atheism, so people who did not identify with an *agama* were regarded as communists and as a threat to the state—in the anti-communist purge between 1965 and 1966, they became the main target of oppression and, after this event, rushed to register an *agama* at government offices (Kipp and Rodgers 1987: 19). In some areas, mass conversion to Christianity occurred (Kipp and Rogers 1987: 19). Furthermore, one of the recognized *agama*, Confucianism, was dropped from the list of legitimate *agama* in 1967 because it was regarded as having strong relationships with communism (Kim 1998: 360; Salim 2007: 116). Many ethnic Chinese who had registered their *agama* as Confucianism converted to Buddhism or Christianity or at least identified themselves as such (Tsuda 2012: 393; Yang Heriyanto 2005: 3). While some regulations in terms of *agama* have loosened in the post-Suharto era, discrimination in terms of atheism, polytheism, and animism remains. In particular, atheism is still regarded as having a relationship with communism, and, indeed, in 2013 a man who declared his atheism was brought to trial for crimes against the law (Paker and Hoon 2013: 159).

It is noteworthy that Confucianism was again recognized as *agama* around 2000 by the central government (Yang Heriyanto 2005: 6). However, at the local government level, it is not recognized in practice. As far as I know, I have never met any Suku Asli or ethnic Chinese in the Bengkalis regency who had a Confucian identification card or claimed the legitimacy of Confucianism.

During the Suharto regime, religious ideologies were enforced through various policies. On national identification cards, people had to fill in a column for '*agama*' and, in 1974, a statute on marriage was enacted (No. 1/1974 on Marriage). This law decreed that marriages should be conducted under the rules of a couple's *agama* (Yang Heriyanto 2005: 3), and their *agama* is stated on the marriage certificate (see Chapter 4). Thus *agama* became the essential identity in people's citizenship.

Agama also plays an essential role in school education. For example, in 1985, it was announced that students progressing from primary school to high school had to take compulsory classes on *agama*. The 'new curriculum,' which was put into practice in 1994, states that elementary school children have to attend *agama* classes for two hours a week (Schiller 1996: 410). In 2013, the government decided to increase the hours of religious education in school, as 'more religious instruction is needed because a lack of moral development has led to an increase in violence and vandalism among youths, and that could fuel social unrest and corruption in the future' (New York Times 2013). Generally, in government schemes, religious education has been associated with the moral development of children. As a result, *agama* was associated with nationalism and social order, and identifying an *agama* became essential in civic life in Indonesia.

The requirement for people to assert one of the recognized universal *agama* associated with Indonesian nationalism, social order, and morals can be seen as partly contradicting the concepts of *adat* or *adat* community associated with locality and diversity. Followers not only of Hinduism and Buddhism but also of Christianity and Islam have to adjust the relationship between *adat* and *agama* through controversies and political actions, while, at a practical level, religious practices and *adat* are difficult to separate (Schiller 1996: 410).

Just after independence, the ideology of state religious politics was unconcerned with the Suku Asli, who lived in a peripheral area and had no political power to claim their traditional religious practices as an *agama*. They had been categorized as 'people who do not yet have *agama*' and, indeed, they would not have identified their practices as an *agama*. However, through the anti-communist purge and the corresponding political requirements for citizenship and education, they confronted the necessity to show that they too had an *agama*—an *agama* they started to construct in and through their involvement with the state and the quest for development.

Contacts with *agama*: passivity and contingency

It is uncertain what meaning the term '*agama*' had in the Siak kingdom and Utan communities before the mid-nineteenth century. However, it seems likely that the term was used generally as a synonym of 'Islam' because, in this region, Islam was overwhelmingly predominant and, even if there were Christians, only a few Dutch settlers and North Sumatran (Batak) immigrants were followers. Therefore, in Utan communities, the term '*agama*' would not have been used, and, even if they had used it, it would have been synonymous with Islam. They did not have contact with Christianity or Buddhism, which could be counterposed with Islam. Only after the 1970s did Christian missionaries arrive in their settlements. Considering the situation of Christian missionaries in Indonesia, the introduction of Christianity to Suku Asli society seems to have been late. There would have been some missionaries who went into their society early on, but I have never heard such stories from Suku Asli elders and, even if some had tried to missionize Suku Asli before the 1970s, the influences were minimal. In the same period, Buddhist followers become organized in the region.

The Utan must have recognized that religious practices and beliefs were related to their social status in the state. As I mentioned in Chapter 1, they were categorized as the lowest class in the Siak kingdom because they were not Muslim. Some Utan communities converted to Islam and obtained the higher status of Malay. In any case, while the concept of *agama* may have been more or less important only in their communication with the Malays, it seems to have had no importance in their communities.

In the latter half of the nineteenth century, the diffusion of the ethnic Chinese population was accelerated from towns to rural areas as a result of the introduction of the *panglong* system. While there would have been some Chinese temples, or *klenteng*, before the nineteenth century, they were concentrated in towns such as Bengkalis and Selat Panjang, where many Chinese traders lived and established communities. However, as a result of immigration, *klenteng* were established in the rural areas as well, and some were founded in areas where the Utan and Akit lived. Such well-known old *klenteng* built in this period include those in Titi Akar, Rupat Island, and Selat Akar, Padang Island. In this process, the Utan and Akit had contact with Chinese folk religions that would be legitimatized and then banned as Confucianism. However, it is improbable that they described Chinese folk religion as *agama* in a way similar to the present meaning, because, in this period, Chinese folk religion was foreign culture and the Islamic Malays would not have intervened in their religious practices.

As I described in Chapter 2, Suku Asli accepted some elements of Chinese religion, mainly ancestral worship, through collaboration with *peranakan* over rituals in their everyday life. However, worshipping at *klenteng* was something outside their everyday life. First, the various *klenteng* were sustained by mutual aid and donations within each Chinese community, the members of which were generally *touke* and their Chinese subjects, who spoke Chinese and identified themselves as Chinese. The 'real' Suku Asli did not live in such communities. Second, in *klenteng*, people pray for various Chinese deities in order to achieve secular desires, such as the success of business and the safety of family. This worship was separated from ancestral worship and the *peranakan* Suku Asli had no obligation to perform this (unlike ancestral worship and their moral relationship with ancestors). *Klenteng* thus did not become the place of worship for 'real' or *peranakan* Suku Asli. Even today, whether one joins in or not is an individual choice. Some *peranakan* Suku Asli who maintain strong social relationships with ethnic Chinese often join the worship at *klenteng*, but most 'real' and *peranakan* Suku Asli do not participate in this worship.

Just after independence, most *peranakan* Chinese and some *peranakan* Suku Asli registered their *agama* as Confucianism. However, before the 1970s, there were few Suku Asli who had fully completed their administrative registration, and so they did not identify their *agama*. A turning point came after the anti-communist purge and the start of Suharto's New Order regime. In accordance with the rise of political pressure to register their *agama* and the prohibition of Confucianism, they confronted the necessity to choose an *agama*. Although Islam was not a choice, as they had maintained their identity and position as non-Muslims, their choice varied from community to community (or even from person to person).

Some Suku Asli registered their *agama* as Buddhism. Just after Confucianism was prohibited, a Buddhist community of ethnic Chinese began activities in Bengkalis town and was recognized by the regency government in 1971. This community, Maitreya Great Tao—which was established in Taiwan in the twentieth century and introduced to Indonesia in the 1940s by a Taiwanese (Brown 1990: 115)—was the first and only Buddhist community in the region. In Taiwan, this community is known as *Yi Guan Dao,* or Unity Sect, and incorporates elements of Confucianism, Daoism, and Buddhism. Yet it is recognized as Buddhist in Indonesia. Between the 1970s and 1980s, this new religious movement rapidly spread through Indonesia and obtained many believers among the ethnic Chinese (Brown 1990). While they have a supreme *Tuhan* (God), this God is not the direct recipient of one's devotion. Instead, Buddha Maitreya, which God sent to the human world, is the main objective of their devotion. This Buddha is represented in the figure of Budai, who has been worshipped as one of the deities of wealth in Chinese folk religion and has been enshrined in many *klenteng* in Indonesia. Therefore, this sect of Buddhism has strong connections with Confucianism, and took the role of a shelter for the Confucians when Confucianism was prohibited. Many ethnic Chinese and some *peranakan* Suku Asli who had identified with Confucians changed their *agama* to Buddhism.

Because Buddhism and these Chinese folk religions are historically associated, believers recognize their similarity. Although this community had an organization and doctrine that fitted with the concept of *agama,* present-day Suku Asli and ethnic Chinese may still use 'Buddhism' as a synonym for 'Confucianism' and vice versa. Furthermore, the community permitted the worship of a Chinese folk religion. For example, in a *vihara* (temple) at Selat Panjang, a large icon of *Kuan-tei* (Guan Yu), who is one of the most popular deities of wealth in Chinese folk religion and often enshrined in *klenteng* in Indonesia, is enshrined together with that of Buddha Maitreya. In addition, as this Buddhist community obtained many Chinese believers in its first stages and accepted the diversity of rituals, it did not actively engage in missionary work. Therefore, Suku Asli could identify themselves as Buddhists without any pressure from the Buddhist community to be 'real' Buddhists. It was much later that the Buddhist community established some *vihara* in Suku Asli settlements. In Teluk Pambang, a *vihara* was first established in 2001. In this situation, more and more Suku Asli have identified themselves as Buddhists, even though such identification may be nominal.

Conversely, quite a few Suku Asli converted to Christianity when the government increased pressure to identify *agama* after the 1970s and various Christian missionaries arrived in Suku Asli communities; for example, Catholic churches were established in the villages of Kelamantan and Bantan Air in the 1970s, and a Pentecostal missionary began activities in Selat Baru in 1987. These churches eagerly engaged in missionary activities and offered support such as medical care and instruction on agricultural techniques and the organization of collective labor. As a result, missionaries obtained a number of converts in each community. Some people who lived in different settlements but had relations with Christians also converted to Christianity and accepted their exhortations.

However, many Christian Suku Asli later changed their *agama* to Buddhism because, according to them, the church prohibited their *adat*, which allows both ways of ancestral worship (i.e. 'real' and *peranakan* Suku Asli ways). For example, missionaries required them to conduct funerals and marriages under the management of the church, and encouraged the *peranakan* Suku Asli to throw away the altars that were in their houses for ancestral worship. Many Suku Asli rejected such interventions in their ancestral religious practices and beliefs. The church in Selat Baru retained most of its believers by permitting some Suku Asli traditional ways to continue. However, this was rather an exceptional case. In Bantan Air, the church lost most of its converts and retreated before the 1990s, and in Kelamantan, while the church has been maintained, only a few dozen households are still Christians. In Teluk Pambang, although the Batak Christian Protestant Church was established in 2001, the church retreated within a year as the villagers had already identified with Buddhists and it could obtain no following at all.

The choice of *agama* in government policies

The government policies that drove Suku Asli to identify with Buddhism were mainly of two kinds. The first concerned the administrative register. According to Koding, village officials visited Suku Asli houses in the 1970s and 1980s and repeatedly questioned the details of family members and their *agama*. At this time, many Suku Asli who had not identified with an *agama* were registered as Buddhists by the officials, who pointed out their kinship with Chinese Buddhists. Second, the identification with an *agama* was necessary for children's education. From around the 1980s, every Suku Asli child began to go to primary school, and during my fieldwork, children took religious education for three hours a week in school classes and went every Sunday for three hours to a *vihara*, where they were taught history, doctrine, and the devotions of Buddhism.

Although they register their *agama* as Buddhism, their devotion to the Buddhist community appears to be limited. For example, the religious community ideally requires believers to conduct temple services at *vihara* three times a day. However, I have never seen any of my friends, adult Suku Asli, visit a *vihara* for the purpose of a temple service. Also, this community encourages believers to be vegetarians, but meat and fish have been and still are largely considered by Suku Asli to be essential foods.

Their choice of *agama* at the beginning seems to have been characterized by passivity and a degree of contingency. Those who had social ties with the ethnic Chinese tended to choose Confucianism, those who had lived in a settlement where a Christian church organized itself became Christians, and others were often identified as Buddhists by village officials. However, after their first choice, Suku Asli generally began identifying with Buddhists, because Confucianism was banned and the Christian church prohibited their *adat*. As a result, most Suku Asli on Bengkalis Island identify themselves as Buddhists at present, except for some Christian 'enclaves' where churches are maintained. Yet their identification as Buddhists is not based on their positive conversion to the doctrine of Buddhism, at least from the perspective of the definition of *agama*, and they rarely join the activities at *vihara*. Rather, it appears to be based on their attachment to their traditional ways and practices, their *adat*, which only Buddhism has permitted without restrictions. This can be seen as a similar process to their rejection of Islam. They have continuously rejected converting to Islam since the precolonial era in order to maintain ancestral worship inherited from their ancestors, or *adat* (see Chapter 2).

However, their recognition of *agama* is changing. Its passive and contingent character is transforming into a positive and necessary one. Suku Asli leaders have begun regarding Buddhism as the exclusive and authentic ancestral *agama* of Suku Asli, and since IKBBSA was established, identifying with Buddhism has become an essential criterion of IKBBSA membership.

Stance and interpretation of *agama*

Let me scrutinize the stance toward and interpretation of the concept of *agama* among Suku Asli before describing the process in which Buddhism became the *agama* of the Suku Asli. The stance and interpretation varies even within a single community. This is not because the significance of *agama* varies among individuals, but because they had to engage with the different backgrounds of religious practices and beliefs—that is 'real' and *peranakan* manners of religious practices and beliefs. Furthermore, the leaders of IKBBSA take a firmer stance on *agama* because they have been involved in political and cultural communications with the government.

A 'real' Suku Asli view of *agama*, *percayaan*, and *adat*

Here I describe the view of *agama* held by Odang, a 'real' Suku Asli who did not engage in political communication with the government. His comments appear to reflect the general view of *agama* among the 'real' Suku Asli without the influences of the recent political movement. Moreover, his comments seem to be more in tune with the historical facts described above than other views that I describe later, and I expect many Suku Asli would agree with his opinion.

One day, I talked with Odang while sitting on the floor of a living room in his house. He was repairing his fishing net with a needle and lines. While I was thinking about what I should ask him, I glimpsed a poster on the wall of the room. The poster was distributed by the Buddhist community, Maitreya Great Tao, and I had seen it several times in Suku Asli houses. The poster showed an icon of Buddha Maitreya with slogans in Chinese characters. Like many other villagers in Teluk Pambang, Odang identified himself as a Buddhist and as a member of the Buddhist community.

Looking at the poster, I asked, 'What was the *agama* of Suku Asli before Buddhism came?' He paused in his work and appeared to catch me looking at the poster. He answered, 'It was *animisme*. We *sembayang* (worshipped) trees, rivers, forests, and so on.' According to him, his father had a certificate that described his *agama* as 'Animism.'[4] When Odang first obtained his own identification card, it stated his *agama* as 'Buddhism.' Although his explanation was convincing to a certain extent, his view of their worship of trees, rivers, and forests as something in the past was slightly strange to me because they still saw 'people' (see Chapter 3) and *datuk* living around and passing through their settlements, and practiced rituals for them. In shamanic séances and dreams, they communicated with these spirits and made offerings. Also, they held rituals at sacred places, *keramat* or *datuk kong*, in which they provided offerings for the spirits. Such rituals were not a past practice—they were practiced much more eagerly than going to *vihara*. For me, these practices and beliefs seemed related to animism. Pointing out some of these facts, I attempted to confirm my observations by asking, 'Don't Suku Asli really believe in animism anymore?' He asserted 'No, animism was our *agama* only in the past. We believe in Buddhism now.' He continued:

> We register our *agama* as Buddhism now. And we believe the existence of Buddha as *Tuhan* (God) *dalam hati* (in our heart). It's enough, we are Buddhists...In the past, we did not know Buddhism. Therefore, our *agama* was animism...Rituals for the spirits are not *agama*. It's *percayaan* (belief). *Percayaan* and *agama* are different. There are such *percayaan* even among Muslims, just like Suku Asli.

According to Odang, the *peranakan*'s offerings at the altar, the séances of Chinese deities, Suku Asli shamanic séances, and sacrifices for natural spirits are all *percayaan*, not *agama* or animism. Although the discussion as to whether one 'really' believes in an *agama* or not can often be a sensitive topic in Indonesia, Odang looked relaxed as usual when he made these comments. For him, 'real' belief in Buddhism was not a sensitive topic that concerned his identity. When I questioned the relationship between *agama* and *acara* (ceremonies) such as marriages and funerals, he said, 'the ceremonies are not *agama* either. It is *adat* that have been inherited from our ancestors.' He stated that Suku Asli *agama* in the past was animism.

Peranakan Suku Asli tend to identify their past *agama* as Confucianism, while 'real' Suku Asli often identify it as 'animism' or say, 'We did not have *agama*.' As I mentioned in Chapter 2, rituals among 'real' and *peranakan* Suku Asli differ, and the *peranakan* way is often described as Confucianism. Generally, for 'real' Suku Asli, Confucianism is the way of the *peranakan*, not their own. Therefore, 'real' Suku Asli do not usually consider Confucianism as their past *agama* or associate Confucianism with Buddhism. In Suku Asli society, as in government circles, the term 'animism,' which was introduced to their society in post-independence state policies, has negative meanings of 'backwardness' or 'primitiveness.' Despite this, Odang presumably identified with animism because he had seen his father's certificate and also because there was no proper term other than 'animism' (in Indonesian or their own language) to express their religious practices and beliefs, although the rituals among *peranakan* could be summarized under the term 'Confucianism.' Therefore, he described their past *agama* as animism, as did the government, emphasizing it was something that belongs in the past.

More importantly, Odang categorized their rituals as *percayaan* and ceremonies as *adat*, differentiating them from *agama*. '*Agama*' does not indicate all religious practices and beliefs. Rather, its meaning is limited. *Agama* is primarily concerned with administrative registration. Odang's identification card labeled his *agama* as Buddhism, and his child, a primary school pupil, was learning Buddhism in school and going to a *vihara* every Sunday. These seem to be the main reasons why he identified himself as Buddhist. Suku Asli *agama* appears to emerge in a limited sphere of everyday life, so Odang's statement that he believes in Buddha 'in his heart' was not necessarily a declaration of his pious belief in Buddha, but showed his ceremonial or performative attitude to Buddhism. His expression might imply that he does not practice any devotions, rituals, or vegetarianism for Buddha in his life but believes only 'in his heart,' which appears 'enough' to identify himself as a Buddhist. Even if it is only ceremonial and performative, this expression seems to be very effective for persuading government officials or Muslims who ask about his *agama* because, although minimal, it is a sufficient explanation to show belief in one God. In the situation that he needed to show his identification with an *agama*, he would have employed this manner of explanation in conversations with outsiders. Still, his belief in Buddhism appears to be political and to belong in the religious politics imposed on Suku Asli. Therefore, the category of *agama* could be seen as something formulated in Suku Asli society in relatively recent years, probably through the *peranakan* registration of Confucianism and the introduction of Buddhism between the 1950s and 1970s.

Odang described the rituals for local spirits as *percayaan* (or *kepercayaan* in formal Indonesian). While he used the term in our conversation above, shamanic séances and sacrifice for the natural spirits were often referred to as *ilmu batin* (or *kebatinan*) (see Chapter 2).[5] These terms were originally conceptualized in the controversies about the definition of *agama* at the national political level in Java. In 1955, scattered 'mystical' groups, primarily among the Javanese, established *Badan Kongres Kebatinan Indonesia* (BKKI; Indonesian *Kebatinan* Organization),[6] which tried to have the government recognize *kebatinan* as an *agama* in the same way as Islam and Christianity (Kim 1998: 363; Kipp and Rodgers 1987: 27). Although *kebatinan* has not been officially recognized, they avoided being labeled as communists during the anti-communist purge and flourished during the New Order. The movement has attracted many government authorities and military leaders (Kipp and Rodgers 1987: 27). As for '*kepercayaan*,' this term was also associated with 'tribal religion,' like 'animism,' and differentiated from *agama* in government religious policies (Kipp and Rodgers 1987: 21; Tsing 1987: 197). However, the word has been continuously used as a simple translation of 'beliefs,' with some connotation of local, individual, and even superstitious ones.

Although Confucianism and animism have been associated with negative meanings such as 'communism,' 'backwardness,' or 'primitiveness,' '*percayaan*' and '*kebatinan*' are relatively neutral and acceptable words in Indonesia insofar as the terms do not violate the official definition of *agama*. Odang's expression of '*percayaan*' is an acceptable expression when he uses it to explain the meaning of rituals to outsiders. These terms are used to indicate practices and beliefs at the essentially vague boundary between legitimate *agama* and illegitimate non-*agama* rituals. By referring to *percayaan*, it comes to be possible that while maintaining their traditional rituals, the Suku Asli can achieve the 'belief in one God' addressed in the Pancasila. In November 2017, the Indonesian Constitutional Court recognized a part of indigenous *kepercayaan* as a legitimatized *agama* (Allard and Damiana 2017; Sapiie 2017), but this has not been fully reflected in administrative policies (Harsyahwardhana 2020; Hindrati 2018). Even in 2019, I saw no Suku Asli who tried to claim full recognition of their *percayaan* as an *agama*.

While *agama* was introduced to Suku Asli society relatively recently, how did they formulate the categories of *adat* and *percayaan* differently? Anne Schiller (1996) describes the process of the conceptualization of *agama* among the Ngaju Dayak, who were regarded as people who 'do not yet have *agama*' but succeeded in having the government recognize their *adat* as *Hindu Kaharingan*, a variety of Hinduism, in the 1980s. Although their *agama* had been involved in *adat*, government policies separated the conceptual categories of *adat* and *agama* based on their definitions formulated in accord with state policies.

Although I cannot say for certain, the Suku Asli distinction of *adat* and *percayaan* was probably formulated throughout the twentieth century in communication with the ethnic Chinese. While it is unknown how the Utan used the term '*adat*' in their community before the twentieth century, the meaning would have been vaguer and would have encompassed *percayaan*. After the ethnic Chinese penetrated their forests, the *peranakan* conducted their rituals related to ancestral worship in the Chinese way under the management of a local *kapitan*. To distinguish the 'real' Utan from *peranakan*, the Utan circumscribed *adat* within their rituals related to ancestral worship. Therefore, *adat* first and foremost indicates the rituals of 'real' Suku Asli (see Chapter 2 and Chapter 5). In the process of their assimilation, *adat* would have been applied to the rituals of *peranakan* in the context of differentiating the Suku Asli from outsiders (see Chapter 5). In contrast, the category of *percayaan* must have been introduced and formulated when Confucianism was dropped as a legitimate *agama*. The practices of Chinese folk religions were partly vindicated by categorizing them as *percayaan*, and 'real' Suku Asli would also have adopted the term to vindicate their rituals for local spirits that may have been problematized as animism.

Percayaan is still separated from *adat* in the recognition of religious practices, which are loosely defined and involve a variety of practices, such as shamanic séance, sacrifice for natural spirits, Chinese spirit possession, and praying in front of a Chinese altar. This sharply contrasts with recent thoughts that the mangrove forests (see Chapter 3) and arts (see Chapter 5) were connected with their *adat* and ancestors. The forests and arts were objectified from their unconscious and subjective world and practices, and arrayed under the coherent and abstract logics of *adat* or ancestor in and through communication with the government that problematized them. Similarly, parts of *percayaan*, especially those related to Chinese folk religion, became involved in the objectifying and abstracting process, and were labeled as Buddhism as a basis for symbolic appropriateness (Geertz 1973: 172). By doing so, they would have tried to summarize the diversity of practices and beliefs that were problematized by governmental religious politics. Geertz (1973) called this a process of orthodoxy; however, parts of *percayaan*, especially sacrifice for local spirits and the shamanic séances of 'real' Suku Asli, did not accomplish this. Even though rituals have the potential to be associated with the manifestation of indigeneity as they are dedicated to local spirits in the specific places in which they live, they have continued as very concrete and detailed practices in Suku Asli lives. This means that *percayaan* has not followed the process of orthodoxy or 'religious rationalisation,' in which the category of *percayaan* takes the role of a kind of shelter for their 'enchanted world,' as discussed by Max Weber (see Hoskins 1987: 158–9).

Conceptualization of *agama* in dialogue: a *peranakan* view

The second example of how *agama* is viewed is a *peranakan* view provided in conversation with Kiat. He took on the role of secretary of IKBBSA, but his participation in communications with government officials was limited. The *peranakan* are often more sensitive about the topic of *agama* than the 'real' Suku Asli because, from their perspective, they actually had their *agama*, Confucianism, in the past and many strongly reject being categorized as people having animism or no *agama*, which is how Muslims often describe the Suku Asli. Like Odang, Kiat identified himself as Buddhist but, in contrast, he thought that Suku Asli *agama* in the past had been Confucianism; in addition, he categorized their everyday worship at the altar as *agama*—Buddhism—as explained below.

During my stay at his house, Kiat sometimes poured out complaints against doubts among the Javanese concerning Suku Asli Buddhism. According to him, his Javanese acquaintances living in a different village often asked whether the Suku Asli 'really' believed in Buddhism. One day, he told me a story about one such question:

> When I was talking with a Javanese, he asked me, 'Why don't Suku Asli go to *vihara* for devotion?' So, I answered, 'I am praying to Buddha every day in my house.'...I know they often say 'Suku Asli *agama* is *agama tepekong* (*agama* for altar).' But we are actually real Buddhists.

The Javanese on Bengkalis Island are generally pious and most go to a mosque several times a day for the purpose of devotions. They consider such behavior necessary for the believers of an *agama*. Therefore, the question to Kiat seems to have involved not only curiosity, but also a degree of accusation and disdain of Suku Asli attitudes to *agama*. In response, he answered: 'I am praying to Buddha every day in my house.' As he was a *peranakan* Suku Asli, he had an altar that enshrined his ancestral spirits and a Chinese deity. Indeed, he prayed in front of it, burning incense sticks three times a day. By demonstrating this everyday worship, he tried to show that he really had an *agama* and that this *agama* was Buddhism. However, in general, such worship was not acceptable for the Javanese sense of *agama* because they knew that altars often enshrined a deity derived from China and ancestors, and it was not necessarily related to one God and Buddhism. Therefore, the Javanese called Suku Asli *agama* an '*agama* for altar,' poking fun at it as worship for altars, not devotion to God.

Kiat often experienced similar questions from Javanese who tried to point out the variance between the doctrines of Buddhism and Suku Asli religious practices, such as those involving beliefs in one God, vegetarianism, and so on. At each opportunity, he tried to persuade them by emphasizing that Suku Asli were really Buddhists who associated Buddhism with their worship of the ancestral spirits and Chinese deities. However, his explanation did not fit the strict doctrines of the Buddhist community. Although the Buddhist community permitted worship at altars, the religious teachers of the community did not regard it as a part of Buddhism. According to a teacher at a *vihara* in Bengkalis town, the worship at altars was part of Confucianism or *percayaan Tionhua* (Chinese beliefs) rather than Buddhism. Moreover, Kiat knew that the worship at his altar was not for Buddha. He and other Suku Asli explained to me that altar offerings were meant for *nenek moyang dan dewa-dewa* (the ancestral spirits and the deities) enshrined in the altar for the purpose of ensuring the safety of the house. Therefore, his association between Buddhism and the altar seems to have been situational. However, this association appears necessary in communications with Muslims because, again, not identifying as a Buddhist may affirm his 'primitiveness,' 'backwardness,' and anti-social personality. Therefore, he tried to explain that Suku Asli everyday worship was part of an *agama*, deviating from the strict doctrine and original meaning of what happens at the altar. In other words, in communication with the Javanese over the role of Buddhism, he attempted to embed *agama* in the everyday life of the Suku Asli.

Thus, once they were officially identified with Buddhism, Suku Asli were required to be 'real' Buddhists, given the pressure of state religious policies. In their society, this process was not directly caused by government policies but by everyday relations with Muslims. Through such constant dialogue with Muslims, they introduced the concept of *agama* or Buddhism to their world by organizing their existing ritual practices in accordance with these concepts.

Although the explanations by Odang and Kiat appear to differ, what they share is that they have tried to embed the national concept of *agama* into their social system. However, the heterogeneity of rituals between 'real' and *peranakan* Suku Asli makes it difficult to construct a common concept of *agama* and, indeed, there are various interpretation of *agama* in Suku Asli society. It is also remarkable that they both seem to be trying to avoid outsiders' interventions in rituals. On the one hand, Odang categorized their rituals as something different from *agama* using the terms '*percayaan*' and '*adat*,' both of which are acceptable in the government category of *agama*. On the other hand, Kiat tried to associate rituals based on Chinese folk religion with recognized Buddhism in order to justify them. Emphasizing that they 'have an *agama*' appears to be an essential way to claim their position is not 'backward' or 'primitive' but legally acceptable. *Agama* has been something that emerged only in the context of communications with outsiders, and it did not become problematic within their community.

Jane Atkinson (1983: 684) argues that the definition of *agama* among the Wana of Sulawesi has been constructed through 'a debate among themselves, with their neighbors, and with the government authorities over what constitutes a religion.' While she sees the Wana concept of *agama* as constructed in the implementation of government policies and ideology, she places more importance on the influences that situationally emerged in ongoing debates between the Wana and others (Atkinson 1983: 684–5), rather than the influences that emerged in fixed controversies between government policies and their historical practices. As a result of such repeated dialogues, the Wana demonstrated their practices, including an assemblage of diet, burial practices, healing rituals, and so on, as directly relevant to 'real' *agama*, and this resulted in their political action to have such practices recognized by the government.

The debates that contain much ideology about belief in an *agama* can be seen as an indirect effect of governmentality. Although the government may not directly engage in this operation, debates with people who have a specific *agama* can configure beliefs about how wrong the ambiguity of *agama* is and how wrong the lack of regular religious services is among people who do not specify an *agama*. Through ongoing dialogues and debates with Muslims, Suku Asli have conceptualized the logic of their own *agama*, not necessarily adhering to the 'true' precepts of Buddhism. Such debates between Suku Asli and Javanese must have been repeated from the past, as with Kiat's experiences. Yet these debates have not driven ordinary Suku Asli to change their stance on *agama*. Because communications between ordinary Suku Asli and Javanese are generally limited, it is usually sufficient to give a situational explanation for persuading the Javanese. Javanese who have continuous communications or friendships with Suku Asli do not typically provoke Suku Asli in terms of *agama*.

However, the situation of Suku Asli leaders is different. After the establishment of IKBBSA, Suku Asli leaders have had opportunities to specify and explain their *agama* not only to the Javanese but also to government officials much more frequently than ordinary Suku Asli. They confronted the necessity to clearly specify a Suku Asli *agama*. Yet, unlike the Wana, they could not persuade the government to recognize their religious practices as *agama*. This is because, first, they have two distinct forms of religious practices and beliefs. As mentioned above, an *agama* should have an integrated doctrine, and they cannot show this integration. Second, and more importantly, religious practices and beliefs among the *peranakan* Suku Asli are associated with Chinese culture, which was the main target of government oppression during the New Order regime. Even though Kiat can justify himself in informal communications with his Javanese acquaintances by pointing out the association between Buddhism and worship at altars, it is risky to argue for this as the basis of political action in formal communications with the government, since it might cast doubt on their indigenous position in this region.

Buddhism as ancestral *agama*: a leader's view

The third view of *agama* is from a leader. Atim was in his late fifties and the village *batin* of Kembung Luar. His grandfather was the last *batin* recognized by the Siak kingdom before independence, and, like Ajui, he was one of the most active leaders of IKBBSA. Although he was a 'real' Suku Asli, he had an altar in his house and conducted day-to-day worship. The description comes from my first interview with him. While his opinion seems to be a far-fetched argument, it reflects the leaders' stance towards *agama*.

I talked with Atim, sitting in a guest room in his house. After chatting for a while, I asked the same question I had asked Odang: 'What was the past *agama* among Suku Asli before Buddhism came?' He looked slightly surprised, and asserted, 'Suku Asli have continuously believed in Buddhism from the past,' which was a strongly worded answer. This response did not fit with the information that I had obtained from other people. Therefore, I told him that I had heard that Maitreya Great Tao was established in the 1970s and its first *vihara* in this area was built in 2001. He answered, 'Yes, it's true. However, we believed in Buddhism before it.' According to him, in the 1970s when he traveled to Titi Akar, Rupat, he saw an idol of Buddha enshrined in the *vihara* that had been established a long time ago, and 'the Suku Asli' (the Akit) living in the village had worshipped the idol. Therefore, the Suku Asli had believed in Buddhism. At first, I felt curious because I had lived in Titi Akar and knew that the *vihara* in Titi Akar had been established at the end of the 1990s. However, I then realized that he was talking about a *klenteng* that was established by the ethnic Chinese at the end of the nineteenth century. Indeed, in the *klenteng*, idols of Buddha were enshrined together with many Chinese deities. So, I said, 'I think it is a *klenteng* of Confucianism, not a *vihara* of Buddhism.' In response, he said, 'It's the same. Whether it is *klenteng* or *vihara*, the Suku Asli have worshipped Buddha from our ancestors. So, we have been Buddhists.'

There was a general tendency for the leaders of IKBBSA to equate Buddhism and Confucianism. When I asked Ajui a similar question, he also asserted that Buddhism had been their ancestral *agama* and pointed out the existence of *klenteng*. However, this view is not common among ordinary Suku Asli. Although there is some ambiguity about the relationship between Confucianism and Buddhism, they generally distinguish *vihara* and *klenteng*, as well as Confucianism and Buddhism. Also, many people regard Buddhism as having been introduced to their society within the past several decades. Furthermore, even if their ancestors had worshipped the icon of Buddha in *klenteng*, they were only Chinese or *peranakan* Chinese. 'Real' Suku Asli and most *peranakan* Suku Asli have rarely engaged in religious practices in *klenteng*.

In spite of these facts, the leaders strongly insisted that Suku Asli have followed Buddhism from their ancestors. The reason relates to the establishment of IKBBSA and their *batin* role. First, their emphasis on historically continuous beliefs in Buddhism among the Suku Asli appeared to be an essential strategy to have the government recognize the position of the Suku Asli in state politics. Kimdi, a regency assembly member and strong supporter of the activity of IKBBSA, told me that the ambiguity of *agama* gave a very bad impression to the government. Giving the example of the Sakai of inland Bengkalis regency, whose *agama* was ambiguous and changeable, he emphasized how the government had a bad impression of Sakai communities because of their flexible *agama*—he also emphasized that Suku Asli *agama* should be integrated and made stable in order to give the government a good impression of their communities. His opinion was shared by other leaders. As the headmen of the Suku Asli, the leaders had met government authorities who asked about the Suku Asli with some curiosity. In such conversations, the question of Suku Asli *agama* is almost inevitable, as *agama* is one of the most important criteria that distinguishes indigenous minorities. At such opportunities, they have clearly described their *agama* as Buddhism by emphasizing historical worship at *klenteng*.

Second, although IKBBSA is their ethnic organization for claiming their position as Suku Asli, it also takes charge of operations on behalf of religious bodies. As I mentioned in Chapter 4, IKBBSA was established for the purpose of issuing marriage letters as substitutes for those issued by religious bodies. Just after its establishment, the leaders of IKBBSA started issuing the letter to anyone of Suku Asli origin who requested it. However, the churches then claimed that Christian Suku Asli should obtain the letter from them, and the government pressured the leaders to issue the letter only to Buddhists. As the basis of the activity of IKBBSA was related to *agama*, they needed to clearly show their *agama*.

Integration of *agama* and Suku Asli

As a result of government pressure, *agama* came up for discussion in the leaders' annual meeting. At a meeting of *batin* headmen in Bengkalis regency in 2011, Ajui suggested that the leaders should issue marriage letters only to Buddhists, not Christians. He insisted that as IKBBSA was an ethnic organization of the Suku Asli, the leaders should issue the letter only to people who practiced marriage in the way of Suku Asli *adat*—that is, Buddhist Suku Asli. However, according to him, as Christians accepted the church's intervention, they should conduct marriages and funerals in a Christian fashion, not in the traditional one; this meant that they did not follow Suku Asli *adat* and thus the leaders should not issue the letters to them. As there was no Christian leader in IKBBSA, all leaders agreed with his suggestion. This meant that Buddhism became a 'proper' *agama* for the Suku Asli in the view of IKBBSA and, indeed, this idea was shared by all the leaders.

It is remarkable that, in the meeting, Ajui would have described Buddhism as their ancestral *agama* without associating *klenteng* and Buddhism. Equating worship at *klenteng* with Buddhism is only a reflection of the manner in which communication with the government officials takes place. Instead of acknowledging this, he described Buddhism as their ancestral *agama* by associating it with *adat*. This logic seems to be plausible only insofar as it excludes Christians from membership in IKBBSA. This is because, as mentioned above, a section of the Suku Asli experienced the church's intervention in their *adat*. Once *agama* is associated with *adat*, it naturally comes to be something concerned with ancestors, because *adat* in Suku Asli society concerns, first and foremost, ancestral rituals and descent. Therefore, for the leaders, *agama* should necessarily be ancestral.

The leaders emphasized the importance of Buddhism as a religion under which ancestral rituals or *adat* could be maintained without undue interventions. Therefore, although Buddhism is regarded as a 'proper' *agama* in IKBBSA, the leaders were not interested in encouraging people to strengthen the faith of Buddhism as led by Maitreya Great Tao. Rather, they strengthened their involvement in the rituals that I described in Chapter 5, which can be categorized as *adat*.

A split with Christians

Until 2019, the matter about IKBBSA issuing marriage letters was essentially settled, and more and more couples held their wedding ceremonies both in their houses using *adat* and in *vihara* using *agama*. Although their attitude toward everyday practices related to Buddhism and *vihara* was apparently unchanged, the fact that new couples held the ceremony in *vihara* reinforced their position as Buddhist in negotiations with the government.

However, the consolidation of their identification with Buddhism appears to have brought about a somewhat negative view of Christians. According to Ajui, following Christianity is *salah* (wrong behavior) because Buddhism is their ancestral *agama*. Although ordinary Suku Asli views are generally more moderate, they also lean toward rather negative opinions of Christians. Kiat stated that the life of Christians was *susah* (difficult). According to him, while people who held Christian marriage ceremonies should obtain the marriage letter from the church, there were many couples who did not hold the ceremony in the church or who had already married when the church entered the community. As they did not have the marriage letter, they suffered much difficulty concerning their children's education or other administrative procedures. In addition to such practical aspects, Buddhists generally see Christians as people who 'do not follow *adat*,' as mentioned above.

On Bengkalis Island, there are a dozen Christian Suku Asli communities. Most of them are small; they generally have between several and a dozen households. The Christian settlement of Selat Baru had sixty households during my fieldwork in 2012, and was one of the largest Christian Suku Asli communities on Bengkalis Island. In this settlement, a Pentecostal church was established by a minister from Sulawesi in 1987. I became acquainted with Atong in this settlement and listened to his stories.

It was very difficult to conduct my research in a Christian community because there was a split between Buddhist and Christian communities. In the ceremonies held in Teluk Pambang, I could not get to know anyone from the Christian community even though there were many people from outside the village. Although I asked my friends in the village to introduce me to someone from the Christian settlement, they answered, 'I don't have friends in the settlement.' Finally, I asked Atang, who first took me to Teluk Pambang and lived in Selat Baru, to introduce someone to me. Although he lived in the village, his house was outside the Christian settlement and he registered his *agama* as Buddhism. He took me to a house in the settlement and introduced me to Atong, who was a Buddhist when I met him in 2012. I visited his house several times and asked him to introduce other people in the settlement, but he did not do so. While I could not confirm the reason, Atang and Atong seemed to hesitate in introducing a Buddhist to Christian Suku Asli. I could obtain the Christian view of *agama* only based on Atong's words.

Atong was born in the settlement and was in his late forties when I met him in 2012. Before 1987, he identified himself as a Buddhist. However, just after the church was established, he converted to Christianity. The reason for his conversion was because he felt that '*pemerintah tawai* (the government laughed at)' their nominal Buddhism. At first, the minister required them to hold rituals such as funerals and weddings under his management. However, many people protested, and using *adat* was permitted to some extent. According to him, he 'really' believed in God, and went to church services once a week together with other Suku Asli. However, several years ago, his wife, a *peranakan* Suku Asli from Teluk Pambang, fell sick and in her dream was called by *Kuat'im*, a Chinese deity. This means that she had to become a Chinese medium, and to have an altar for the deity in the house. Atong consulted the minister whether he could continue to be a Christian, but the minister gently encouraged him to become a Buddhist. Therefore, he returned to Buddhism.

In terms of *agama*, the views of Odang, Kiat and Atim, and Atong not only demonstrate diversity but also imply the different degree of their incorporation into the nation that the Indonesian government imagines. Odang said that he believed in *agama* only in his heart, putting Buddhism at a distance from his everyday practices. He essentially does not follow the way of life required by the Indonesian government. Kiat and Atim tried to label their everyday practice as *agama* and claimed they were following the nation's ways of life. However, when Atong was a Christian, he applied Christian practices and beliefs to his everyday life. Christians embody the way of life that the government recommends, and can incorporate their identity into the nation state more easily than Buddhists.

Buddhist Suku Asli with similar views to Odang, Kiat, and Atim share everyday experiences because their practices have remained unchanged and can be regarded as common. However, people who have Christian views changed their everyday lives to adopt new perspectives and ways of life. Here the split of everyday life between Buddhists and Christians emerges. According to Atong, he converted to Christianity because 'the government laughed at' their Buddhism. Although it was not addressed, Christian Suku Asli seem to regard those who identify with Buddhism as not really having an *agama*. This gap between Buddhist and Christian communities is based on differences in what counts as 'real' belief and emerged when the church was established in the settlement. The gap deepened when IKBBSA decided that Buddhism was its *agama*. As previously mentioned, *batin* did not issue marriage letters to Christians or support other official procedures. Some Buddhists said that marrying a Christian was inappropriate because of the different *agama*. This split was also evident in their everyday friendships. I did not see any Buddhist in Teluk Pambang attend ceremonies held in the Christian settlement.

This split may also be due to the emergence of the orthodoxy of *agama* and *adat* in Suku Asli society. Through the activities of IKBBSA, *agama* and *adat* have been politicized within their community. The leaders avoided having their religious practices and beliefs problematized by government policies and have changed them with the necessity of integrating their society as the Suku Asli—that is, as an indigenous ethnic group.

The fact that distinction based on *adat* extended the split between Buddhist and Christian communities contrasts with the fact that *adat* brought conciliation to former conflicting groups in North Halmahera. Although serious violence occurred between Christians and Muslims in North Halmahera around 2000, the Tobelo and neighboring groups of different religious affiliations have conciliated through discussion and creation of the concept of *Hibua Lamo* (big house), a philosophy and organization based on their common *adat*. The reason *adat* led to the split in Suku Asli society seems to be because it was understood and used critically to distinguish between, rather than to connect, people. As IKBBSA deputized the religious body and showed its differentiated position, IKBBSA leaders failed to objectify the commonness of *adat* across Buddhist and Christian communities.

The abstraction of everyday practices and the conceptualization of indigeneity

Suku Asli attitudes to and manipulation of *agama* are somewhat different from other indigenous communities. Although most Suku Asli identify their *agama* with the newly introduced Buddhism, this is not a simple 'conversion' like the Forest Tobelo that I mentioned at the beginning of this chapter. Moreover, they do not directly claim their traditional rituals as *agama* or positively politicize them in relation to the government in the way the Ngaju Dayak and the Wana do. Their choice of Buddhism relates to their two kinds of rituals (Suku Asli and *peranakan* ways). They could not simply demonstrate one way as their *agama*. Furthermore, the *peranakan* way of rituals, which is seen as deriving from China, contradicts the image of *orang asli* that both they and the government have held, and is even potentially risky, as the government oppressed Chinese culture during the Suharto era. Therefore, they chose a way that has allowed them to continue with their religious practices and beliefs under the name of Buddhism, which accepts the diversity of religious practices in a passive manner. However, in the process of trying to claim their position as an indigenous ethnic group, they confronted the necessity of having to demonstrate their position in terms of *agama*. As a result, they actively identify themselves as Buddhists and exclude Christian Suku Asli.

Geertz (1973) describes 'internal-conversion' among the Balinese before the 1960s, quoting Max Weber's famous argument about 'traditional' and 'rationalized' religions. Describing the situation within which the Balinese strengthened religious concerns and systemized the doctrines of Hinduism, he demonstrates that, although their religion had been based on the correct practice of ritual, it was objectified and increasingly became based on the 'correct belief' through their experiences of reading religious publications and discussing the meaning of belief among themselves. In other words, their understanding of their religion shifted from a stress on orthopraxy, or the right kind of practice, to orthodoxy, or the right kind of belief. Suku Asli adoption of Buddhism cannot be seen as internal-conversion. They are not seeking a systematized doctrine or a way of correct belief in Buddhism. Moreover, they try to maintain their traditional religious practices—*adat*—and avoid the religious body's interventions. Rather, they identify themselves as Buddhists in relation to the state religious policies and neighboring Muslims. Therefore, their adoption of Buddhism can be seen as performative in the same way as some elements of their *adat,* which I described in Chapter 5.

Instead of internally pursuing the systematized doctrine, Suku Asli objectification of their practices in terms of *agama* follows a particular kind of logic—that is, a logic that demonstrates their legitimate position in relationship to government religious policies and Muslim perceptions of *agama*. For now, their focus seems to be on manipulating the image of themselves held by others through identifying with Buddhism. This is directly connected to their claims regarding their position as an indigenous ethnic group distinguished from Islamic populations, a position that avoids serious conflicts with government policies. In other words, we can observe the emergence of indigeneity as the reflection of outsiders clearly through the Suku Asli adoption of Buddhism.

Nevertheless, I would like to suggest that Buddhism is becoming an important part of their identity, because Buddhism is something abstracted from their religious practices and beliefs according to their cultural logic. Their Buddhism is different not only from the 'orthodox' version of the religious Buddhist community but also from their actual religious practices. However, they summarize the maintenance of *adat*, belief, and other religious practices, which include diverse and individual interpretations, with a 'Buddhism' label and, indeed, most of them accept it as their *agama*. Thus even though it would be wrong to suggest that their practice has been rationalized or shifted to orthodoxy, Suku Asli conceptualizations of *agama* seem to indicate leaving behind certain elements of practices—that is, the very beginning of a shift from orthopraxy, a shift that has brought about a much more explicit emphasis on their tradition and identity as distinct signs of being Suku Asli.

The abstraction of their everyday practices, or shift from their orthopraxy, can be seen not only in their adoption of *agama* but also in the other spheres of their identity that I have described in previous chapters. They have abstracted their various heterogeneous, ancestral backgrounds in order to start creating a common past. They have objectified the hinterland as 'land for descendants' and started treating the mangrove swamps as 'ancestral land,' stressing their connection with particular spaces. They have strengthened the existence of the 'Suku Asli' through IKBBSA's activities. They have started to integrate their diverse *adat* into the form of 'art.' In these processes, their unconscious, small-unit, actual practices and associations, which can be summarized by the term 'indigeny,' are objectified and abstracted, and more conscious, comprehensive, and imagined concepts are constructed. It is important to keep in mind that these operations may well be the beginning of a change that will eventually take them from a universe of orthopraxy to a universe of orthodoxy—a beginning more than apparent in the way in which their practices have started to be seen as an embodiment and manifestation of a distinct 'indigenous' and 'ethnic' identity. Their identity and categorization, which were characterized by relational 'non-

Islamic alliance,' appear to be transforming into a distinct identity that includes substantiality, integration, and criteria as Buddhists.

Furthermore, this change brings about a change of their tribal position in terms of modernization. As I mentioned in Chapter 2, one of the reasons why the Suku Asli were marginalized and discriminated as 'tribal people' was because of their non-Islamic religious practices. Because they have not adopted Islam, they have been seen as 'backward' and 'primitive.' Therefore, when their *agama* is specified and recognized by Muslims, they can start to amend the image of their 'backwardness' and 'primitiveness' to a considerable extent. In other words, by specifying an integrated *agama*, they can accomplish the beginning of their transition to modernization. The leaders of IKBBSA have tried to configure their position as an indigenous ethnic group and an *adat* community by adopting the government image; in this process, the specification and integration of a Suku Asli *agama* have been essential. Although their Buddhism was not adequately recognized by dominant Muslims during my fieldwork, they are on their way to becoming what they ought to be—that is, an *adat* community.

Conclusion

The Ongoing Quest for Indigeneity

Indigeneity is not something to be understood as a primordial and static connectedness between specific people and a place but as a dynamic and relational process that emerges in relationships and dialogues between people and others. The complex history of people's movements throughout history, especially in Asia and Africa, makes it impossible to activate a categorical definition of people, but it is necessary to consider the people's situation in the particular context of each case. If we understand indigeneity from a relational perspective, it is similar to ethnicity and is 'fundamentally not a thing *in* the world, but a perspective *on* the world' (Brubaker 2004: 65). This is especially the case for indigenous peoples themselves, who are not really conscious of indigeneity in everyday life. Instead, they live according to their perspectives and practices that have been forged in their unconscious and subjective connectedness with the land—that is, indigeny. However, in communicating with others, indigeneity as a perspective emerges and may be problematized. In this dialogue, people objectify and abstract a part of their world or practices sustained by their indigeny and explain it to others, a part of which may be embodied in the forms of institution, organization, document, and so on. This process and perspective as a whole can be understood as indigeneity.

Following the conceptualization of indigenous peoples at an international level and the rise of decentralization at a national level, the indigenous movement has dramatically developed in Indonesia since 1998. Local people whose lands had been exploited by the centralized government began exercising the movement based on the concept of *adat* community, which had been legitimized by the Dutch colonial government and was revived by the AMAN NGO. The government accepted the concept of the *ada*t community and formulated various legislation. In the same period, the government began implementing development programs for people in marginalized and tribal positions and attempted to govern them by stimulating their aspirations and desires with policies of governmentality. While people now have more opportunities to access recognition and support from the government, they face the necessity of manifesting their position as an *adat* community. In this communication, their practices and perspectives are often problematized by the government and supporting NGOs.

This process influenced the emergence of indigenous identity in Suku Asli society. Their indigeny can be characterized by their fluid and extensive identity across *peranakan*, Akit, and Rawa, dependency on resources in the mangrove forests, flexible, open, and loose social relationships summarized by open aggregation, *adat* without fixed institutions, and the ritual practices of the worship of natural spirits and Chinese folk religion. These perspectives and practices are destabilized and problematized under the government image and politics of the *adat* community. As a result, they embody their indigeny with the compartmented mangrove forests as their ancestral forest, with IKBBSA as an ethnic organization or *adat* institution, with documents to identify their ethnicity as Suku Asli, with *adat* to underscore arts, and with Buddhism as their ancestral religion. In this process, while referring to their logic and perspectives formulated through indigeny, they have objectified their unconscious and subjective perspectives and practices under the government's frame of *adat* community, abstracted their heterogeneous perspectives and practices, and expressed them in coherent logic. In short, they became Suku Asli, which connotes their distinctive and recognized indigeneity and ethnicity in and through the exchange between their indigeny, which was forged in their life, and indigeneity, which was brought to their society through government development programs, including governmentality.

It should be demonstrated here that the categories and practices that were introduced and formulated in and through the communication have not completely been internalized within all individuals. In the Suku Asli case, the term '*adat* community' was known only by some IKBBSA leaders, and most of the people did not participate in the activities led by the ethnic organization (see Chapter 4). As described in the ethnographic sketch in the introduction, Kiat identified himself as 'Suku Asli,' which was recognized by the government while rejecting people's history as the Utan. Odang accepted the historical name of the Utan and preferred to use '*orang asli*,' which is rather conventional and covers more flexible and extensive identity across the Suku Asli, Akit, and Rawa. In 2019, when I again visited the village, there were no dramatic changes in the activities of OPSA and IKBBSA. OPSA was managed as a cooperative group to maintain the 'ancestral forest' and obtained subsidies occasionally from the regency government. The ethnic festivals and *batin* meetings by IKBBSA were still held annually at various villages, obtaining subsidies and recognition from the regency government, and part of the ordinary people have joined the organization. Many people still refer to themselves as '*orang asli*,' which demonstrates that, while they have actually embodied their indigeny through communication with the government, they have not completely established the unified ethnicity and indigeneity that was imagined by the government. Through employing an assemblage of non-specified strategies, or 'war machine,' they have tried to maintain personal autonomy and reject the internalization of state identification based on their agency.

Indigeneity can be seen as a perspective formulated in and through the objectification, abstraction, and embodiment of indigeny in the process of communications with exogenes. While I have focused on indigeneity in a modernization context, if we consider the long-term political process of constructing indigenous identity, it is not a one-way process. The categories and practices, which were imagined and imposed by exogenes, can constitute an essential part of people's non-articulated, unconscious, and subjective world through their accumulation of related practices and inherited memories. In Suku Asli history, for example, such transformations were evident in cases where the state category of '*suku*' was naturally connected with their ethnic identity and where the *peranakan* rituals have been accepted as a version of Suku Asli *adat*. Therefore, indigeneity can be seen as a hybrid of indigeny and exogeny in and through dynamic but long-term transactions so that a distinctive and well-bounded indigenous identity is formulated.

Association and separation: the potential of *adat* community

In the era of decentralization in Indonesia, not only people in an autochthonous position but also various kinds of local people have opportunities to access land and resources (Henley and Davidson 2007: 1–5; Rhee 2009: 46–56). This may cause land competition for survival, and when people are involved in such competition, they face the necessity of at least objectifying their indigeneity and demonstrating their *adat* and the legitimacy of their ancestral land. Li (2000: 151) suggests that 'a group's self-identification as tribal or indigenous is not natural or inevitable.' This view seems to be the case in the sense that rural communities may have some room for choice in their identities. This was especially so just after 1998 when the Indonesian polity changed and national or international activists began the indigenous movement in the scheme of struggling with the state. However, in present-day Indonesian politics, increasing numbers of people participate in the land competition, the room for choice has narrowed, and a group's self-identification as indigenous seems to have become more inevitable for people in tribal or marginalized positions.

In this process, many people seek recognition and support by adopting the key concept of *adat* community, which has been used as a weapon by the locals against the centralized authority and is now recognized by the government to a certain extent. It is remarkable that the concept has the strong power of both association and separation among people. On the one hand, *adat* community associates people by summarizing and abstracting different backgrounds, histories, beliefs, and practices beyond everyday experiences of individuals; on the other hand, it separates people by creating distinctive others and boundaries and recognizing exclusive authority and legitimacy for a part of the people. Like ethnicity (Brubaker 2004), *adat* community attracts the loyalty and aspiration of people and mobilizes them to reinforce the 'groupness.'

The influence that the concept exerts seems to be more evident among peoples in tribal and marginalized positions because their social relationship is often flexible and vague, and they do not have concrete norms or institutions in terms of *adat*. Such people have actually experienced dramatic change in their groupness through the adoption of the concept. For example, a Wana community of Central Sulawesi faced a resettlement plan by the government and asked an NGO to support its land claim between 2011 and 2012. While their effort to embody the concept dramatically associated the Wana with the NGO staff and consolidated the community, it also caused rivalry within the community in terms of knowledge and practice of *adat* community (Grumblies 2013). Similarly, the Suku Anak Dalam of Batin Sembilan in Jambi associated with landless immigrants and national and international NGOs to organize a resistance group in order to resist encroachment on their ancestral land by an oil palm company. They claimed and occupied a section of an oil palm plantation from which they had been expelled in the 1980s, and violent conflicts occurred (Steinebach 2013). Through the adoption of the concept, people not only build up their networks and create consolidation within a community, but also set up others within and outside their community—and they manifest indigenism and indigenousness, which are self-conscious political stances that organize the related people collectively and allow them to claim a certain degree of collective autonomy from the state (Benjamin 2016a: 516, 2016b: 363–9).

The Suku Asli case has also involved both association and separation. Through their commitment to their indigenous movement, they were associated with many *peranakan* Chinese on their ethnic certification and the leaders extended their network beyond villages; on the other hand, the split between Buddhist and Christian communities expanded. However, it seems that the concept has the potential to emphasize only the connection of people, as in the case of the Tobelo and their neighboring groups, to reconcile the conflict between them (Müller 2013). It can be understood that *adat* may dissimilate people as others and create boundaries between people because the concept of *adat* or *adat* community is one of a small number of tools with which people in marginalized and tribal positions can resist the centralized power. It should be claimed against a limited range of counterparts, and underscores the aspect of association and cooperation among the people.

At the end of 2012, the west part of the village (where there were many Suku Asli houses) was separated from Teluk Pambang and the new administrative village of Suka Maju was established. Although Suku Asli became the majority of the population in the new village, a Javanese won the seat of village headman in the July 2017 election. When I revisited the village in 2019, a *peranakan* leader living in a *dusun* (sub-village) began negotiating with the Javanese headman to again separate the *dusun* from Suka Maju. He pointed out that although the village annual budget had dramatically increased since 2014 based on the Law on Administrative Village (No. 6/2014 on Administrative Village), its allocation was unequal and his *dusun* had little support. In his request to the headman, he emphasized his hope to establish a new village based on the administrative recognition of an *adat* law community. According to him, as there were no Javanese in the *dusun*, it might be possible to establish the new village if he applied to the regency government with the headman's approval. Ajui, who lived in a different *dusun*, did not engage in this movement and avoided commenting on the problem. This negotiation had only just begun and the result was unpredictable during my visiting.

Again, the concept of *adat* community involves the power of both association and separation. Through the negotiation of the concept, I hope the villagers can reach an agreement for a favorable solution.

Glossary

acara	event; ceremony; ritual
adat	tradition or custom; customary law; norms; ancestral ritual
agama	religion; in particular, universal religion legitimated by the state
bakau	a species of mangrove trees, the Rhizophoraceae family
batin	indigenous title of headman, mainly for *orang asli* groups
bomo cina	spirit medium possessed by Chinese deities, similar to *kiton* in Chinese
datuk	a title of headman in Malay kingdoms; spirit living in the natural world and being able to control other spirits
datuk kong	shrine for local spirits related to Chinese folk religion; synonym of *keramat* in Suku Asli communities
daulat	charismatic power of the ruler; sovereignty
dukun	shaman employing spirits in Suku Asli culture, equal to *bomo asli*
empat suku	literally 'four clans,' a class/set of people with Minangkabau origins in the Siak kingdom
hamba raja	literally 'king's subjects'; a class of Malay peasants in the Siak kingdom
ilmu	magic, knowledge
imlek	New Year's feast based on the Chinese lunar calendar
kacu	mixed; not pure
kepala	head; leader; chief
kepercayaan	belief; indigenous faiths, equal to *percayaan*
keramat	sacred place in Malay and Suku Asli culture; synonym of *datuk kong* in Suku Asli community
kertas mas	mock money to be burned in *peranakan*/Chinese rituals
klenteng	Confucian temple
masyarakat adat	literally '*adat* community'
masyarakat terasing	literally 'isolated community,' a label given to tribal people who were the main target of government development programs
orang	people; non-physical humans in cosmology
orang asli	literally 'real/genuine people'; indigenous people; tribal people
orang bunyian	invisible human beings; people of sounds
panghulu	a title of regional/lineage head among the Minangkabau
panglong system	a system to delegate timber harvesting to Chinese merchants
penghulu	role of administrative village head after the independence of Indonesia until the 1960s in Riau
peranakan	mixed-ancestry Chinese; acculturated Chinese; one having Chinese patrilineal descent
percayaan	belief; indigenous faiths

rakyat banang	a subclass/set of *rakyat raja* in the Siak kingdom for non-Muslims and the forest or coastal dwellers, i.e. the Sakai, Akit, Utan, and Rawa
rakyat raja	literally 'king's folk,' a lower class in the Siak kingdom composed of *rakyat tantera/banang*
rakyat tantera	a subclass/set of *rakyat raja* in the Siak kingdom for Muslims in peripheral regions, including the Orang Suku Laut, Petalangan, and some Malays
reformasi	reformation, the slogan of the Indonesian political movement in the post-Suharto era
silat	traditional martial art; martial art demonstration performed in rituals
sirih box	a box containing *sirih* (betel leaves), tobacco, areca nuts, and other luxuries used at Malay and Suku Asli rituals
suku	clan in Minangkabau; tribes in modern Indonesian; regional group based on fictive kinship in rural area of Riau; administrative unit based on region in the Siak kingdom
suku-suku terasing	literally 'isolated tribes,' a label of tribal people in the government development program replaced by *masyarakat terasing* in the 1970s
tepekong	(Chinese) altar put in each house of the *peranakan* Suku Asli and Chinese
totok	China-born ethnic Chinese; 'newcomer'; Chinese who maintain their Chinese culture and identity
touke	(Chinese) middleman; trader
tujuh likur	New Year's feast held based on the Islamic calendar
vihara	Buddhist temple

Notes

Introduction

1 Individual names that appear in this book are all pseudonyms.

2 The term 'indigenous peoples' was first translated into '*masyarakat adat*' through the meetings held by *Jaringan Pembelaan Hak-hak Masyarakat Adat* (the Indigenous Peoples' Rights Advocacy Network) in 1993 (Moniaga 2007: 281–2).

3 'Indigenous people' and 'tribal people' are different categories, although they are often confused because the United Nations definition of 'indigenous peoples' includes 'cultural distinctiveness' and 'the experience of marginality' (Saugestad 2004: 264). In terms of the difference, see Benjamin (2016a: 516, 2016b: 364).

4 The Sultan of Johor recognized the Orang Suku Laut for their loyalty and granted them the hereditary feudal right to possess 'the seas and what floated on them' (Trocki 2007 [1979]: 68; Chou 2020: 221).

5 Although the term 'Sakai' has the strongly negative meaning of 'slavery and debt bondage' (Porath 2000: 177), it is accepted by the people to a certain extent at present (Porath 2003: 4).

6 The categorization of *masyarakat terasing* or KAT varies according to the source cited (see Persoon 1998: 289). For example, Noerbahrij Yoesoef (1992: 9) lists six groups of *masyarakat terasing* in Riau (the Sakai, the Akit, the Bonai, the Talang Mamak, the Kuala, and the Laut) at the beginning of the 1990s. However, Benjamin (2002: 23) quotes data about *masyarakat terasing* between 1990 and 1995 provided by the Department of Social Affairs in Jakarta, which say that there were eight groups of *masyarakat terasing* in Riau (the Orang Suku Laut, the Talang Mamak, the Bonai, the Utan, the Akit, the Sakai, the Kuala/Laut, and the Bertam).

7 I calculated total populations based on an estimation of seeing that one household has an average of five people. This estimation is derived from fragmented data in the survey by the regency government (Dinas Sosial Kabupaten Bengkalis 2010).

8 '*Batin*' is an Arabic term that means 'inner' and is generally used in the Malay world. However, in Suku Asli usage, it always indicates 'headman.' I use this term in the meaning of 'headman' in this book (see also note 5 in Chapter 6).

9 At the end of 2012, which was the end of my main fieldwork, the village of Teluk Pambang was divided into three different administrative villages, in which the western part of Teluk Pambang, which was my main field, became the new village of Suka Maju. As the new village had no administrative function during my fieldwork, I describe the situation of Teluk Pambang in this book.

10 The focus of this fieldwork was an investigation into shamanic practices among the Akit. The thesis was submitted to Tokyo University of Marine Science and Technology as a master's dissertation (Osawa 2009).

Chapter 1

1 Despite my dilemma about using the term (see Chapter 1), I decided to use it as many *orang asli* themselves seem to use it in a neutral and positive sense.

2 Andaya (2008: 241) uses '*Malayu*' instead of '*Melayu*,' as the former is more commonly used in historical inscriptions and documents, and for the purpose of discussing diverse Malay societies prevailing around the Malacca Strait.

3 The 'Malay world' is the term used to indicate the region where the kingdoms of the Malays existed; that is, the coasts of Borneo, the east coast of Sumatra, and the Malay Peninsula (Benjamin 2002: 7).

4 The autonomy as reflected in the nomadism of certain tribal groups was significant for the expansion of the Malay world. Indeed, Malay rulers relied on the seafaring skills of the Orang Suku Laut to maintain and extend their power (Chou 2020: 221).

5 Bengkalis was the capital of Eastern Coast Province between 1875 and 1887, before the capital was moved to Deli in North Sumatra, present-day Medan.

6 The words used for the pursuit of the new economic opportunities on the river and sea coasts were '*merantau*' and, for the migrants, '*perantau*.' '*Rantau*' means 'reaches of the river' or 'shore-line' (Andaya 2008: 89–90; see also, Barnard, T. 2003: 13–15, Kathirithamby-Wells 1997: 40).

7 Bezoar is a stone (calculus) found in an organ or duct of an animal's body. It was collected in the forests, exported to the Middle East and Europe, and used as a medicine or antidote. Benzoin is a resin used for making perfumes and some types of incense.

8 Van Anrooij (1885) does not mention the translations of these categories, and I could not confirm the meanings of '*tantera*' and '*banang*' in this usage.

9 '*Hinduk*' is also frequently used to mean 'clan' or 'community' in the *Bab Al-Qawa'id*. Although the difference between '*hinduk*' and '*suku*' is unclear, these terms would have been differentiated based on the *negeri propinsi* (subdivision) of the kingdom (see Junus 2002: 71). Tenas Effendy (2002: 364) implies that '*hinduk*' indicates a subdivision group under '*suku*.'

10 Edwin Loeb (1934: 29) asserts that the term originated from the Minangkabau, pointing out that '*suku*' in Malay meant 'leg' or 'fourth part.' The Orang Suku Laut in the Riau-Lingga Archipelago also used the term '*suku*' to denote subdivision of groups. However, this use indicated mainly territorial and hierarchical occupational groups in the Riau kingdom, not matrilineal clan (Chou 2010: 20–5).

11 The Minangkabau spelling of *panghulu* differs from the Riau Malay *penghulu*.

12 Although a matrilineal clan no longer coincides with a region, matrilineal and exogamy clan—*suku*—is still maintained among the Minangkabau, Malays, and some *orang asli* groups living in inland parts of Riau.

13 Their history was recorded in two reports. One is the *Proyek Pembinaan Kesejahteraan Masyarakat Terasing Hutan Panjang* (Development and welfare project of isolated community in Hutan Panjang) edited by the Department of Social Affairs in Pekanbaru (Kantor Wilayah Departemen Sosial Propinsi Riau 1979). Another is *Mengenang Sejarah Perjuangan Batin Pantjang di Kampung Titi Akar* (Memoir of the history of Batin Patjang's struggle) edited by the village office of Titi Akar at the beginning of the 1980s (Kantor Desa Titi Akar n.d.). Both reports were based on interviews with Akit elders at the time. The description given here is based on these two reports and my interviews during my fieldwork in Titi Akar and Hutan Panjang, Rupat, between 2006 and 2007.

14 In different versions, they came to the mouth of the Siak River from the region of Mandau, which is upstream of Siak River. This had been the region of the Sakai. Indeed, there was a region in upstream Siak where people known as the Akit (Akit Penguling) lived (van Anrooij 1885: 302–03, 350–1). However, the relationship between them is unknown.

15 Orang Rempang would be related to people from Rempang Island near to Batam Island. According to the oral history, after giving the land to the Akit, they moved to islands around Batam.

16 Although it is usual for the population of both villages to identify themselves as Orang/Suku Akit, the people in Titi Akar may refer to themselves as Orang/Suku Akit-Hatas.

17 According to the report of Titi Akar, the first *batin* in Titi Akar took the role between 1816 and 1883, though these years are obviously estimated ones. In addition, the role of the Datuk Laksamana in Bukit Batu was established in the latter half of the eighteenth century by Raja Ismail of the Siak kingdom (van Anrooij 1885: 332–3). Therefore, this event would have occurred around 1800.

18 Some colonial records state a different view of the origin of the name—that the name *Orang Akit* was derived from their custom of building a house on a raft and living in it (van Anrooij 1885: 303; Loeb 1935: 294), and Max Moszkowski (1909: 36) took a photograph of such a house at the midstream of the Siak River at the beginning of the twentieth century. According to some Akit elders in Rupat, they have never seen such houses on rafts. Moszkowski's photograph was probably of the people called the '*Orang Akit Penguling*' (van Anrooij 1885: 303) who lived in midstream Siak. While van Anrooij (1885: 358–9) states that the '*Orang Akit Penguling*' also immigrated to Rupat, together with the Orang Akit and Orang Hatas mentioned above, I did not find people who identified themselves as the Orang Akit Penguling in Rupat during my fieldwork.

19 The influences of the worldwide depression and the Japanese incursion were disruptive even in this peripheral area. Some Suku Asli elders remember that their standard of life dropped disastrously before and just after the Japanese occupation.

20 In the government category of *masyarakat terasing* or KAT, the Rawa, who are clearly mentioned in past records and live in present-day Siak regency, are always omitted. They would be included in the Akit or Utan. The government often confuses them even today.

21 The *Rancangan Undang-Undang Pengakuan dan Perlindungan Hak Masyarakat Hukum Adat* (Draft Law on the Recognition and Protection of the Rights of *Adat* Law Community).

22 In Riau, although AMAN engaged in the support of the Talang Mamak, it stopped activities several years ago because of internal affairs (personal communication with an NGO member in Pekanbaru).

Chapter 2

1 The Sakai, who live in the upstream region of the Siak River, are usually not included in this category as they do not have communication with the Utan, Akit, and Rawa.

2 The 'Teochew' people came from the historical Chaozhou prefecture, now the Chaoshan region, of eastern Guangdong province in China.

3 Van Anrooij (1885: 324–5) states that the distinction between *hamba raja* and *rakyat raja* was becoming less strictly protected around that time and points out that there were some cases of marriages between them. While this seems to have been the case for part of the *rakyat raja*, who became the Malays in the following period (including the Petalangan and the Orang Suku Laut) and part of the Sakai, this was not applicable to Suku Asli, Akit, and Rawa.

4 In the past, the criteria distinguishing the *peranakan* Chinese and *peranakan* Suku Asli seem to have been, first, whether one could speak the Chinese language or not, and, second, whose community one lived in. In addition, the criterion distinguishing 'pure' and *peranakan* Chinese must have been whether one had mixed ancestry or not. However, these criteria have become vague. This is because, in recent years, more and more *peranakan* Chinese (and even some of those who seemed to be 'pure' Chinese) who spoke the Chinese language within their families and lived in Chinese communities have identified themselves as (*peranakan*) Suku Asli because they have obtained Suku Asli certificates from IKBBSA (see Chapter 4); also, more and more 'pure' Chinese who have no kinship connections with the natives have identified themselves as *peranakan* (Chinese) in state policies related to the ethnic Chinese (see the later part of this chapter).

5 I surveyed 185 households of Suku Asli in Teluk Pambang (according to the 2010 census there was a total of 346 Suku Asli households in Teluk Pambang; see Dinas Sosial Kabupaten Bengkalis 2010), in which 141 households had Chinese surnames, while 44 households did not. In Titi Akar in Rupat, I surveyed all 275 households of the Akit in 2006; in this survey, 102 households had Chinese surnames (42 percent). While I investigated the number in other villages with smaller samples, it was only in Teluk Pambang that the percentage of *peranakan* was higher than non-Chinese-descended *orang asli*.

6 Strictly speaking, '*datuk kong*' is a combination of Malay and Chinese words. '*Datuk*' means elder or grandfather in Malay and '*kong*' also means grandfather in Chinese. The ethnic Chinese in the Malay world generally call sacred places by this name, and some are also shared by the Malays in different areas (Tong 1998).

7 Some Sakai people accepted Chinese ancestry. There are the people called '*Sakai Cino*' or Chinese Sakai, and they are descendants of Sakai women and Chinese merchants. Their number is limited, and the population concentrates on a trading center in the region. They engage in business and are wealthier people in the region (Porath 2003: 5, 31).

Chapter 3

1 The cosmological order based on the binary relationship between *laut* and *darat* is also general among the Malays in Malaysia (see Endicott 1970).

2 Teluk Pambang was divided into three villages in 2012, and its western half became the new village of Suka Maju. The border was drawn on the Tengah River and extended from south to north. According to a village monography in 2019, the new village has an area of eighteen square kilometers and a population of 2190 people, of which 1359 were Buddhist. The Buddhist population roughly numbers the same as the Suku Asli.

3 It is unknown when the ethnic Chinese first entered this region. Some Suku Asli told me that the households of *peranakan* or the Chinese had already been involved with the first Suku Asli migrants, but some told me otherwise. If involved, Chinese traders who pursued forest products would have been the main agent of Suku Asli immigration to this region.

4 The Dutch colonial government resettled the Javanese for the purpose of ensuring workforces in plantations in Malaysia (Li 2007b: 39–40).

5 *Bakau* is a kind of mangrove tree. The English term 'mangrove' is used to indicate various plants and vegetation growing in tidal forests (Giesen et al. 2006: 1). However, the locals distinguish each species. *Bakau* indicates a species of the Rhizophoraceae family. In the Kembung Luar River, *bakau putih*, or *Rhizophora apiculata*, is dominant.

6 The trunk of the young *bakau* is a straight pole five to six centimeters in diameter. If one cuts its branches and thrusts it into the ground, it pierces the tropical peat a few meters in depth and provides a stable pier.

7 *Jalor* is a dugout canoe three to four meters in length. They could make it on their own using axes and adzes. A *sampan* is made by putting planking together (four to five meters in length). Suku Asli bought *sampan* from Malay, Chinese, or Suku Asli who had the skills to build them. At present, *jalor* have already disappeared and *sampan* are used in general. Suku Asli handle these boats with two sculling oars standing at the front or back.

8 'Jl.' is the abbreviation of '*Jalan*,' which means 'Street.'

9 Suku Asli essentially regard the ethnic Chinese living in towns as outsiders. Therefore, this could be seen as the instrumental deployment of an ethnic boundary (see also Chapter 2).

10 The exportation of charcoal from other islands, such as Rupat Island and Rangsang Island, was still permitted in 2012.

11 The government provides free rice for each *Rukun Warga* (RW; neighborhood association: a political unit under the administrative village) twice a year. This support is not only for Suku Asli, but everyone living in the designated RW.

Chapter 4

1 According to Skeat and Blagden (1966 [1906]: 494), this title was mainly found among Orang Asli societies of 'the Jakun' or 'proto-Malays' in the Malay Peninsula. Conversely, Semang rarely used it.

2 *Antan*, *tongkat*, and *monti* are the titles of the assistant roles. They have no direct English translation.

3 Strictly speaking, this letter is different from the *surat pernikahan* issued by religious bodies. '*Pernikahan*' means marriage legitimized by the national laws, whereas '*perkawinan*' indicates de facto marriage recognized by the community. Therefore, the birth certificate issued with the *surat perkawinan* deals with the child as the mother's child out of wedlock. Although it was possible to give parents' names on the birth certificate if the parents obtained a *ketipan akta perkawinan* (certificate of de facto marriage), Suku Asli rarely obtained this as it also needed cumbersome and costly procedures to obtain the document at the subdistrict office. This means that almost all Suku Asli are children born out of wedlock on the related official documents.

4 The *batin* system among the Akit on Rupat Island does not have these systems of hierarchical order and voting.

Chapter 5

1 A 'Culture System' is a system in which peasants were forced to cultivate cash crops such as coffee, indigo, sugar cane, and gambier for exportation. This suppressed the cultivation of self-supporting crops among the peasants, and they fell into serious poverty.

2 *Hak ulayat* was adopted from a Minangkabau term and generalized across the Netherlands East Indies by van Vollenhoven (Henley and Davidson 2007: 20).

3 This draft law has not yet been passed, though the discussion continues (see Nugraha 2019; Chapter 1).

4 It should be noted here that there is a sequel to the 'ancestral land.' When I visited Teluk Pambang in 2019, Ajui referred to the mangrove forest that was recognized as 'ancestral land' as *hutan adat* (*adat* forest), although he had not used the words in 2012. It seems to be that the concept is adopted from the government category of '*adat* forest,' through which the government allows the permanent customary use of the land (see Chapter 3).

Chapter 6

1 '*Agama*' is generally translated as 'religion.' However, I use the term '*agama*' with the strong implication of political construction and monotheism in state politics, distinct from 'religion' or 'religious practices and beliefs' that have been practiced in each local community.

2 The Indonesian Constitutional Court decision (No. 97/PUU-XIV/2016) provides that the Civil Administration Law of 2006 (No. 23/2006 on Civil Administration) and its revised law of 2013 (No. 24/2013 on the Revision of the Law No. 23/2006), which regulate the registration of *agama*, contradict the Indonesian Constitution of 1945. In November 2017, the court recognized 'indigenous beliefs' as an *agama*, and a few dozen indigenous beliefs have obtained the legal position, but the full recognition of its administrative position is still in process (Allard and Damiana 2017; Harsyahwardhana 2020; Hindrati 2018; Sapiie 2017).

3 Although the words 'Belief in one God' were the fifth principle at the beginning, they were given the first position after controversies between Muslims and non-Muslims (Kim 1998: 357).

4 This must have been the *Surat Tanda Kewarganegaraan Indonesia* (Indonesian Citizenship Certificate) that was used between 1945 and 1947.

5 The words '*ilmu batin*' (or '*ilmu kebatinan*') in Suku Asli dialect seem to be derived from '*kebatinan*' in Indonesian. However, Suku Asli do not appear to recognize this. '*Batin*' means 'inner' in Arabic, and '*kebatinan*' is an abstracted form of the word; the term in Indonesian is thus translated as '(supernatural) internal power' or, more often, 'mysticism.' However, in Suku Asli dialect, *batin* means, first and foremost, their traditional headman. Therefore, they tend to vaguely recognize '*ilmu batin*' as 'headman's technique.' The Indonesian expression '*ilmu kebatinan*' was probably introduced to Suku Asli society in the past several decades in communication with the Malays or Javanese and later connected with their traditional headman.

6 Although it is difficult to define the word '*kebatinan*,' it can be summarized as 'mysticism' or 'a belief system which mixes indigenous religious elements with influences of Hinduism, Buddhism and Islam, and emphasizes the Human spirituality' (Kim 1998: 363).

References

Abdurrahman, H. (2015), 'Draft laporan penkajian hukum tentang mekanisme pengakuan masyarakat hukum adat,' Pusat Penelitian Dan Pengembangan Sistem Hukum Nasional, Badan Pembinaan Hukum Nasional, Kementerian Hukum Dan Hak Asasi Manusia R.I. Retrieved 15 April 2020 from www.bphn. go.id/data/documents/mekanisme_pengakuan_masy _hkm_adat.pdf

Acciaioli, G. (1985), 'Culture as art: from practice to spectacle in Indonesia,' *Canberra Anthropology*, 8 (1–2), pp. 148–72.

Acciaioli, G. (2007), 'From customary law to indigenous sovereignty: reconceptualizing masyarakat adat in contemporary Indonesia,' in J. S. Davidson and D. Henley (eds), *The Revival of Tradition in Indonesian Politics: The Deployment of Adat from Colonialism to Indigenism*, London: Routledge, pp. 295–318.

Allard, T. and J. Damiana (2017, November 7), 'Indonesian court recognizes native religions in landmark ruling,' *World News*. Retrieved 10 April 2021 from www.reuters.com/article/us-indonesiareligion/Indonesian-court-recognizes-native-religions-in-landmark-rulingidUSKBN1D71J2

Andaya, L. Y. (2008), *Leaves of the Same Tree: Trade and Ethnicity in the Strait of Melaka*, Honolulu, HI: University of Hawai'i Press.

Anderson, B. (1990), *Language and Power: Exploring Political Cultures in Indonesia*, Ithaca, NY: Cornell University Press.

Antaranews (2020, February 29), 'Riau miliki dua hutan adat yang diakui pemerintah,' *Antaranews*. Retrieved 26 April 2020 from www.antaranews.com/berita/1326538/riau-miliki-dua-hutan-adat-yang-diakui-pemerintah

Arizona, Y. and C. Cahyadi (2013), 'The revival of indigenous peoples: contestations over a special legislation on *masyarakat adat*,' in B. Hauser-Schäublin (ed.), *Adat and Indigeneity in Indonesia: Culture and Entitlements between Heteronomy and Self-ascription*, Göttingen: Universitätsverlag Göttingen, pp. 43–62.

Arumingtyas, L. (2019, March 27), 'Penetapan hutan adat hanya 1% dari realisasi perhutanan sosial,' *Mongabay*. Retrieved 26 April 2020 from www.mongabay.co.id/2019/03/27/penetapan-hutan-adat-hanya-1-dari-realisasi-perhutanan-sosial/

Atkinson, J. M. (1983), 'Religions in dialogue: the construction of Indonesian minority religion,' *American Ethnologist*, 10 (4), pp. 684–96.

Badan Restorasi Gambut (2018), 'Peta Indikatif Restorasi (PIR) Gambut: Provinsi Riau.' Retrieved 18 April 2020 from https://brg.go.id/program-kerja/#&gid=1&pid=1

Banks, M. (1996), *Ethnicity: Anthropological Constructions*, London: Routledge.

Barnard, A. (2006), 'Kalahari revisionism, Vienna and the "indigenous peoples" debate,' *Social Anthropology*, 14 (1), pp. 1–16.

Barnard, T. P. (1998), 'The timber trade in pre-modern Siak,' *Indonesia*, 65, pp. 86–96.

Barnard, T. P. (2001), 'Texts, Raja Ismail and violence: Siak and the transformation of Malay identity in the eighteenth century,' *Journal of Southeast Asian Studies*, 32 (3), pp. 331–42.

Barnard, T. P. (2003), *Multiple Centres of Authority: Society and Environment in Siak and Eastern Sumatra, 1674–1827*, Leiden: KITLV Press.

Barnard, T. P. (ed.) (2004), *Contesting Malayness: Malay Identity across Boundaries*, Singapore: NUS Press.

Barnard, T. P. (2014), '"We are comfortable riding the waves": landscape and the formation of a border state in eighteen-century island Southeast Asia,' in P. Readman, C. Radding and C. Bryant (eds), *Borderlands in World History, 1700–1914*, London: Palgrave Macmillan, pp. 83–100.

Barth, F. (1969), 'Introduction,' in F. Barth (ed.), *Ethnic Groups and Boundaries: The Social Organization of Culture Difference*, Bergen: Universitets Forlaget, pp. 9–38.

Barth, F. (1994), 'Enduring and emerging issues in the analysis of ethnicity,' in H. Vermeulen and C. Govers (eds), *The Anthropology of Ethnicity: Beyond 'Ethnic Groups and Boundaries'*, Amsterdam: Het Spinhuis, pp. 11–32.

Bedner, A. and S. van Huis (2008), 'The return of native in Indonesian law: indigenous communities in Indonesian legislation,' *Bijdragen tot de Taal-, Land- en Volkenkunde*, 164 (2), pp. 165–93.

Benda-Beckmann, F. von (1979), *Property in Social Continuity: Continuity and Change in the Maintenance of Property Relationships through Time in Minangkabau, West Sumatra*, Hague: Marinus Nijhoff.

Benda-Beckmann, F. von and K. von Benda-Beckmann (2011), 'Myth and stereotypes about adat law: a reassessment of Van Vollenhoven in the light of current struggles over adat law in Indonesia,' *Bijidragen tot de Taal- en Volkenkunde*, 167 (2–3), pp. 167–95.

Benjamin, G. (1968), 'Headmanship and leadership in Temiar society,' *Federation Museums Journal*, 13 (New Series), pp. 1–43.

Benjamin, G. (2002), 'On being tribal in the Malay world,' in G. Benjamin and C. Chou (eds), *Tribal Communities in the Malay World: Historical, Cultural, and Social Perspectives*, Singapore: International Institute of Asian Studies, pp. 7–76.

Benjamin, G. (2016a), 'Indigeny–exogeny: the fundamental social dimensions?,' *Anthropos*, 111, pp. 513–31.

Benjamin, G. (2016b), 'Indigenous peoples: indigeneity, indigeny or indigenism?,' in C. Antons (ed.), *The Routledge Handbook of Asian Law*, London: Routledge, pp. 362–77.

Benjamin, G. (2019), 'Music and the cline of Malayness: sounds of egalitarianism and ranking,' in N. Porath (ed.), *Hearing South East Asia: Sounds of Hierarchy and Power in Context*, Copenhagen: Nias Press, pp. 87–116.

Biezeveld, R. (2007), 'The many roles of adat in West Sumatra,' in J. S. Davidson and D. Henley (eds), *The Revival of Tradition in Indonesian Politics: The Deployment of Adat from Colonialism to Indigenism*, London: Routledge, pp. 203–23.

Bisnis.com (2019, June 13), 'KLHK Targetkan Penetapan Hutan Adat Seluas 6,53 Juta Hektare,' *Bisnis.com*. Retrieved 26 April 2020 from https://ekonomi.bisnis.com/read/20190613/99/933374/klhk-targetkan-penetapan-hutan-adat-seluas-653-juta-hektare

Bloch, M. and J. Parry (1989), 'Introduction: money and the morality of exchange,' in J. Parry and M. Bloch (eds), *Money and the Morality of Exchange*, Cambridge: Cambridge University Press, pp. 1–32.

Bort, B. (1927), 'Report of Governor Balthasar Bort on Malacca 1678,' M. J. Bremner (trans.), *Journal of the Malayan Branch of the Royal Asiatic Society*, 5 (1), pp. 1–232.

Bourchier, D. (2007), 'The romance of adat in the Indonesian political imagination and the current revival,' in J. S. Davidson and D. Henley (eds), *The Revival of Tradition in Indonesian Politics: The Deployment of Adat from Colonialism to Indigenism*, London: Routledge, pp. 113–29.

Bowen, J. R. (2000), 'Should we have a universal concept of "indigenous peoples' rights"?: Ethnicity and essentialism in the twenty-first century,' *Anthropology Today*, 16 (4), pp. 12–16.

Breman, J. (1983), 'The village on Java and early colonial state,' *Journal of Peasant Studies*, 9 (4), pp. 189–240.

Bronson, B. (1978), 'Exchange at the upstream and downstream ends: notes toward a functional model of the coastal state in Southeast Asia,' in K. L. Hutterer (ed.), *Economic Exchange and Social Interaction in Southeast Asia: Perspectives from Prehistory, History, and Ethnography*, Michigan Papers on South and Southeast Asia 13, Ann Arbor, MI: Centre of South and Southeast Asian Studies.

Brown, I. (1987), 'Contemporary Indonesian Buddhism and monotheism,' *Journal of Southeast Asian Studies*, 18 (1), pp. 108–17.

Brown, I. (1990), 'Agama Buddha Maitreya: a modern Buddhist sect in Indonesia,' *Contributions to Southeast Asian Ethnography*, 9, pp. 113–24.

Brubaker, R. (2004), *Ethnicity without Groups*, Cambridge: Harvard University Press.

Burns, P. (1989), 'The myth of adat,' *Journal of Legal Pluralism*, 28, pp. 1–127.

Burns, P. (2007), 'Custom, that is before all law,' in J. S. Davidson and D. Henley (eds), *The Revival of Tradition in Indonesian Politics: The Deployment of Adat from Colonialism to Indigenism*, London: Routledge, pp. 68–86.

Cadena, M. de la and O. Starn (2007), 'Introduction,' in M. de la Cadena and O. Starn (eds), *Indigenous Experience Today*, Berg: Oxford, pp. 1–30.

Chan, Kwok-Bun (2005), *Chinese Identities, Ethnicity and Cosmopolitanism*, London: Routledge.

Chandler, D. and J. Reid (2018), '"Being in being": contesting ontopolitics of indigeneity,' *European Legacy*, 23 (3), pp. 251–68.

Chou, C. (2003), *Indonesian Sea Nomads: Money, Magic and Fear of the Orang Suku Laut*, London: Routledge.

Chou, C. (2010), *The Orang Suku Laut of Riau, Indonesia: The Inalienable Gift of Territory*, London: Routledge.

Chou, C. (2013), 'Space, movement and place: the sea nomads,' in S. Chandra and H. P. Ray (eds), *The Sea, Identity and History: From the Bay of Bengal to the South China Sea*, New Delhi: Manohar, pp. 41–66.

Chou, C. (2020), 'On being Orang Suku Laut in the Malay world,' in J. Levin (ed.), *Nomad-state Relationships in International Relations: Before and after Borders*, Cham: Palgrave Macmillan, pp. 217–38.

Chou, C. and V. Wee (2002), 'Tribality and globalization: the Orang Suku Laut and the "growth triangle" in a contested environment,' in G. Benjamin and C. Chou (eds), *Tribal Communities in the Malay World: Historical, Cultural, and Social Perspectives*, Singapore: International Institute of Asian Studies, pp. 318–63.

Chua, C. (2004), 'Defining Indonesian Chinese under the New Order,' *Journal of Contemporary Asia*, 34 (4), pp. 465–79.

Clarke, I. (2000), 'Ancestor worship and identity: ritual, interpretation, and social normalization in the Malaysian Chinese community,' *Sojourn: Journal of Social Issues in Southeast Asia*, 15 (2), pp. 273–95.

Colombijn, F. (2003a), 'The volatile state in Southeast Asia: evidence from Sumatra, 1600–1800,' *Journal of Asian Studies*, 62 (2), pp. 497–529.

Colombijn, F. (2003b), 'When there is nothing to imagine: nationalism in Riau,' in P. J. M. Nas, G. A. Persoon and R. Jaffe (eds), *Framing Indonesian Realities: Essays in Symbolic Anthropology in Honour of Reimar Schefold*, Leiden: KITLV Press, pp. 333–65.

Conklin, B. A. (1997), 'Body paint, feathers, and VCRs: aesthetics and authenticity in Amazonian activism,' *American Ethnologist*, 24 (4), pp. 711–37.

Coppel, C. A. (2013), 'Diaspora and hybridity: *peranakan* Chinese culture in Indonesia,' in Tan Chee-Beng (ed.), *Routledge Handbook of the Chinese Diaspora*, London: Routledge, pp. 345–58.

Dampier, W. (1906), *Dampier's Voyages*, Vol. II, New York: E. P. Dutton.

Davidson, J. S. and D. Henley (eds) (2007), *The Revival of Tradition in Indonesian Politics: The Deployment of Adat from Colonialism to Indigenism*, London: Routledge.

Dethia N. S., R. Agustina and F. X. Arsin (2020), 'Surat Keterangan Ganti Rugi (SKGR) sebagai janiman dalam perjanjian utang piutang,' *Indonesian Notary*, 2 (3), pp. 425–47.

Dinas Sosial Kabupaten Bengkalis (2010), 'Blueprint pembangunan mapan Komunitas Adat Terpencil (KAT) di kabupaten Bengkalis,' Pekanbaru: PT. Yasra International.

Dove, M. (2006), 'Indigenous people and environmental politics,' *Annual Review of Anthropology*, 35, pp. 191–208.

Dove, M., D. S. Smith, M. T. Campos, A. S. Mathews, A. Rademacher, S. Rhee and L. M. Yoder (2007), 'Globalisation and the construction of Western and non-Western knowledge,' in P. Sillitoe (ed.), *Local Science vs Global Science: Approaches to Indigenous Knowledge in International Development*, New York: Berghahn Books, pp. 129–54.

Duncan, C. (2003), 'Untangling conversion: religious change and identity among the Forest Tobelo of Indonesia,' *Ethnology*, 42 (4), pp. 307–22.

Duncan, C. (2004a), 'Legislating modernity among the marginalized,' in C. R. Duncan (ed.), *Civilizing the Margins: Southeast Asian Government Policies for the Development of Minorities*, Ithaca, NY: Cornell University Press, pp. 1–23.

Duncan, C. (2004b), 'From development to empowerment,' in C. R. Duncan (ed.), *Civilizing the Margins: Southeast Asian Government Policies for the Development of Minorities*, Ithaca, NY: Cornell University Press, pp. 86–115.

Effendy, T. (1997), 'Petalangan society and changes in Riau,' *Bijdragen tot de Taal-. Land- en Volkenkunde*, 153 (4), pp. 630–47.

Effendy, T. (2002), 'The Orang Petalangan of Riau and their forest environment,' in G. Benjamin and C. Chou (eds), *Tribal Communities in the Malay World: Historical, Cultural, and Social Perspectives*, Singapore: International Institute of Asian Studies, pp. 364–83.

Endicott, K. (1970), *An Analysis of Malay Magic*, Oxford: Clarendon Press.

Erni, C. and S. Stidsen (2006), 'Indonesia,' in S. Stidsen (ed.), *The Indigenous World 2006*, Copenhagen: The International Work Group for Indigenous Affairs, pp. 300–08.

Fasseur, C. (1994), 'Cornerstone and stumbling block: racial classification and the late colonial state in Indonesia,' in R. Cribb (ed.), *The Late Colonial State in Indonesia: Political and Economic Foundations of the Netherlands Indies, 1880–1942*, Leiden: KITLV Press, pp. 31–56.

Fasseur, C. (2007), 'Colonial dilemma: Van Vollenhoven and the struggle between adat law and Western law in Indonesia,' in J. S. Davidson and D. Henley (eds), *The Revival of Tradition in Indonesian Politics: The Deployment of Adat from Colonialism to Indigenism*, London: Routledge, pp. 50–67.

Fitzpatrick, D. (2007), 'Land, custom, and the state in post-Suharto Indonesia: a foreign lawyer's perspective,' in J. S. Davidson and D. Henley (eds), *The Revival of Tradition in Indonesian Politics: The Deployment of Adat from Colonialism to Indigenism*, London: Routledge, pp. 130–48.

Foucault, M. (1991), 'Governmentality,' in G. Burchell, C. Gordon and P. Miller (eds), *The Foucault Effect: Studies in Governmentality*, Chicago, IL: University of Chicago Press, pp. 87–104.

Geertz, C. (1960), 'The Javanese Kijaji: the changing role of a cultural trader,' *Comparative Studies in Society and History*, 2 (2), pp. 228–49.

Geertz, C. (1963), *Agricultural Involution: The Process of Ecological Change in Indonesia*, Berkeley, CA: University of California Press.

Geertz, C. (1973), *The Interpretation of Cultures*, New York: Basic Books.

Geertz, C. (1983), *Local Knowledge: Further Essays in Interactive Anthropology*, New York: Basic Books.

Gibson, T. and Sillander, K. (2011), 'Introduction,' in T. Gibson and K. Sillander (eds), *Anarchic Solidarity: Autonomy, Equality, and Fellowship in Southeast Asia*, Monograph 60, New Haven, CT: Yale University Southeast Asia Studies, pp. 1–16.

Giesen, W., S. Wulffraat, M. Zieren and L. Scholten (eds) (2006), *Mangrove Guidebook for Southeast Asia*, RAP Publication 2006/07, Food and Agriculture Organization of the United Nations & Wetland International. Retrieved 25 April 2020 from www.fao.org/docrep/010/ag132e/ag132e00.htm

Gonda, J. (1973), *Sanskrit in Indonesia*, New Haven, CT: HRAF Press.

Gooszen, H. (1999), *A Demographic History of the Indonesian Archipelago 1880–1942*, Singapore: Institute of Southeast Asian Studies.

Gow, P. (1995), 'Land, people and paper in Western Amazonia,' in E. Hirsch and M. O'Hanlon (eds), *The Anthropology of Landscape: Perspectives on Place and Space*, Oxford: Clarendon Press, pp. 43–62.

Graham, L. R. and H. G. Penny (2014), 'Performing indigeneity: emergent identity, self-determination, and sovereignty,' in L. R. Graham and H. G. Penny (eds), *Performing Indigeneity: Global Histories and Contemporary Experiences*, Lincoln, NE: University of Nebraska Press, pp. 1–31.

Gramberg, J. S. C. (1864), 'Reis naar Siak,' *Tijdschrift voor Indische Taal-, Land- en Volkenkunde*, 39, pp. 497–530.

Grumblies, A.-T. (2013), 'Being Wana, becoming an "indigenous people": experimenting with indigeneity in Central Sulawesi,' in B. Hauser-Schäublin (ed.), *Adat and Indigeneity in Indonesia: Culture and Entitlements between Heteronomy and Self-ascription*, Göttingen: Universitätsverlag Göttingen, pp. 81–98.

Hamidy, U. U. (1987), *Rimba Kepungan Sialang*, Jakarta: Balai Pustaka.

Hamidy, U. U. (1991), *Masyarakat Terasing Daerah Riau di Gerbang Abad XXI*, Pekanbaru: Universitas Islam Riau.

Harsyahwardhana, S. (2020), 'Akibat hukum putusan MK no. 97/PUU-XIV/2016 tentang judicial review UU administrasi kependudukan terhadap penghayat aliran kepercayaan,' *Area Hukum*, 13 (2), pp. 369–87.

Hathaway, M. (2010), 'The emergence of indigeneity: public intellectuals and an indigenous space,' *Cultural Anthropology*, 25 (2), pp. 301–33.

Hauser-Schäublin, B. (2013), 'Introduction: the power of indigeneity: reparation, readjustments and repositioning,' in B. Hauser-Schäublin (ed.), *Adat and Indigeneity in Indonesia: Culture and Entitlements between Heteronomy and Self-ascription*, Göttingen: Universitätsverlag Göttingen, pp. 5–12.

Henley, D. and J. S. Davidson (2007), 'Introduction: radical conservatism—the protean politics of adat,' in J. S. Davidson and D. Henley (eds), *The Revival of Tradition in Indonesian Politics: The Deployment of Adat from Colonialism to Indigenism*, London: Routledge, pp. 1–49.

Heryanto, A. (1988), 'The development of "development",' *Indonesia*, 46, pp. 1–24.

Hindrati, E. (2018), 'Majelis Agama Kaharingan Indonesia Mendesak Pemerintah Indonesia Agar Mengakui Kaharingan Menjadi Agama,' Aliansi Masyarakat Nusantara. Retrieved 10 April 2021 from www.aman.or.id/2018/10/majelis-agama-kaharingan-indonesia-mendesak-pemerintah-indonesia-agar-mengakui-kaharingan-menjadi-agama/

Hirtz, F. (2003), 'It takes modern means to be traditional: on recognising indigenous cultural communities in the Philippines,' *Development and Change*, 34 (5), pp. 887–914.

Hoadley, M. C. (1988), 'Javanese, Peranakan, and Chinese elites in Cirebon: changing ethnic boundaries,' *Journal of Asian Studies*, 47 (3), pp. 503–17.

Hobsbawm, E. and T. Ranger (1992), *The Invention of Tradition*, Cambridge: Cambridge University Press.

Hoskins, J. (1987), 'Entering the bitter house: spirit worship and conversion in West Sunda,' in R. S. Kipp and S. Rodgers (eds), *Indonesian Religions in Transition*, Tucson, AZ: University of Arizona Press, pp. 136–60.

Isjoni (2002), *Komunitas Adat Terpencil: Tersingkir di Tengah Gemerlap Zaman*, Pekanbaru: Penerbit Bahana Press.

Isjoni (2005), *Orang Talang Mamak: Perspektif Antropologi Ekonomi*, Pekanbaru: Unri Press.

Josselin de Jong, J. P. B. de (1948), 'Customary law: a confusing fiction,' *Mededelingen Koninklijke Vereniging Indisch Instituut*, 80, pp. 3–8.

Junus, H. (2002), *Sejarah Kabupaten Bengkalis: Sebuah Tinjauan Paling Dasar*, Bengkalis: Pemerintah Kabupaten Bengkalis.

Kähler, H. (1960), *Ethnographische und linguistische Studien über die orang darat, orang akit, orang laut und orang utan im Riau-Archpel und auf den Inseln an der Ostküste von Sumatra*, Berlin: Dietrich Reimer.

Kahn, J. (1993), *Constituting the Minangkabau: Peasants, Culture, and Modernity in Colonial Indonesia*, Providence: Berg.

Kantor Desa Titi Akar (n.d.), *Mengenang sejarah perjuangan batin Pantjang di Kampung Titi Akar Kecamatan Rupat Kabupaten Riau*, Titi Akar, Bengkalis: Kantor Desa Titi Akar.

Kantor Sensus and Statistik Propinsi (1972), 'Riau dalam angka 1972,' Pekanbaru: Pemelintah Kabupaten Riau.

Kantor Wilayah Departemen Sosial Propinsi Riau (1979), *Proyek pembinaan kesejahteraan masyarakat terasing Hutan Panjang, Kecamatan Rupat, Kabupaten Bengkalis, Propinsi Riau*, Pekanbaru: Kantor Wilayah Departemen Social Propinsi Riau.

Kartomi, M. (2019), 'The nobat ensemble in the Riau-Lingga sultanate, its colonial era demise and its recent sonic re-invention,' in M. Kartomi (ed.), *Performing the Arts of Indonesia: Malay Identity and Politics in the Music, Dance and Theatre of the Riau Islands*, Copenhagen: Nias Press, pp. 77–105.

Kathirithamby-Wells, J. (1993), 'Hulu-hilir unity and conflict: Malay statecraft in east Sumatra before the mid-nineteenth century,' *Archipel*, 45, pp. 77–96.

Kathirithamby-Wells, J. (1997), 'Siak and its changing strategies for survival, c. 1700–1870,' in A. Reid (ed.), *The Last Stand of Asian Autonomies: Responses to Modernity in the Diverse States of Southeast Asia and Korea, 1750–1900*, London: Macmillan Press, pp. 217–44.

Kementrian Lingkungan Hidup dan Kehutanan (2019), 'Peta indikatif dan areal perhutanan sosial provinsi Riau: Revisi III,' Kementrian Lingkungan Hidup dan Kehutanan.

Kenrick, J. and J. Lewis (2004), 'Indigenous peoples' rights and the politics of the term "indigenous",' *Anthropology Today*, 20 (2), pp. 4–9.

Kim, Hyung-Jun (1998), 'The changing interpretation of religious freedom in Indonesia,' *Journal of Southeast Asian Studies*, 29 (2), pp. 357–73.

Kipp, R. S. and S. Rodgers (1987), 'Introduction,' in R. S. Kipp and S. Rodgers (eds), *Indonesian Religions in Transition*, Tucson, AZ: University of Arizona Press, pp. 1–31.

Kuper, A. (2003), 'The return of native,' *Current Anthropology*, 44 (3), pp. 389–402.

Lee, R. B. (2005), 'Power and property in twenty-first century foragers: a critical examination,' in T. Widlok and W. G. Tadesse (eds), *Property and Equality Volume 2: Encapsulation, Commercialization, Discrimination*, New York: Berghahn Books, pp. 16–31.

Lenhart, L. (1997), 'Orang Suku Laut ethnicity and acculturation,' *Bijdragen tot de Taal-, Land- en Volkenkunde*, 153–4, pp. 577–604.

Li, T. L. (1999), 'Marginality, power and production: analysing upland transformations,' in T. M. Li (ed.), *Transforming the Indonesian Uplands: Marginality, Power and Production*, Amsterdam: Harwood Academic Publishers, pp. 1–44.

Li, T. M. (2000), 'Articulating indigenous identity in Indonesia: resource politics and the tribal slot,' *Comparative Studies in Society and History*, 42 (17), pp. 149–79.

Li, T. M. (2001), 'Masyarakat adat, difference, and the limits of recognition in Indonesia's forest zone,' *Modern Asian Studies*, 35 (3), pp. 645–76.

Li, T. M. (2007a), 'Adat in Central Sulawesi: contemporary deployments,' in J. S. Davidson and D. Henley (eds), *The Revival of Tradition in Indonesian Politics: The Deployment of Adat from Colonialism to Indigenism*, London: Routledge, pp. 337–70.

Li, T. M. (2007b), *The Will to Improve: Governmentality, Development, and the Practice of Politics*, Durham: Duke University Press.

Loeb, E. (1934), 'Patrilineal and matrilineal organisation in Sumatra,' *American Anthropologist*, 36 (1), pp. 26–56.

Loeb, E. (1935), *Sumatra: Its History and People*, Vienna: Institut für Völkerkunde der Universität Wien.

Long, N. (2009), 'Fruits of the orchard: land, space, and state in Kepulauan Riau,' *Journal of Social Issues in Southeast Asia*, 24 (1), pp. 60–8.

Long, N. (2013), *Being Malay in Indonesia: Histories, Hopes and Citizenship in the Riau Archipelago*, ASAA Southeast Asia Publications Series, Honolulu, HI: University of Hawai'i Press.

Lye Tuck-Po (2005), 'The meanings of trees: forest and identity for the Batek of Pahang, Malaysia,' *The Asia Pacific Journal of Anthropology*, 6, pp. 249–61.

Macdonald, C. (2011), 'A theoretical overview of anarchic solidarity,' in T. Gibson and K. Sillander (eds), *Anarchic Solidarity: Autonomy, Equality, and Fellowship in Southeast Asia*, Monograph 60, New Haven, CT: Yale University Southeast Asia Studies, pp. 1–16.

MacRae, G. (2003), 'The value of land in Bali: land tenure, land reform and commodification,' in T. A. Reuter (ed.), *Inequality, Crisis and Social Change in Indonesia: The Muted Worlds of Bali*, London: RoutledgeCurzon, pp. 145–68.

Masuda, K. (2009), 'The reconstitution of adat in a dual level land conflict: a case study of a village community under forest development schemes in Sumatra,' Afrasian Centre for Peace and Development Studies Working Paper Series 61, Otsu: Afrasian Centre for Peace and Development Studies.

Masuda, K. (2012), *Indonesia: Mori no Kurashi to Kaihatsu*, Tokyo: Akashi Shoten.

Masuda, K., K. Mizuno and K. Sugihara (2016), 'A socioeconomic history of the peatland region: from the trade to land development, and then to conservation,' in K. Mizuno, M. S. Fujita and S. Kawai (eds), *Catastrophe and Regeneration in Indonesia's Peatlands: Ecology, Economy and Society*, Singapore: NUS Press, pp. 148–84.

Merlan, F. (2009), 'Indigeneity: global and local,' *Current Anthropology*, 50 (3), pp. 303–33.

Mizuno, K., M. S. Fujita and S. Kawai (eds) (2016), *Catastrophe and Regeneration in Indonesia's Peatlands: Ecology, Economy and Society*, Singapore: NUS Press.

Moniaga, S. (2007), 'From bumiputera to masyarakat adat: a long and confusing journey,' in J. S. Davidson and D. Henley (eds), *The Revival of Tradition in Indonesian Politics: The Deployment of Adat from Colonialism to Indigenism*, London: Routledge, pp. 275–94.

Moor, J. H. (1837), *Notices of the Indian Archipelago and Adjacent Countries: Being a Collection of Papers Relating to Borneo, Celebes, Bali, Java, Sumatra, Nias, the Philippine Islands, Sulus, Siam, Cochin China, Malayan Peninsula &c.* Singapore: (Publisher unknown).

Moszkowski (1909), *Auf neuen Wegen durch Sumatra: Forschungsreisen in Ostund Zentral- Sumatra*, Berlin: Reimer.

Mujiburohman D. A., T. Arianto and R. Riyadi (2014), 'Kajian yuridis tumpeng tindih pemilikan tanah di Kabupaten Kampar Provinsi Riau,' in D. W. Pujiriyani and W. H. Puri (eds), *Penataan dan Pengelolaan Pertanahan yang mensejahterakan Masyarakat: Hasil Penelitian Strategis PPPM-STPN*, Yogyakarta: Pusat Penelitian Pengabdian kepada Masyarakat Sekolah Tinggi Pertanahan Nasional, pp. 169–95.

Müller, S. (2013), 'Adat as a means of unification and its contestation: the case of North Halmahera,' in B. Hauser-Schäublin (ed.), *Adat and Indigeneity in Indonesia: Culture and Entitlements between Heteronomy and Self-ascription*, Göttingen: Universitätsverlag Göttingen, pp. 99–114.

Ndlovu, M. (2019), *Performing Indigeneity: Spectacles of Culture and Identity in Coloniality*, London: Pluto Press.

New York Times (2013, January 6), 'Indonesia envisions more religion in schools,' *New York Times*. Retrieved 29 April 2020 from www.nytimes.com/2013/01/07/world/asia/in-indonesia-science-may-give-way-to-religion.html?pagewanted=all&_r=0

Nicholas, C. (2002), 'Organizing Orang Asli identity,' in G. Benjamin and C. Chou (eds), *Tribal Communities in the Malay World: Historical, Cultural and Social Perspective,* Singapore: International Institute for Asian Studies, pp. 19–136.

Niezen, R. (2003), *The Origin of Indigenism: Human Rights and Politics of Identity*, Berkeley, CA: University of California Press.

Nugraha, I. (2019, December 13), 'RUU masyarakat adat masuk prolegnas 2020, berikut masukan para pihak,' *Mongabay*. Retrieved 9 December 2021 from www.mongabay.co.id/2019/12/13/ruu-masyarakat-adat-masuk-prolegnas-2020-berikut-masukan-para-pihak/

Osawa, T. (2009), 'Shamanistic practices among the Akit of eastern Sumatra,' Master's thesis, Tokyo University of Marine Science and Technology.

Osawa, T. (2016), 'At the edge of mangrove forest: the Suku Asli and the quest for indigeneity, ethnicity and development,' PhD thesis, The University of Edinburgh.

Osawa, T. (2017), 'Rejection and acceptance of the state: the attitude toward power in tribal societies of eastern Sumatra,' *Japanese Journal of Cultural Anthropology,* 81 (4), pp. 567–85 (in Japanese).

Ota, M. (2011), 'Implementation of the Community Forest (Hutan Kemasyarakatan) scheme and its effects on rural households in Gunungkidul district, Java, Indonesia: an exploration of the local agrarian context,' *Tropics* 19 (3), pp. 123–33.

Paker, L. and Chang-Yau Hoon (2013), 'Secularity, religion and the possibilities for religious citizenship,' *Asian Journal of Social Science,* 41, pp. 150–74.

Pemerintah Kabupaten Bengkalis (n.d.), 'Statistik Kabupaten Bengkalis: Luas wilayah dan penduduk.' Retrieved 18 April 2020 from https://statistik.bengkaliskab.go.id/jumlahluaspenduduk/tahun/9

Pemerintah Propinsi Riau (2005), 'Profil Komunitas Adat Terpencil: di Kabupaten Indragiri Hilir, Indragiri Hulu, Pelalawan, Rokan Hulu, Bengkalis,' Pekanbaru: Pemerintah Propinsi Riau Badan Kesejahteraan Sosial.

Persoon, G. (1998), 'Isolated groups or indigenous peoples; Indonesia and international discourse,' *Bijdragen tot de Taal-. Land- en Volkenkunde,* 154 (2), pp. 281–304.

Picard, M. (2011), 'Balinese religion in search for recognition: from agama Hindu Bali to agama Hindu (1945–1965),' *Bijidragen tot de Taal-, Land, en Volkenkunde,* 167 (4), pp. 482–510.

Porath, N. (2000), 'The re-appropriation of Sakai land: the case of a shrine in Riau (Indonesia),' in A. Abramson and D. Theodossopoulos (eds), *Land, Law and Environment: Mythical Land, Legal Boundaries,* London: Pluto Press, pp. 176–90.

Porath, N. (2002a), 'A river, a road, and indigenous people and an entangled landscape in Riau, Indonesia,' *Bijdragen tot de Taal-. Land- en Volkenkunde,* 158 (4), pp. 769–97.

Porath, N. (2002b), 'Developing indigenous communities into Sakais: South Thailand and Riau,' in G. Benjamin and C. Chou (eds), *Tribal Communities in the Malay World: Historical, Cultural, and Social Perspectives,* Singapore: International Institute of Asian Studies, pp. 97–118.

Porath, N. (2003), *When the Bird Flies: Shamanic Therapy and the Maintenance of Worldly Boundaries among an Indigenous People of Riau (Sumatra),* Leiden: CNWS Publications.

Porath, N. (2010), '"They have not progressed enough": development's negated identities among two indigenous peoples (*orang asli*), in Indonesia and Thailand,' *Journal of Southeast Asian Studies,* 41 (2), pp. 267–89.

Porath, N. (2019a), 'Embodied knowledge, numinous power and comedic sounds in the healing aesthetics of the Orang Sakai of Riau,' in N. Porath (ed.), *Hearing South East Asia: Sounds of Hierarchy and Power in Context*, Copenhagen: Nias Press, pp. 140–73.

Porath, N. (2019b), 'The ensoundments of hierarchy and power in Southeast Asia,' in N. Porath (ed.), *Hearing South East Asia: Sounds of Hierarchy and Power in Context*, Copenhagen: Nias Press, pp. 1–86.

Reid, A. (2004), 'Understanding *Melayu* (Malay), as a source of diverse modern identities,' in T. Barnard (ed.), *Contesting Malayness: Malay Identity across Boundaries*, Singapore: NUS Press, pp. 1–24.

Reid, A. (2009), 'Escaping the burden of Chineseness,' *Asian Ethnicity*, 10 (3), pp. 285–96.

Rhee, S. (2009), 'The cultural politics of collaboration to control and access forest resources in Malinau,' in M. Moelino, E. Wollenberg and G. Limberg (eds), *The Decentralization of Forest Governance: Politics, Economics and the Fight for Control of Forests in Indonesian Borneo*, London: Earthsca, pp. 43–60.

Riauonline (2019, June 1), 'Pertama di Riau: Masyarakat sampaikan usulan hutan adat,' *Riauonline*. Retrieved 26 April 2020 from www.riauonline.co.id/lingkungan/read/2019/06/01/pertama-di-riau-masyarakat-sampaikan-usulan-hutan-adat

Salim, A. (2007), 'Muslim politics in Indonesia's democratisation: the religious majority and the rights of minorities in the post-New Order era,' in R. H. McLeod and A. Macintyre (eds), *Indonesia: Democracy and the Promise of Good Governance*, Singapore: Institute of Southeast Asian Studies, pp. 115–37.

Sandbukt, Ö. (1984), 'Kubu conception of reality,' *Asian Folklore Studies*, 43, pp. 85–98.

Sapiie, M. A. (2017, November 7), 'Constitutional court rules indigenous faiths "acknowledged" by state,' *Jakarta Post*. Retrieved 15 December 2021 from www.thejakartapost.com/news/2017/11/07/constitutional-court-rules-indigenous-faiths-acknowledged-by-state.html

Saugestad, S. (2004), 'Discussion: on the return of the native,' *Current Anthropology*, 45 (2), pp. 263–4.

Schiller, A. (1996), 'An "old" religion in "New Order" Indonesia: notes on ethnicity and religious affiliation,' *Sociology of Religion*, 57 (4), pp. 409–17.

Scott, J. (1998), *Seeing like a State: How Certain Schemes to Improve the Human Condition Have Failed*, New Haven, CT: Yale University Press.

Scott, J. (2009), *The Art of Not Being Governed: An Anarchist History of Upland Southeast Asia*, New Haven, CT: Yale University Press.

Singapore Chronicle (1827, February 15), 'Sago,' *Singapore Chronicle*, p. 2.

Skeat, W. W. (1900), *Malay Magic: An Introduction to the Folklore and Popular Religion of the Malay Peninsula*, London: Macmillan.

Skeat, W. W. and Blagden C. O. (1966 [1906]), *Pagan Races of the Malay Peninsula, Vol. 1*, London: Frank Cass & Co. Ltd.

SKEPHI and R. Kiddell-Monroe (1993), 'Indonesia: land rights and development,' in M. Colchester and L. Lohmann (eds), *Struggle for Land and the Fate of the Forests*, Penang: World Rainforest Movement, pp. 228–63.

Skinner, W. G. (1959), 'Overseas Chinese in Southeast Asia,' *Annals of the American Academy of Political and Social Science*, 321, pp. 136–47.

Skinner, W. G. (1996), 'Creolized Chinese societies in Southeast Asia,' in A. Reid (ed.), *Sojourners and Settlers: Histories of Southeast Asia and the Chinese*, Sydney: Allen & Unwin, pp. 51–93.

Steedly, M. M. (1999), 'The state of culture theory in the anthropology of Southeast Asia,' *Annual Review of Anthropology*, 28, pp. 431–54.

Steinebach, S. (2013), '"Today we occupy the plantation—tomorrow Jakarta": indigeneity, land and oil palm plantations in Jambi,' in B. Hauser-Schäublin (ed.), *Adat and Indigeneity in Indonesia: Culture and Entitlements between Heteronomy and Self-ascription*, Göttingen: Universitätsverlag Göttingen, pp. 63–80.

Stevens, A. M. and A. E. Schmidgall-Tellings (2004), *Kamus Lengkap Indonesia-Inggris*, Ohio: Ohio University Press.

Suryadi (2019, July 19), 'Mencari solusi selamatkan pulau Bengkalis dari abrasi,' *Mongabay.* Retrieved 22 April 2020 from www.mongabay.co.id/2019/07/19/mencari-solusi-selamatkan-pulau-bengkalis-dari-abrasi/

Suryadinata, L. (1978), *Pribumi Indonesians, the Chinese Minority and China*, Kuala Lumpur: Heinemann Educational Books.

Sylvain, R. (2002), '"Land, water, and truth": San identity and global indigenism,' *American Anthropologist*, 104 (4), pp. 1074–85.

Tan Chee-Beng (1982), 'Peranakan Chinese in northeast Kelantan with special reference to Chinese religion,' *Journal of Malaysian Branch of the Royal Asiatic Society*, 55 (1), pp. 26–52.

Tan Chee-Beng (1983), 'Chinese religion in Malaysia: a general view,' *Asian Folklore Studies*, 42 (2), pp. 217–52.

Tan Chee-Beng (1988), 'Structure and change: cultural identity of the baba of Melaka,' *Bijdragen tot de Taal-, Land- en Volkenkunde*, 144 (2–3), pp. 297–314.

Tan Chee-Beng (2004), *Chinese Overseas: Comparative Cultural Issues*, Hong Kong: Hong Kong University Press.

Tan Giok-Lan (1963), *The Chinese of Sukabumi: A Study of Social and Cultural Accommodation*, Ithaca, NY: Cornell Modern Indonesia Project Series.

Tan, Mely G. (1997), 'The ethnic Chinese in Indonesia: issues of identity,' in L. Suryadinata (ed.), *Ethnic Chinese as Southeast Asians*, Singapore: Institute of Southeast Asian Studies, pp. 33–71.

Tan Yao Sua and Kamarudin Ngah (2013), 'Identity maintenance and identity shift: the case of the Tirok Chinese Peranakan in Terengganu,' *Asian Ethnicity*, 14 (1), pp. 52–79.

Tideman, J. (1935), *Land en Volk van Bengkalis*, Mededeeling 9 van het Encyclopaedisch Bureau van de Koninklijke Vereeniging 'Koloniaal Instituut,' Koninklijk Nederlandsch Aardrijkskundig Genootchap.

Tong, C. H. (1998), 'The sinicization of Malay keramats in Malaysia,' *Journal of the Malaysian Branch of the Royal Asiatic Society*, 71 (2), pp. 29–61.

Trigger, D. and C. Dalley (2010), 'Negotiating indigeneity: culture, identity and politics,' *Reviews in Anthropology*, 39, pp. 46–65.

Trocki, C. A. (1997), 'Chinese pioneering in eighteenth-century Southeast Asia,' in A. Reid (ed.), *The Last Stand of Asian Autonomies: Responses to Modernity in the Diverse States of Southeast Asia and Korea, 1750–1900*, London: Macmillan Press, pp. 83–102.

Trocki, C. A. (2007 [1979]), *Prince of Pirates: The Temenggongs and the Development of Johor and Singapore: 1784–1885*, Singapore: NUS Press.

Tsing, A. L. (1987), 'A rhetoric of centers in a religion of the periphery,' in R. S. Kipp and S. Rodgers (eds), *Indonesian Religions in Transition*, Tucson, AZ: University of Arizona Press, pp. 187–210.

Tsing, A. L. (2007), 'Indigenous voice,' in M. de la Cadena and O. Starn (eds), *Indigenous Experience Today*, Berg: Oxford, pp. 35–68.

Tsintjilonis, D. (2004), 'The flow of life in Buntao: Southeast Asian animism reconsidered,' *Bijdragen tot- de Taal-, Land- en Volkenkunde*, 160 (4), pp. 425–55.

Tsuda, K. (2012), 'The legal and cultural status of Chinese temples in contemporary Java,' *Asian Ethnicity*, 13 (4), pp. 389–98.

Tyson, A. D. (2010), *Decentralization and Adat Revivalism in Indonesia: The Politics of Becoming Indigenous*, London: Routledge.

Ufford, P. Q. van (1987), 'Contradictions in the study of legitimate authority in Indonesia,' *Bijdragen tot de Taal-, Land- en Volkenkunde*, 143 (1), pp. 141–58.

van Anrooij, H. A. H. (1885), 'Nota omtrent het rijk Siak,' *Tijdschrift voor Indische Taal-, Land- en Volkenkunde*, 30, pp. 259–390.

Warman, K. (2014), 'Peta perundang-undangan tentang pengakuan hak masyarakat hukum adat.' Retrieved 26 April 2020 from https://procurement-notices.undp.org/view_file.cfm?doc_id=39284

Warren, C. (2007), 'Adat in Balinese discourse and practice: locating citizenship and the commonweal,' in J. S. Davidson and D. Henley (eds), *The Revival of Tradition in Indonesian Politics: The Deployment of Adat from Colonialism to Indigenism*, London: Routledge, pp. 170–202.

Wawrinec, C. (2010), 'Tribality and indigeneity in Malaysia and Indonesia,' *Stanford Journal of East Asian Affairs*, Winter, pp. 96–107.

Wee, V. (1985), 'Melayu: hierarchies of being in Riau,' PhD thesis, Australian National University, Canberra.

Wee, V. (2002), 'Ethno-nationalism in process: ethnicity, atavism and indigenism in Riau, Indonesia,' *Pacific Reviews*, 15 (4), pp. 497–516.

Wilkinson, R. J. (1957), *A Malay–English Dictionary*, London: Macmillan & Co Ltd.

Willmott, D. E. (1960), *The Chinese of Semarang: A Changing Minority Community in Indonesia*, Ithaca, NY: Cornell University Press.

Winstedt, R. O. (1961), *The Malays: A Cultural History*, 6th edn, London: Routledge and Kegan Paul.

Wollenberg, E., M. Moelino and G. Limberg (2009), 'Riding the rapids: synthesis and conclusion,' in M. Moelino, E. Wollenberg and G. Limberg (eds), *The Decentralization of Forest Governance: Politics, Economics and the Fight for Control of Forests in Indonesian Borneo*, London: Earthsca, pp. 281–98.

Yang Heriyanto (2005), 'The history and legal position of Confucianism in post-independence Indonesia,' *Marburg Journal of Religion*, 10 (1), pp. 1–8.

Yang, Shu-Yuan (2011), 'Cultural performance and the reconstruction of tradition among the Bunun of Taiwan,' *Oceania*, 81, pp. 316–31.

Yoesoef, N. (1992), *Masyarakat Terasing dan Kebudayaan di Propinsi Riau*, Pekanbaru: UP. Telagakarya.Index

Index

Subjects

Personal names

Place names